West Indian Yarns

George Hammond Hawtayne

WEST INDIAN YARNS

BY

'X. BEKE.'

NEW EDITION, REVISED AND ENLARGED.

DEMERARA:
J. THOMSON, "ARGOSY" PRESS.
LONDON:
E. A. PETHERICK & CO., 38, PATERNOSTER ROW.

1890.

TO

LIZZIE

PRESS NOTICES.

Reprints from Colonial papers are not as a rule distinguished by originality either in matter or manner. On the contrary if they have any quality which is peculiarly their own, it is an exceptional turn for making the new book old and the interesting dull. West Indian Yarns by X. Beke, (Demerara, James Thomson,) is to a considerable extent an exception. X. Beke has not written a possession for ever, nor even a possession for many years, but his yarns are tolerably smart reading, and may be recommended to whomever has them at hand in an idle hour. They are of very various degrees of merit, and one or two short sentimental stories among them are naught. For the most part they are sketches of negro and creole habits. To judge from X. Beke, all the West Indies which is not negro, is Scotch, and if he gives the talk of the former as he gives that of the latter, it must be very good indeed. There is a long-winded genealogical Scotchman who is excellent. So is another Scot who offered to work without pay on the ground that "on a big estate like o this there's plenty of orra things aboot, and I'd be aye picking up something till ye found it convenient to allot me a sailary." Strange to say the planter would have nothing to do with this model of honesty. X. Beke has also some fairly amusing stories of negro dignity.—*Saturday Review.*

The *Argosy* press of Georgetown, Demerara, is now setting up a second edition of 'West Indian Yarns,' by Mr. G. H. HAWTAYNE, a Government official in that colony. In these 'Yarns,' of which the first edition has become exhausted, the writer describes with much knowledge and humour a state of things that is fast passing away in the social life of some of the island colonies. As photographs in black and white of society a generation ago, Mr. HAWTAYNE's amusing sketches will preserve for present and future dwellers in those colonies many shades of existence which would otherwise disappear. Persons who intend avoiding the winter by taking a trip to the West Indies will find much to amuse them in the 'Yarns.'—*New York Nation.*

CONTENTS. Page.

CONTENTS.	PAGE.

CONTENTS.	PAGE.

WEST INDIAN YARNS.

UNDER THE BATTERY.

MY introduction to the West Indies was accompanied by what in its way was a "baptism of fire" as the Emperor Louis Napoleon would have called it.

It was many years ago when the Royal Mail Company had not attained the punctuality which is now so remarkable, and I took passage on a "first trip" steamer. We had bad weather moreover; and this with heated bearings delayed us, so that on our arrival at St. Thomas we found the inter-colonial boat had gone. Of course the Company's agent had a bad time of it, but ultimately the ocean steamer was despatched one way, and a vessel chartered to take the rest of us on our route.

This boat, as it turned out, was of Yankee origin, called, if I recollect rightly, the *Ben Franklin.* Her Captain and crew were a very unsatisfactory lot and her fittings, to say the least, peculiar. She was to all appearance a passenger steamer, but the ports were large and capable of further enlargement, and the cabins, &c., all of a very temporary and makeshift character. However anything was better than to stay in St. Thomas, and we all hastened hurriedly on board. A portion of the provisions brought in the ocean boat was hustled on to the *Franklin's* deck, poultry, pigs, ice, vegetables, meat, &c., &c., all in admired confusion, and after sun-down we started. Just as we got opposite a small fort at the entrance of the harbour, bang! went a gun, followed by another. What could it mean? A third followed, and then the Captain was requested to stop, but he wouldn't, "he'd let her rip," but a fourth shot, with a thud which shook the vessel, appeared an unanswerable argument, and we stopped. A lady rushed from below screaming that all in the cabin "was smashed save the baby and a cake of soap," and matters did indeed look serious. A boat was lowered and a Bishop and a Colonial Governor, with one or two others, put off to parley with the gunners of the fort. I, who had to duck when one of the balls whizzed over my head, thought I might as well see the fun. In the dark we slowly neared the fort and were challenged. Some sort of reply was given, and then we all began to clamber over the wet stones towards the battery. The Bishop, a fine specimen of the muscular christian, rolled up his sleeves and prepared to do battle, and the Governor, a tall wiry man, seemed able to give a good account of any half dozen of the puny Danes; and I think it was the Governor's Secretary who kept me company, discreetly moving up as supports to our champions. There was a parley and a reference to the Danish Governor, then a long pull back under arrest to the town, and a tiresome tramp through the town to the Consul's house. We were all in great terror of the myriads of dogs that yelped and barked at every step we took. The Consul received us in his dining room, in his "robe de nuit," and promised all should be enquired into and redressed. We did a little of the "Civis Romanus Sum" business which was then in fashion, and on our return were received on board the *Franklin* by our grateful fellow-passengers. It turned out that the despatch had been sent out to St. Thomas to receive on board her armament sent before by a sailing vessel ostensibly laden with coal; she was then to take part in a liberating expedition to Venezuela, or some other of those South American republics which are ever in a ferment; but, this being discovered, the *Franklin* was not allowed to leave the harbour. The gunners at the fort had orders to sink her if she attempted to go out. These orders, through some blunder, had not been countermanded, and we all might have been sent to the bottom.

There was a Lieutenant of Artillery on board, now, I dare say, a Major General, from whose attention and professional knowledge a very pretty and very frightened young lady derived much comfort in this trying time; and a Barbadian matron, who was irritating from the way in which she demanded why all sorts of things, which she declared would have been done had we been in Barbados, had not been at least attempted. At daybreak the two shot holes we had received were caulked, and steam being got up, we proceeded and at length reached Barbados.

NAMES.

THE predilection which negroes have for grand names, alluded to by Marryatt in one of his novels, is well known. In some of the West India Islands every darkie has a play-name or name for common or every day use, which is as a rule, short and so to speak, handy. Their baptismal names, on the contrary, are lengthy and romantic, being borrowed from the pages of "Standard novels" or from the heroes and heroines of "penny dreadfuls." In the olden days, Shakespeare was greatly resorted to as a sponsor, and sable Hamlets, Othellos, Romeos, and Macbeths abound among the older negroes. Often in the desire for a polysyllabic name its uncomplimentary or inappropriate character is overlooked, and hence some more or less worthy people are found whose names bear the prefixes of Mendacious, Abnormal, Abdominal, Ananias, &c. One man I know, christened Hobbledehoy, tries to conceal the unfortunate name by a strong accent on the second syllable. I have even known a Camomile Brown.

"Massa," said a respectable dark gentleman to a Registrar of Births, &c., "Massa, me make you for know dat for me wife confine Tuesday gone, and she gie me twin, both of dem boys, and me ax you be so kind as gie me name for dem."

"Well," said the Registrar, "let us see, I think you had better call one 'Waverley' and the other 'Guy Mannering.'"

"Tank you, me massa, dem name fustrate, but me beg

you write dem on a 'crip of paper, else me no member dem." The Registrar did so and Mr. Pompey went away rejoicing. Some weeks after, the following conversation was overheard between Pompey and a friend :—

"Well buddie (brother) and how does dem two picknie get on?"

"Fustrate! hearty," replied Pompey.

"Dey is christened yet?"

"Oh! yes, dey baptize last Sunday at chapel."

"And what name you gie dem?"

"Well, me friend, for tell de troot, me scarce able for get my tongue round de words, but de name well handsome. Ah! dey call um 'Waberley' and 'Guy Maddering,' someting so."

"Eh! me fadder!" said Pompey's friend, "where ebber you get dem name?"

"Registrar gie um, and write um down for no make mistake."

"And parson take um?"

"Yes, me friend. Fust he say he nebber hear Guy Maddering before, but he know Waberly been one pusson as write plenty good book, so he speck praps dey been brudders, and so he receibe de name for me picknies and dem." The 'parson' no doubt was one of the locus preacher tribe whose reading did not extend to Scott.

Two black girls, labourers on a friend's estate in the island of St. Maria, returning from work, met on the road. They had but a scanty amount of clothes, but each had a baby in her arms. There was some quarrel between them and a wordy combat ensued. At its close one damsel, turning away, said, "Well I don't want no more discoorse wid you "Miss Terăsa."

"Me make you for know, marm," retorted the other girl, "that for me name no Terăsa, but Tereesa."

"Well, me dear," was the reply, "Terăsa else Terėesa both de same, for me name a better name than for your own, for me name Diana de Goddess of Chaste;" and Diana strutted off with a swing of her tattered skirt and toss of the head that would have become a duchess.

A negro often takes as his "bragging" or "play" name that of his master, and in their social gatherings these names alone are used, while the gait and manner, or any other peculiarities of their employers, are also imitated.

Servants and labourers are addicted to bestowing on their offspring the names of their masters and mistresses, and often when, as is the custom in some of the colonies, a son takes as his surname the christian name of his father, the result is embarrassing. For instance, if Mr. Brown Robinson's groom, Jack Cæsar, calls his child "Robinson Cæsar," the latter, when he has a son, will probably christen him as "Brown," and the child is not known as "Brown Cæsar," but as "Brown Robinson," so that proper minded persons are apt, on finding the aristocratic name to be borne by a small coloured boy, to shake their heads and make edifying reflections on the morality of the original Robinson.

This mark of respect or of admiration for the name, and sometimes the rank of a superior, was curiously exemplified some years ago in, as I think, Jamaica, where the wife of a black military labourer marched up to the font with her infant, and, in the presence of a scandalized congregation, gave its intended name as "George Frederick Augustus Snodgrass Adjutant."

Coolie Immigrants when converted and baptized often assume as their new names those of the persons—generally the owners or managers of estates or their wives or relatives—who stand as sponsors on the occasion.

Two neighbours, a proprietor and a middle aged maiden lady, had a desperate quarrel over a disputed right of way. They had not gone to law, but from being excellent friends they had become bitter foes, and the small society of the parish was deeply interested in each phase of the dispute. Mr. P. employed on his estate several coolies; and two of them, a driver or superintendent, Sahye, and his wife Jebuseeah, having become converted to Christianity, were about to be baptized. Sahye applied to his employer to be his sponsor, and Jebuseeah, who was a protégée of Miss W., obtained permission to take her name. The unhappy feud between the sponsors prevented the double ceremony taking place on the same day, as nothing would induce the one to meet the other under any circumstances; and so the Coolies were baptized on different days.

Of course a marriage, according to the rites of the Church, was to follow; and one fine Sunday, when the quarrel between Mr. P. and Miss W. was at its climax, the congregation in the church were astounded at hearing the banns of marriage published between Philip James P., widower, and Arabella W., spinster. The gentleman and lady rose simultaneously as if to forbid the banns, the greatest excitement prevailed, when their eyes met, and it flashed across their minds that the banns were those of their Coolie protégées, a smile lit up the face of each, and the incident was the means of a mutual explanation, and afforded an opportunity for a happy adjustment of the disputed right of way.

A young official, who was in some way connected with affairs matrimonial and had to issue licenses or certificates, was once applied to by an aged pair for the required paper.

"Your intended wife's name I see is Raffle," he observed to the ancient bridegroom.

"Yes sah! Meloina Raffle."

"Aha!" observed the clerk, "old man going to take a chance in a Raffle; expect a prize, eh!"

"I don't know, me massa. I hab she dear love, and dat is all de prize I want" was the touching reply.

SMIFF THE OVERSEER.

"NEVER," once said a friend, "call a negro drunk," and he gave his reasons as follows:—One night just as my wife and I were preparing to go to bed, I heard a sound as of some animal in my garden, and looking out saw to my disgust, a black man on a mule careering all over the flower beds and making sad havoc with my pet roses. I was out in a minute regardless of having no hat on and being thinly clad for so wet an evening.

"Beg pardon, Sah," said my visitor coming to a halt and then backing into an allamanda bush, "Beg pardon, but Massa Smiff de obersheer, he dead Sah! he fall down in de gutter" (gutter was the term for a lovely fern-clad ravine just below my house).

Now "Massa Smiff, de obersheer," was a dreadful creature who was always in scrapes, and with whom I had been at loggerheads for a long while; however one could not leave him in the "gutter." My horror at the accident made me forget my injured plants, and so calling out a small Portuguese boy and bidding him bring a lantern, and followed by two curiosity-driven servant girls, on I went. It was, as I said, a rainy night, and the ground was slippery in the extreme, and as I slid and stumbled I made several, I dare say, rough remarks on "Mr. Smiff." "Here he mule, Sah!" suddenly said our guide, as we came up to the animal which was nibbling away at the grass by the road-side.

"And here be Massa Smiff, Sah!" And there was Mr. Smith, sure enough. He had evidently fallen over the brink of the road, his weight had made a regular shoot down the side of the ravine for some thirty feet or more, and he lay on his back, with his feet a long way above his head, which rested against the spiny trunk of a gru gru palm that had arrested his further descent. He seemed unconscious; his eyes were open, and reflected the light of the lantern in a most startling way.

"Mr Smith!" I called out. No reply. "Go down to him," said I—"Mr. ———"

"My name, Sah, is Herod, Hamlet Herod, Sah."

"Well, help up Mr. Smith. Here, Antonio! Give a hand."

Mr. Herod and Antonio set about the task, and, after a

great deal of labour, Mr. Smith was dragged up like a log to the road side, when he suddenly shewed signs of life by biting Antonio in the arm, and as Antonio let him go with a yell, down he slid till he was brought up with a bang by the gru gru palm, and lay staring as before.

I was wet through, and the wind blew in terrible gusts down the valley. The strange light in Mr. Smith's eyes, the grotesque shadows of our party on the bank behind us, and the weird figures of the negro girls with their white skirts thrown over their heads, and the two men trying to get Mr. Smith once more up the incline, made a wonderful picture. Another effort was made. The drunken creature was again hauled up to the road, where he once more made a snap with his teeth at Antonio, who ran home, and Mr. Smith slid down to his former position, dragging with him his friend Herod. Herod, however, had lost patience with Mr. "Smiff," and he began to beat him about the head with his fists. This, of course, could not be allowed, so I scrambled down to the two men and, holding Herod's uplifted arm, called on him to desist. "You'll kill the man" I said.

"Why, Sah, he's drunk, beastly drunk."

"Well," I said, "and so I suspect are you."

Mr. Herod was indignant at this unfortunate remark; he crawled slowly up the side of the ravine, drew himself up when he reached the road, and said in a most impressive manner: "Well, Sah! If I'm drunk I can be of no use to you, Sah. I wish you, and for *you drunken friend Smiff de obersheer*, good night," and mounting his mule away he rode.

It was a long weary time before I got help and had

"Smiff de obersheer" taken to a place of safety. He was almost sobered by that time, but on parting he would shake hands and thank me for "a most 'greeable evening." I caught a cold, and was taught a lesson to be careful when and how I next said a man was drunk.

A LOVING BROTHER.

THE following scene shows a degree of fraternal devotion which throws all similar stories of ancient days into the shade, and proves that where fraternal love is concerned "iron bars do not a prison make."

A Portuguese dealer, whose shop was but small, had been convicted of an irregularity, some one of those breaches of the law into which a too ardent pursuit of trade leads people. He was brought before a magistrate, and the case was fully proved.

"Jose Antonio," said the magistrate, "you are convicted on this charge, and as it is not your first offence of the same kind, you must be imprisoned for one month."

"Prison? You no take fine?"

"No!"

"'Scuse me, me worship, but spose me go jail, how me shop go sell."

"I cannot help that. You must put some one to look after it. You have a brother, Manuel."

"Yes, me worship, but before me go put he a mind shop, better me shut 'em up. Manuel! me worship, me no able for trus' him with one bit candle—"

"Well then, you must stand down."

"Yes, me worship, but you could let me talk to Manuel a little bit?"

"Constable! take this man down."

Presently Jose re-appears. "Beg pardon, me worship, but me settle um all right."

"What do you mean?"

"Manuel 'gree with me, he go jail in me place and I go mind de shop; if you please, me worship."

But his worship did not please.

A LESSON.

OF all the hospitable Scottish planters I ever knew, the foremost was my old friend K —— who owned an estate in Santa Maria, a lovely spot with a house that might have been built of India rubber, for there was apparently no limit to the accommodation it could give. and the beds its owner could make up.

Nothing pleased him more than when a dozen friends, or, for a matter of that, strangers, dropped in and remained as long as they liked. At the time I speak of, there were stationed in the colony a considerable number of troops, and one favourite excursion of the officers was to ride down to old "Dunvegan" (as the planter was called from the estate on which he resided), and spend what they called a quiet Sunday. The fare was always ample if plain, but there was no place where you could find a fatter haunch of mutton, far different to the ordinary tough and skinny stuff which so sorely tried our patience and our teeth at other tables. The liquors were plentiful and of various kinds: Madeira, brown sherry, strong Scotch ale (in those days we knew nothing of pale sherry or pale ale, and we drank brown brandy, and knew not Hennessy), champagne, and some especially good claret, all were at our command—the only drawback being that we were expected in "common ceveelity," as our host expressed it, to drink much more than was good for us, to correct the mixture with just a dram of rum shrub, and to "top up" with a big draught of rum and water, "My own particular distilling, Sir," to refuse which would have given mortal offence.

One evening, some half-dozen had come down from the garrison, and the dinner had been a very jovial affair; still no one was the worse for what he had taken, except a very small and young ensign, and he was only affected to the extent of being moved to incontrollable laughter at the accent in which our old host spoke. It certainly was stronger after the Madeira had gone round three or four times than before. but whenever he commenced a story, he was interrupted by a roar of laughter from young Mr. Verdant. In vain did the rest of us endeavour to keep the boy in order. As soon as he was quiet, and old Dunvegan recommenced, out would come a peal which drowned our host's voice. He stood this very patiently for a while, then getting up from the table, he beckoned to Verdant and said, "I want to tell you something, come with me."

Verdant pulled himself together and followed the old man out to the stables. Arrived there, Dunvegan took the ensign by the hand and said, "I'm just going to treat ye as I'm sure your ain faither would if he were here, and I'll no doubt if ever ye tell him of it, he'll thank me. D'ye know it's no very ceevil of ye to laugh and mock at me in my ain house before my freends, me that's auld enough to be your grandfaither, aye I may say your great-grandfaither, so ye'll jest take what I am going to give you in a faitherly way;" and so saying the old fellow gave his young guest a box on each ear with his big hands, much to the astonishment of the 'officer and gentleman.'

"Noo," he continued, "we'll go back and finish our wine and say nae mair aboot it."

VERY OFFICIAL.

WHEN a head of an official department adopts a particular style in his correspondence, it is safe to be copied by all his subs down to the messenger; and the youngest clerk chides his washer for lost handkerchiefs or ill ironed collars in a "minute" which has quite the official ring affected by his chief.

I once fell in with a letter addressed by a police corporal at head quarters to a solitary constable stationed on the northern coast of Barataria, who had allowed a vessel to communicate with the shore during quarantine. It was written on official paper on which the stamp of the department was duly impressed, and it ran thus:—

Sir,—I am directed by the Inspector General to order you to report the surcumstences under which you did allow the skuner "Nancy Bell" to land peoples at —— Bay. Such conduck being all together contrairy to the rules and regulashuns of the island of Barataria and its dependents.—I have, &c., SOLOMON BOBB, Corporal in charge.

To P. C. WILLIAM ULYSSES, in charge of —— Station.

But Bobb, though an official, was human, and he had a private liking for his friend the Constable which asserted itself even on a grave occasion like this, so he added a postscript.

P.S. Privit and confidentshul.

Dear Bill,—I am really surprise how you could make such a dam fool of yourself. you best come up and make your pease with the General, and no more at preasant

"MY SUSPEESHUNS!"

ANGUS and Jeanie MacDuff were a quiet couple whom I knew in St. Maria. Angus came out as an indentured ploughman with four huge Clydesdale horses and a ponderous plough that was to tickle the tenacious lands of Rosedale, and bring about the growth of unprecedented canes; but the experiment did not succeed. The horses could not stand the climate. The plough got "masshiated" as a labourer expressed it, in other words broken, and when I knew Angus, he and some monstrous horse shoes nailed on the stable door were all that remained of this essay at implemental husbandry. But Angus had thriven; he had become overseer, then manager, and soon after, marrying the daughter of an old planter, who was an heiress, he bought an estate and made money.

Prices went up for a couple of years, and Angus was lucky enough to make a "big haul," which he put by, and, when prices fell again and estates went into the market, he bought one at the other side of the island as a great bargain.

One evening I was at Montrose, and Mrs. MacDuff was telling me what a trial this newly acquired property was. It required Mr. MacDuff's frequent presence, and it was a long way off. "Indeed Jeanie," said Augus, "it's no' a bad road. I'll tak' ye there some day."

"Weel! weel! but ye ha'e to stop there a' day and come hame the next, and ye canna get yer food nicely and comfortably."

"Noo, my dear Jeanie, mak' yoursel' easy. I assure you that Susan, that is auld Mrs. Pompey, is a very decent auld body and cooks remarkably weel, auld as she is, and I jist get a fowl and a bit fish—and Su—that is, auld Mrs. Pompey does what she can; of coorse it's no' like hame."

Some days after, Mrs. MacDuff was driven by her husband to Sandy Mount, as the new property was called, in an antiquated gig which was Angus's first and only carriage. I happened to overtake them near the house. The day was very warm, and I was tired and thirsty, and I thought the accident of meeting with the old couple promised well for a drink, so I drew nigh. As we reached the door, out came Mrs. Pompey, a very sprightly and good-looking black woman of about thirty, who bobbed and curtsied and wished good morning to her "massa and missis."

But Mrs. MacDuff looked most sternly at Angus, who gave one glance at his wife, and then found some sudden difficulty with the reins which prevented his looking up.

"Angus! Mr. MacDuff!" But there was no reply to Mrs. MacDuff's address.

"Mr. Macduff!"

"Yes, me dear."

"Is this woman Mrs. Pompey?—*auld* Mrs. Pompey, that ye say maks ye sae comfortable?"

"Weel, yes my dear, this"—

"Then Mr. MacDuff, a' I ha'e to remairk is that she's nane so auld, *nane so auld* Angus, and I ha'e my suspeeshuns."

So saying Mrs. MacDuff got out of the gig, pushed Mrs. Pompey aside, and hustled into the house with an expression on her face that was the "storm signal" in the MacDuff household; and I concluded, as the Yankees say, to go on my journey.

THE "GENERAL."

THERE was a man in St. Maria (and "manager out of employ" seemed to be his only calling, for he never kept a situation long,) who, for some reason or another, had acquired the sobriquet of "General," not that Mr. Ratoons was at all military in figure or appearance. On the contrary, he was a knock-kneed shambling fellow with round shoulders and a red nose. With nothing to do, Ratoons was always ready to run after anything new; and the advent of a Swedish corvette, and an intimation that the captain would kindly allow an inspection of the vessel, was more than enough to induce the "General" and a chum of his to present themselves on board. They were shewn round the ship and afterwards were seated in the captain's cabin discussing a glass of Madeira. Ratoons would have remained all day, especially with a bottle before him, but his more discreet companion, after a second glass, said "Well, General, we must be going." As he said so, an officer of the ship started up and left the cabin.

After a few minutes, the captain and another officer rose and escorted their guests on deck, where a guard of marines was drawn up. The men presented arms to the bewildered Ratoons.

"Pardon, Monsieur le General," explained the captain, "but had we been aware of your distinguished rank I should have taken care"—

"Oh, don't mention it," said Ratoons, waving an adieu with a large cotton umbrella.

"That Madeira's got into the captain's head" said Mr. Ratoons to his friend as he got into the boat.

"These English Colonial Generals do not seem distinguished," remarked the captain to his lieutenant.

A BAILEE.

A COOLIE once consulted a lawyer, a clever fellow, but a little fond of expressing himself in a style which, to say the least of it, was "high-falutin," about obtaining satisfaction for a goat that a countryman, to whom he had entrusted it, had killed and eaten. The lawyer enquired if he had *given* the goat to his friend.

"No! Sahib; me no goat give 'um for he self—me goat give 'um supposing goat make pickney, he one pickney take, he one pickney give me—suppose goat no make pickney he sell 'um, half money keep, half money give me." So, in mixed Hindo-Creole-English was the case stated.

"Ah then," said the lawyer, "you entrusted the animal to this individual to keep half the usufruct, the produce, or in case of sale to divide the proceeds?"

"Yes, Sahib—Yes! so me give 'um."

"And I am to understand that the man killed it and ate it. Well! now you see he was what we term the *bailee*—do you understand?"

"Yes, Sah! *bailee*, he eat 'um *belly*, head, body, ebery ting eat um."

CAUGHT.

THERE was an excellent magistrate in Barbados, the terror of the Bridgetown rascals, who was somewhat eccentric and usually wore a buff waistcoat which had to be made of rather an extra size, and gained for him among the lower orders a well-known sobriquet. One day an old offender was brought before him for some offence and convicted. The prisoner immediately became most penitent and begged the magistrate to be lenient. "Do! Mr. G—, do! I beg you Sir, do my kind master! Have mercy Mr. G—!"

"Look you here," said the magistrate, "to-day it's Mr. G—; yesterday when I met you in the Roebuck it was "yaller bellied-Kit." Three months—take him down."

A NEW BOOK.

I ONCE was in a country Police Court when a sprightly negress, gorgeously attired, tripped up to the magistrate's table to be sworn as a witness. Either from nervousness, or for some other reason, she giggled immensely, and when the Testament was placed in her hands she nearly burst out laughing. The magistrate, a solemn "beak" in his way, reproved her for her levity, and after reminding her in a most impressive manner that she was about to call her Creator to the truth of her statement, &c., enquired, "Do you know what book that is you have in your hand?"

"Oh yes, my Worship, it be de book of Matrimony."

The magistrate collapsed, and I left the Court lest I should be ordered into custody for contempt.

A HUMANE EMPLOYER.

ANY one who is connected with an estate must be more or less frequently before the magistrate, and the sayings and doings heard and seen in Court are often very amusing.

I once was present at the début, as magistrate, of a

friend—a stranger to the colony and its people—the planters of whose district were good fellows, and some of them extremely sharp witted. One in particular, a worthy old Highlander, had worked his way from a humble station to that of proprietor of several estates. He became a Justice of the Peace and was quite a "local magnate." On the occasion referred to, he was in Court, and was invited to a seat on the bench alongside my friend, who began to investigate a charge of wife-beating preferred against a young black man. The case was clearly made out and the assault was proved to have been of a somewhat aggravated character.

The magistrate in his zeal inflicted no fine, but imposed a term of imprisonment with hard labour as punishment. "Weel," said the old Justice, in a stage whisper, "Mr. —— you'll no mind my remarking that "yon's a very decent mon, generally speaking. I've known him ever since he was a lad, and his faither before him, and I am sorry to see him in this predeecament. I'd be sorry to see him go to jail,—jail is but a bad school for the likes of them."

"Yes," said the magistrate, "that may be, but you see, an example must be made."

"Weel, weel, I'll not go altogether against ye in that, but the wife is a regular bad one—ye may call her a perfect deevil, and ye don't know these black women, they are enough to drive a man daft once they get in their tantrums."

"Possibly; but they must be protected."

"Yes! just so—but I assure ye, I think if you put a money fine on the fellow and speak to him somewhat severely, and gie him a bit of advice and warning as to what will befall if he comes back here again on any such conduct, it will be better than putting him in jail. I don't like jail."

"Well," said the magistrate, "of course your experience is greater than mine" (the young rascal had then none at all) "so I do not mind altering the sentence."

"Here! Quashie Othello! Mr. Mac has spoken in your behalf, and given you a good character, so I will allow you this time to pay a fine, but recollect if, &c., &c., &c.,—you will pay ten dollars."

"Thank ye, my dear Sir," again whispered the Justice, "I'm much obleeged to ye—ye'll find you have done right. I tak' an interest in the fellow and I'll pay his fine, he will repay me. Ah! weel, now he's dischairged, I don't mind mentioning that he's my head boiler, and I could not have gone about" (*i.e.*, putting the sugar mill to work) "without him on Monday. I'll wish you good morning."

The magistrate's face was a picture.

A SICK-BED FRIEND.

MY friend and neighbour Carew, who managed his own estate in St. Molasses, had a young overseer named McGregor, a strong well-made young Highlander, who learned his duties quickly, and was a faithful servant; one day, however, he sickened, and fever set in; there was in those days no district medical officer and McGregor was sent off in a canoe to town so as to be under proper care and treatment. Carew gave up his own rooms, and enlisted the sympathies of old Jane who looked after them, and a better nurse than that thin frail-looking old mulatto woman no one could desire.

In a day or two, the doctor reported that poor McGregor's was a case of yellow fever, one of those sporadic cases which will crop up now and then apparently without cause. Carew, who received the message some days later, at once hurried up to town, and I went with him. There could be no doubt as to the poor overseer's condition, but some days had elapsed since the crisis, and McGregor was reported better, but in need of stimulants, especially champagne.

My friend, who was annoyed that he had not been earlier sent for, gave *carte blanche* for everything that could be required, and then left, promising soon to return.

Now in St. Molasses there was a fellow called Plantagenet who was a Government employé,—a "fellow of infinite wit" but of very infinitesimal principles. He managed to live on a couple of hundreds a year in a style which cost other people thrice as much, or more. He was, however, always ready to proffer his services in a most generous fashion; often undertook a troublesome task, volunteered assistance when ever he thought he could be of use, and so laid a foundation on which he could venture at some subsequent period to base a request. Many of his friends paid for these little services by a loan, "just until Tuesday," which day never seemed to arrive; or by an endorsement, "only as a matter of form," which resulted in a matter of hard cash. Plantagenet has been known to saunter into the Ice House at the heels of some couple who had gone in to get a drink, and ask the barman in an apologetic tone for a glass of iced water.

"Anything in it, Mr. Plantagenet?"

"Not to-day, Cyrus, thank you—not to-day—I am not in cash as it happens, and I, as you know, never run a tick for drink" (there were reasons beyond Plantagenet's control for this). "Plain water with a big lump of ice if you can spare it—thank you, Cyrus!"

But before the glass was raised to his lips he would, of course, be asked to join the other drinkists, and I am told that his firm refusal, then hesitation, followed by a graceful surrender, and a murmured, "whatever you're taking, thank you"—was a study.

As Carew and I went home in our canoe that night, and he leant back in the stern steering with the yoke lines over his shoulders, and his face turned up to the sky, he said "I have had a lesson to-day, old man!"

"Yes," I replied, "what's that?"

"Merely that, in every fellow, there's some good which, bad as the man's nature may otherwise be, atones for much of that badness. I used to think and speak of Plantagenet as a mean, selfish snob, without one particle of real good in him; but I was wrong."

"What has occurred to make you alter your opinion?"

"Well! would you believe it? old Jane says nobody had been near poor McGregor, everybody funked yellow Jack, except Plantagenet, and he has been round daily of late, reading to the poor fellow and cheering him up. So there must be some good in him, must there not?"

I assented, and we glided in the moonlight along the coast, where the sea was like glass. We did not chat much, and the silence was broken only by the thud of the oars against the thole pins, and the swish of the water as it rushed past us in silvery flashes.

A few days after, we were again in town and found McGregor better. Old Jane was quite perky on having brought her patient through, for she knew well that the nursing is more than half the battle in such cases.

"Is there anything you want Jane?" asked Carew as the two came down the entrance steps.

"Yes, massa! I s'pose Mr. Mac will want another case shampang."

"Another case of champagne! Why, Jane, it was only last week you had one."

"Dat for true, massa; but no 'member massa Plagynet he come ebbry day and read de 'cripture to he too nice, but den he get dry, and he look for drink, and de way dat buckra take de shampang—Aou! my goodness, he go down he troat same like water down a ratta hole!"

I walked away, but as I went I heard Carew giving an order for another supply of the "fizz," coupled with one for the exclusion of Plantagenet.

VERY SAD!

THE Revd. Peter Simple once excused himself for being late at some clerical meeting, by the circumstance of his having been detained at the death-bed of a certain married woman. Mr. S.

was very young and very zealous, and he dwelt at some length on the many virtues of the deceased. She had been one of the leading members of the congregation, so thoroughly pious and consistent, &c.

"What did she die of?" asked the Archdeacon.

"Oh! a sad death, sir, she died giving birth to a still-born child."

"Oh! Indeed!"

"Yes; and what makes it more sad is that, two years ago, her husband cruelly deserted her and went to Trinidad and has never been heard of since!"

CHEAP GLASS WARE.

THE ladies had left the table, and had swept out in a picturesque file into the adjoining drawing room, and we men drew closer to our host Talboys, who sent the decanters round. Talboys was Dealer of Suits in the Government of Barataria, a snug office with some £800 to £1,000 a year, and duties which, with the altered fortunes of the island, had become less and less each year. In Talboys' father's time (for the post had descended from sire to son) the income was larger, but in those palmy days the work was somewhat more onerous. The family was an ancient one, and had been settled in the colony for a hundred years and more, and in Barataria we thought a good deal of the "first families," and looked on the men who had had a great grandfather in the Island as fit to rank with any one who, like Christopher Sly, had ancestors that came in with "Richard Conqueror." Families in the West Indies, however, get poorer as they get older, and the Talboys had lost estates and houses and money, until a Government office was a welcome refuge from the grim wolf, poverty. But old families have old habits that cling to them thro' all changes, and if Percy Talboys, round whose table we sate, did not keep race horses or fighting cocks, or play whist at guinea points, and a doubloon on the rubber, as his forbears had done, he had the family failing of spending more than he got, I cannot say, earned. To cut his coat according to his cloth was a wretched thing to do, and Percy was never out of debt. He was gifted, however, with a wonderful power of cajoling a creditor; no one ever was angry with him, and the fiercest dun would leave his house or office with a grin on his face and a pledge to give Percy another month.

With European creditors he had, as Mrs. Glass says, "another way." It is on record that Talboys would saunter down to the Post Office when the mail came in, take his letters, look at the addresses, remark that this was "from that confounded tailor," and coolly write across it "Dead" and drop it back into the box. The next, which was from "that greedy fellow the bootmaker" would be returned with "try Antigua" or "Jamaica" across it. How the Postmaster allowed it I do not know, but Mass' Percy was a privileged being, and in those days postmasters were sympathetic.

But I must return to Talboys' dinner; we had passed the claret (and it *was* claret) round, when Graylin—he owned an estate near town—remarked: "These slender stemmed glasses of yours, Talboys, remind me of Judge Buster's old butler. You know how he is kept on, though old and worse than useless, because he once was Greville's butler, somewhere in the twenties, and went home with Greville and actually waited on the Prince Regent, whom his master was fool enough to entertain to his severe loss. Well, old Harklees had always been used to the sturdy thickset glasses of that age, and regarded the straw stemmed ware his master got out last month with some degree of awe; but he began to wipe them in the good old style, holding the foot firmly in the one hand, and giving the bowl a brisk rub round with the cloth, when lo! bowl and stem became dis-severed. Harklees tried another with the same result, and then he slowly shook his head and remarked, 'What next white man do? Me gad! he make wine glass to unscrew'; and Harklees duly proceeded to 'unscrew' each of the two dozen glasses and place the foot and bowl of each in due order along the table. You can imagine the great delight of the Judge, who happened to look at the dinner table as Harklees had concluded his task."

"Excuse me, Talboys," said Jones, a medico, and a good fellow, "but what splendid glass you have. I have been admiring it all dinner time."

"Yes," said Talboys, "it *is* good. I don't care to drink out of common glass, your wine don't taste the same; just as soon drink porter out of an earthen tea cup. I once knew a fellow who did that, but he died afterwards—of beer. This glass was a present."

"Lucky fellow!" we all observed.

"Yes, and a costly one—worth three hundred dollars they said."

"By Jove!" was all we *could* say under the circumstances.

"Yes," said Talboys, "we West Indians pride ourselves on, and are credited with, a good deal of generosity, but it isn't real. We creoles, and creolised Englishmen too, in nine cases out of ten are lazy, not generous; it's so much more easy to say 'take,' than to say 'no,' and have a jaw over it; but when a London merchant makes a handsome present like this glass, well it is all the more flattering a gift, because, dy'e see, those fellows are not impulsive and don't give except after mature thought."

"And what was your especial virtue, Talboys, that called forth this splendid gift?" asked Murray a small man, and a magistrate.

"Well, if you want to know, it happened thus," replied Talboys, tossing off a glass of Chateau la Rose: "When I was at home last year, I wanted some glass, and one day I strolled into Breakit and Smashem's place in Bond Street, just to look round, you know. I happened to be at the end of my leave and was deuced hard up. They showed me no end of things, and of course you'll say I ought to have gone out of the place, or better still, never have gone in. Well, I saw this set, *Veni, Vidi et victus fui.* I ordered it, told them to send it out to me, told them who I was and my address and went off. In due time the glass arrived in that fine old tub, the *Dover*, and by a mail before that, I got the invoice, amount £62 5s. 10d., and of course a hint that a remittance by return would oblige.

"Well, I thought, honesty is the best policy, and I at once wrote explaining that the price was far more than I had anticipated, and saying that I could not afford to pay more than £25, which I would remit on receipt of Breakit and Smashem's reply. I got the reply, old Breakit wrote himself. He began at first as if he was riled, and said something about a person in my position ordering expensive and elegant glass which I could not pay for; I expect then that he relented, no doubt sympathising with a man whose love for art out-stepped his means, and so he generously added that rather than take £25, he would make me a present of it. Of course, I wrote back a letter of thanks and gratitude, and I sent the old fellow a turtle. He never acknowledged letter or turtle, but I am sure he was satisfied. I know *I am.* Have another glass of claret? Well, a whitewash, and then we will join the ladies."

"BOTTS!"

ONE of the largest stores in ——— was kept by a worthy German named Bötz, or, as it was Englished, Botts. He had a large face of extraordinary whiteness, which contrasted strongly with his black eyes and hair. Every day, and all day, from the hour his store opened until it closed, Botts would saunter to and fro under the gallery before its doors, clad in white, always with a cigar in his mouth, which cigar however was never lighted. He was quite a character, and none of us ever went into town without paying a visit to old Botts.

Once we had an accession to the garrison staff in the the shape of Lieut. Colonel Sir Utterly Utter, Bart., who was one of the stiffest, most pompous fools I ever met. No one in the regiment caıed for him. His conversation consisted entirely of references to the aristocratic connections of the Utterly Utters and the glories of Utter Towers. To have to listen to a long disquisition on these subjects, delivered with a drawl and half closed eyes, was terribly trying to one's patience. Sir Double U, as we nicknamed him, was however a very fine looking fellow, but his face, like Botts', was singularly white. He used to tell us, the Utters had been always famed for the "marble pallor of their complexion," and the subs swore he preserved the peculiarity by a nightly application of cold cream.

I was staying with an old friend at an estate called "Pomme d'or," when Sir U., along with some other officers, was invited to spend a couple of days there and see the beauties of that side of the island. A very pleasant affair it promised to be; we younger people made several excursions, and left Sir Double U. to the care of our host, who, poor dear fellow, had to listen *nolens volens* to his guest's maundering talk about his family.

There was of course a big dinner; and our host, who was a bachelor, got very nervous about the preparations, but the resources of Pomme d'or were, as usual, equal to the occasion, and but for our principal guest's either haughty silence or absurd references to his favourite topics, we should have got on capitally.

Now, near Pomme d'or, there lived a good-natured, good-for-nothing district doctor named Mike Maguire. How he lived no one knew, his official pay was small, and a good deal of it went in drink,—in truth he was rarely sober. A more disreputable figure never was seen than that Maguire generally represented. His linen and clothes were grimy and shabby, and he wore a battered old hat which generally bore about it evidence of having recently come in contact with mother earth. My friend used to invite Maguire occasionally to his house and try and lead him into better courses, but any improvement was but temporary.

On the evening of the dinner party, and just as the cloth was removed and the wine was being passed round, we were all disconcerted by Maguire opening the door and rushing up to our host. "Me boy" said the doctor stretching out both hands and then grasping a chair so as to steady himself. "Ah! ye mean divil, to forget poor Mike Maguire " when ye invited your friends."

"Dr. Maguire"—our host had risen from his chair—"you must really excuse me."

"Faix and since ye apologize for the omission, Mike Maguire's not the boy to bear malice, and by token——"

"But I must beg—"

"Whist man! not another word; tell them to bring me a chair and—ah! here's a glass and begorra I'll make up for lost time."

"Dr. Maguire, your conduct—"

"Me conduct is it ye want to make remarks on? I'd

let ye know"—and here the doctor drew himself up, but unluckily his eye fell on the very disgusted Sir Utterly Utter. "What!" he called out, "Botts! old cock, Botts!"

"My name, sir, said the Baronet, "is not Botts. I am called Utter, Utterly Utter."

"And a d——d ugly name it is too" said Maguire, "but it suits your appearance to a T. D'ye know ye're very like Botts, jest the same white face."

By this time our host had got two or three of us to assist in removing the wretched intruder; he was escorted to the door and consigned to the care of the servants with orders to have him put off the premises.

When we resumed our seats our host began to offer some apology to Sir Utterly, who, we could all see, was boiling with rage. Just as our host was stammering out a few conciliatory words, the door opened quietly and Maguire, putting in his head, yelled out—"By all the powers ye're the image of Botts."

We all burst out laughing, save Sir U. U., who rose from his chair, trembling with indignation. The doctor was dragged back by the servants, and some of us followed to see the wretched fellow put on his pony and started off.

The serjeant of police was sent for and asked to have the doctor conducted home. But the evening's entertainment was done for, and conversation was at an end. We had all of us great difficulty, whenever we looked at Sir U., in repressing a laugh, and, ultimately, that worthy made some excuse and went to his room. Before he left us, however, and as we were standing in the gallery upstairs bidding him good night, we heard people passing behind the garden hedge and saw the doctor with the serjeant riding homewards. He was arguing away, and still insisting that if it wasn't Botts, or Botts' ghost, it was very like Botts.

A CARELESS POSTMAN.

OUR parish church in Barataria was an unpretending building, perched on a knoll at the back of a town or village, whichever title you chose to give to a collection of houses, some of brick or stone, and others wooden, which clustered between the hills and the sea. It had, like most West Indian towns, seen better days, and boasted of a parade ground which, at the time I speak of, was only used for cricket, and pasturing skinny goats and gaunt sheep. Along the bay could still be seen the half sunken, tumble down walls of the old barracks and fort; and in the sand a half dozen old, red, and rusty 32-pounders lay like some stranded monsters of the deep. We used to come round of a Sunday evening in our canoes when it was moonlight, and go to church. It was very enjoyable pulling under the shadow of the cliffs that rose perpendicularly out of the sea, and which in the daytime were seen to be striped with variegated strata, and bedecked with long pendant plants and vines, with here and there a white flowered frangipanni tree, or a tall carata standing sentinel-like at some cranny in the face of the rock; but the moonlight reduced all these varied tints to grey and white. The water as it lapped against the rocks, or went swirling from the oars, sparkled and flashed as if its drops were diamonds. Then, as the canoe emerged from the shelter of the cliff, it would glide across some tiny bay with its fringe of sandy beach and dark back ground of wooded hills,—a fresh scene lit up with all the glory of the moonlight one sees nowhere but in the tropics. The parson was a hard working zealous man, whose untiring industry commanded respect even if we did not always accept his doctrines or his ritual. He always had on hand some obscure saint who required celebrating, and he confessed people at any hour. His services were very frequent, and so sometimes he, as it were, got hard up for a subject, and then preached a sermon either below par, or one unsuited to the bulk of his congregation, who were chiefly of the peasant class. One night he preached about guardian angels—dear me! How earnestly he did impress upon us that there were these angels around, and near us at all times, as if any one doubted it. Then he quoted from some book a long story about a postman, who used to cross Dartmoor, or some other moor in England, alone at all hours of the day or night, and who, when asked by his priest if he were not afraid, said "No; that he used to sit down beneath a particular rock on the moor, when his guardian angel would sit alongside of him and the two would sing hymns till he was refreshed, and then he would continue his tramp." It was very pretty, and, I daresay, true that some postman had said so, but when on our way home, I asked Solomon Sam, my stroke oar, what he thought of the sermon, he replied, "De discoorse berry good me massa, but da postman wha carry de letta and dem, and 'top in de way wid de hangel fo' sing hymn, he muss ha' been drunk, else he see jumbie. I speck he get in trubble 'bout dem self letta."

SPOTTING HER!

CREOLES have a lazy habit, which, indeed Europeans after a short residence in the West Indies acquire, of using a peculiar sound which can be produced by saying M (slowly) with the lips closed, to signify, according to the inflection, assent or dissent, surprise, &c., &c. A gentleman and lady were purchasing some articles in a London draper's shop, and the lady asked for "netting." The shopman shewed a variety of such goods but none satisfied her. He then asked if there was anything else he could shew her. The lady in reply shook her head, also using the sound of negation above mentioned. "Oh!" said the man, "you wanted mosquito netting?" "How do you find that out?" asked the gentleman. "The way the lady answered me told me she comes from the West Indies," was the reply, "and I wasn't four years in Berbice without knowing what mosquito nets are."

A NEW APPLICATION OF AN OLD TEXT.

"WHAT went ye out for to see?" is, of course, a very common text. In Barataria we had a very worthy, but rather eccentric parson, who had charge of a parish in the hills. One of the churches he served was a small edifice perched on an elevation beside the road, with its enclosure marked by dragon's blood bushes, and a clump or two of bamboos. It was not too much frequented; the people round about belonged to another denomination, and the Reverend Charles Chaunter was a good deal disheartened at having on some Sundays to preach to half-a-dozen listless inattentive hearers.

But one fine day the Reverend gentleman took unto him a wife, and combining duty with pleasure, he spent his honeymoon at a place not far from St. Swithin's. That part of Barataria, by the way, had a wonderful rainfall. Well, the first Sunday after his wedding, the little church, contrary to custom was filled to the doors; and poor Mrs. Chaunter was the subject of every one's remarks, and the object of everybody's stare. The Reverend Charles gave out as his text the words above quoted, and then said, "I'll tell you what ye have come out for to see,—my wife, Mrs. Chaunter;—there she is in that pew and when you have done looking at her perhaps you'll attend to me." With a less unsophisticated congregation, this would probably have called forth a titter, but Chaunter knew his people, and with a scarcely suppressed "Yes me massa" they all turned their attention to him.

AN UNKNOWN TITLE.

IT is said that a young man designed for the ministry once came out to Barbados, and, having called at Bishop's Court, received a very kind letter, signed "T. Barbados," inviting him to call on the writer, and that the poor lad went about asking the waiters at the hotel if they knew where "T. Barbados lived." This may or may not be true.

A GOOD EXCUSE.

As you come down the hill at St. Molasses and enter the town, you pass a house with white walls and a little enclosure in front of it, where grow, or grew, a few rose bushes, and the palings of which were covered with flowering creepers.

It was in, as it were, a nook and somewhat out of the track of travellers who rode or walked in a very intermittent way to or from the little town.

A very worthy old Scotch parson lived there with his wife. They were rather a frugal couple, and a good many jokes used to be told at their expense, and rumour said that the Revd. Angus was put on an allowance of stimulants, which his better half never allowed him to exceed.

One evening just at sunset, I came in from a rather long walk, and met the old man pacing up and down before his house with his hands folded behind him and his head bent as if in meditation.

"Good evening" said I, raising my hat.

"Ah! Good evening to ye, Mr. Beke. Good evening, ha'e ye been far?"

"Only as far as —— "

"Eh! but ye'll be dry after such a walk as that, wull you come in and ha'e a glass?"

"No, thank you."

"It'll do ye good. It is very little I tak' myself, and ane too often sees the ill effects of over indulgence, but jist a drap after your walk, and when you're heated."

"I am much obliged but —— "

"It's bad to get a chill, ye ken, Mr. Beke, and ye must be careful—come up noo."

"Really," I begun, "if you will excuse me —— "

"Well, betwixt the twa o' us, it'll be doin' me a kindness if ye wull. I am feelin' mysel' as if a drap would do me good, but Mrs. McKenzie—weel it's only when a body calls in that I get a chance, so I beg o' you come —— "

I yielded, and it was amusing to remark the half shy way in which old Angus mentioned to his wife that he had asked me in to have a glass because I looked fagged, &c., and the keen look of his wife that told me the excuse was rather "thin,"—worn thread-bare I expect. However Angus joined me and had a "fleeting pleasure."

NOTHING LIKE PRINCIPLE.

IT was "earthquake weather," not a brêath of wind, a cloudless sky and a burning blistering sun; there was no shade in the market square of St. Maria in which my office was situated; a few parched red leaves still appeared on the almond trees and the silk cottons were bare. Above the low brick work of some of the houses, the atmosphere flickered and waved as it does over a heated boiler. The fruit and cake sellers had removed their trays to the shade under the galleries, and men on the opposite side to the ice house paused and faltered before crossing that fiery square, even though ice and thirst-relieving compounds lay on the other side. My work was over for the day, and it was my hour for going home, but I dawdled about as if something would occur to render the heat less oppressive, and while thus waiting, who should come in sight, making for my den, but Simpson.

Simpson?—He was a country magistrate; most people knew but little of him, he was retiring, and entertained but rarely, but I had seen a good deal of him and I rather believed in Simpson. Of late he had become a temperance man, not a teetotaller or Good Templar, but he was always preaching about fellows taking drinks too often. Spirits he condemned in toto, and laid down for every one a sort of drink-by-rule plan which he said he stuck to; he had the profoundest contempt for a man who could not keep to rules, nothing, he used to say, is so despicable as a man who makes a rule only to break it, &c., &c. As I said before, I admired Simpson, and it was for this perhaps, because I—if I have a fault—am too prone to yield to others, and I used to set up Simpson as a model, a man with a principle (with a big P) that he ever lived up to, never swerved from.

He had come to me on business that did not keep us long; he would not dine with me as he had another engagement. "Would he come and have a cocktail?" I asked this because I wanted to be able to say I had tried and proved Simpson.

"You know I never take anything."

"Yes, but it's an awfully hot day, and one will do you good."

"There's gin or some other spirit in a cocktail and I never—"

"I know, but I'm going over, won't you come?"

"Well I'll go with you, but don't ask me to drink."

And then we sauntered to the ice house. It was a small bar with no very great accommodation or variety of temptations. A small black boy was the presiding genius, and he had been taught how to compound some of the best known drinks.

It would take too long to tell how I seduced Simpson into confessing he *would* take something; it *was* hot, unusually hot, and there *were* occasions where a man *was* justified in departing from a rule when considerations of health, &c., rendered a strict adherence to it unadvisable. Pride in my powers of persuasion tempered the regret I felt at finding that Simpson was but human, and at length, Joe, who was awaiting the close of our discussion, at which he seemed somewhat amused, was told to make two cocktails.

"Very little gin in mine" said Simpson; "perhaps it would be better without any, eh?"

"Mass Simpson, me nebber make cocktail without foundashin, Sah, gin, or rum, or brandy."

"Very well then," sighed Simpson like a martyr, "only, not much, you know Joe, not much, you know."

"Yes me know, Mass Simpson."

Simpson and I took our cocktails, looked at each other, turned up our little fingers perpendicular to the axis of our glasses, nodded, said "here's luck;" went, in short, through the absurd "drink exercise" and down went the cockstails.

"Ah!" said Simpson, putting down his glass and feeling in his pocket, "no doubt it's very nice, but I do hate breaking through a principle. What's to pay, boy?"

"No," said I, "that's my business." So we squabbled over who was to pay and then decided on tossing. "Tails" said Simpson. "Heads" said I, and heads it was.

"Well, boy?" enquired Simpson.

"A shillin', Sah; and the two brandies and sodys you had last night and a co'pse revivah dis marning and anodder brandy and sody, will make———"

I did not look at Simpson! We left the temple of Bacchus. Somehow, we neither were inclined for conversation. Since then I have thought doubtingly, regretfully, that *perhaps* Simpson might be, after all, the humbug other men said he was.

THE GOOD OLD DAYS!

WE have all heard of the young West Indian heiress, who, on succeeding to her property, was applied to by her Attorney for instructions about the cultivation of her estate, and who directed him to take out all those troublesome canes and cultivate the land for a crop of guava jelly.

There was another damsel of a more practical turn of mind, who, in the good (or bad) old days, owned several slaves. Her agent wrote to tell her of one old fellow who had bad legs which defied all treatment, and as he was unsaleable, he was a source of expense and loss to the estate. He presumed he must be kept on until either he got better or died. But the proprietress, with a shrewd eye to profit, wrote back to have the man's legs amputated, and to teach him tailoring!

SUSCEPTIBLE HENS.

ALTHOUGH these yarns are amusing, or intended so to be, I think it not improper to add to them one anecdote of a scientific character; because it shews either the extraordinary effects of thermal influences on the susceptibility of the females of the *gallus vulgaris* kind, in other words, of hot weather on a hen, or else the fertility in excuses of the elderly black woman.

I once was in a small island, of which the food products were very scanty in number, and poor in quality, consisting chiefly of conchs, ground corn, pigs (very gaunt and sickly), fowls of a degenerate breed, and eggs.

As an adjunct to my breakfast one morning I chose as the safest food, eggs. Could I have any?

"Oh yes, me massa," replied the old woman who had charge of the 'great house' of the estate of which I had the temporary use, "how much you does want?"

I said two, but she brought four, "poached" as she called it, but in reality still in their shells at the bottom of a bowl of hot water.

I was not well, and I cared for none of the other things, potted this and tinned that, which I had brought with me, and I turned gladly to the eggs, but—No. 1 was not fresh;

No. 2 was very stale;

No. 3, well—smelt—;

No. 4 seemed to contain a sample (for analysis) of Demerara lees.

I called the old lady, who came with a smile.

"Woman!" said I, striving to keep down my wrath and—well other things besides—"woman these eggs are bad! stale! old!!"

"Me massa if you choose to believe me, dey was all lay dis morning, ebbery one."

"This morning? impossible! Look at them! Smell them! Taste them! Don't tell me a falsehood—"

"Oh me massa! you don't member how hot de wedder be! de sun so hot dis time, de fowl does lay their egg so; they can't help—"

The reply rather staggered me; I can't say I was satisfied; but yet it may be worth recording as a possible truth, worthy of investigation.

OBEAH.

WHEN Mrs. ——— came to stay with us she brought her maid, a black girl some 22 years of age. One day on my return home, I was informed that "Blossom," the girl in question, was in deep distress, because Wellington (my groom) had "obeahed" her.

Now, obeah, pure and simple, and unaccompanied with the administration of poison, only does harm by affecting the imagination; but the negro who believes that obeah has been worked against him, often pines away from sheer fright.

Sometimes he has recourse to some obeah practitioner who undertakes to counteract the evil, and when the patient believes this has been done, he recovers. The mere punishment of a detected obeahman by a magistrate does the victim of the fraud no good; the law cannot undo the mischief.

I interviewed "Blossom" who was in a terrible state of agitation, trembling like a leaf. Wellington had got some of her hair and wore it round his waist and was working obeah for her. "He want for marry me, but me no want him."

I rode off to the stables where I found Mr. Wellington. I made him stoop on some pretext, when his jersey rose up, and round his waist I saw a string with "bobs" of wool,—Blossom's hair, tied at intervals. I collared the fellow and sent for Blossom; told her to bring me a white handled razor, and made her cut off the string, because I informed her only an unmarried person must do that. She followed my directions, but her hand trembled and Wellington wriggled so that he narrowly escaped a slash. We then formed a small procession to the house, the girl carrying the string with outstretched arm. A coal pot was brought and the magic cord and hair duly burned. Wellington, however, still protesting his innocence, a bottle of ether was brought by Blossom and was dubbed, after the Chinese method, "lie water." Wellington agreed with much hesitation to the ordeal, and Blossom poured what was intended to be a few drops, but what her trembling hand caused to be near a spoonful on Wellington's extended tongue;—a yell, as he dashed from my side, followed, and the last

I saw of Wellington for many months was my gentleman bounding like a deer through the guinea grass. He spread my fame as a head obeahman, and Blossom recovered her spirits and health. It afterwards occurred to me that I had been practising "an occult art" and had rendered myself liable to fine or imprisonment.

These obeahmen are often called upon by those who should know better, to assist in recovering stolen property, and persons too, whose education should have taught them better, often stand in dread of these practitioners. A clergyman once applied for a warrant against one Archie Sam, who, to a legitimate business as cooper, no doubt added that of obeah doctor.

I asked what was the offence—and the circumstances.

It turned out that the reverend gentleman had gone down the coast the previous Sunday to officiate at a church usually served by his curate. On his arrival, he ran against Mr. Archie Sam who lived in a different part of the island. Just before ascending the pulpit, the rector took a glass of water from a "goglet" in the vestry room, and shortly after commencing his sermon was attacked by a feeling of dizziness, which, however, soon passed off.

I explained that I did not see how anything could be charged against Archie, but Mr. ——— got very angry, and said there were the facts of the appearance of the obeahman in the village far from his home—and the unusual effect of the glass of water; for his part he thought the case was clear.

I differed, and declined to issue a warrant. The rector

complained to the governor, who reported the circumstances to the bishop, from whom the parson received an admonition, *vulgò*, a wigging.

The materials used are of various kinds—bone, needles tied crosswise with black thread and rubbed with tallow, nails, wire, coals, salt, a looking-glass, cards, and earth from a grave. There is nothing which may not be employed. In the incantations, a white cock, and, of course, rum, are indispensable. I knew an old fool who was cheated out of all his earnings, and ultimately out of his house and home, by a rascal who assured him there was much hidden treasure in his garden, and, who drew heavily on him for the materials necessary for its discovery.

The practice of obeah was kept up in many places by men of the W. I. regiments who were recruited in Africa, and, who, on being pensioned, added to their means by setting up as obeahmen.

I remember several years ago, a rascal being brought before me charged with practising obeah. The police corporal, however, who was somewhat hasty and premature, had arrested the man before he had actually done any act which constituted that offence.

The prisoner was an important character, as he was firmly believed in by the country people, and I felt that his acquittal would be considered as a striking instance of his powers rather than as the result of the corporal's precipitancy.

I could not convict him, but I determined he should not go scot free. Pointing to a small bag he wore suspended from his neck by a dirty cord, I asked him what was in it?

"No harm, me washup, it only one ting I does wear fo' keep away pain."

I insisted on its being taken off his neck and placed on the table, and ordered the fellow to open it. This he refused to do.

A group of the townspeople had edged up to my table, every one of whom had been repudiating all belief in obeah, and in undertones expressing wonder how anybody could be so foolish "as believe in such a thing." To one of these gentry who was a churchwarden, and in some respects a well educated man, I handed one of the prisoner's razors with a request that he would cut open the little packet. A very decided "no" was the result, and so with each of the non-believers who shrank back from the mysterious oddments spread before me. In the end I cut it open myself, and, as I expected, found it filled with earth probably taken from a grave.

"What is this stuff?" I asked the obeahman.

"Dat no harm, Sah, he no poison."

"Then," said I, "you will eat it."

"Eat it my washup?"

"Yes, eat it up—you say it is no harm."

"Me eat it?"

"Yes, eat it up."

I shall never forget the man's face as I fixed my eyes on his and uttered these words. I subsequently found that he had been told I was a chief obeahman, and whether he fancied my powers were real and greater than his I do not know, but gazing steadily at me, he began to tremble, and, eventually stretching out his hand, grasped the bag, which he then raised very slowly from the table. "Eat it up," I repeated.

By degrees he raised it to his lips, and placing the contents between his lips, he swallowed them.

As he finished I said "Now be off; if ever you return to this district you shall be severely punished."

I waved my hand to him, and, darting through the door, he made his exit. I have since heard that he still lives, and that the above occurrence has been handed down to present times, when small boys delight in dubbing the obeahman, "Eat it up."

VERY IMPROPER!

"DRY goods stores" (*anglicè*, drapers' shops) in the West Indies are almost invariably conducted by shopmen, or clerks as they are called. A woman behind the counter is almost unknown. I remember a grave official going to a store where, contrary to custom, a dark lady was employed and a very dignified, not to say severe, looking damsel she was. The honourable Mr. Dray purchased some handkerchiefs and, then, referring to a memorandum, said, "And now I want to look at your stockings."

"Mistah Dray, sah! you are rude, and your language is most impraper. Dis young man will serve you, sir." And off she bounced before my friend could explain or apologize.

CREOLE WHALERS.

THERE is, or was, every year a large number of American whaling schooners visiting Dominica and St. Vincent, Grenada and other Islands, where the catch at times is very remunerative. At Dominica they lay in their stock of vegetables preparatory to cruising about. The boat hands are also recruited from young creoles of the different islands, as they all row well, and can stand exposure to the sun better than the Yankee.

A good number of these lads continue in the vessels till they return to Massachusetts, and thence they ship for various parts. In time they come home, wonderfully improved by having had to work hard, and being under discipline. Food too of a better kind than the yam and salt fish of their native place has produced good results, and it is difficult to recognise in a strong muscular sailor well clad, the owner of a huge pair of boots, and his speech strongly marked with the Yankee accent, the thin-legged ragged, ill-nurtured lad, one's boatman or fisherman of the previous year or so.

I once heard two of these men talking of their respective skippers, both of whom had been drowned.

"We lost our Captain," said one, "Captain Ezekiel T. Jones, off Dominica; he fell overboard trying to clear a line we had out. We got his body, and the mate he headed it up in *ile* to take home to his widow. He was a good man, Captain Jones was."

"Ah,' said the other, "when I was in the Nancy Bell, our Captain, Hosea Bell, he got in a row ashore at Cariacou, and he must have got a lick on the head or something, for he died aboard three days after, ravin' mad. We headed him up in *sperm* though for he was a good Captain to us.

It is to be supposed that the more precious sperm was used as a greater compliment.

One of these sailor lads, as black as your boots, was very fond of telling his adventures in New York and London. He always declared that "niggers" were the worst-treated people in New York, except Irishmen, and that in London every one was kind and considerate. He had been an inmate of some Sailors' Home, the comforts of which he thoroughly appreciated, but the chief charm of the institution lay in his having had a white man at his beck and call. "Yes buddy! they only charge me four dollar a week and you get lodging and board, and more-over when I been there, sposin' I choose, I only got to ring a bell and dey send me up a white man, a parson too, wid black coat and white tie, all regular for read de scripture to me, and every time I want him he force fo' come, and all for the four dollar! De way dat parson read all troo Rebbelashuns to me was fuss' rate."

VERA SATEERICAL.

I was cantering home along a flat, that was the prelude to a long, weary, scramble up a mountain road, to be followed by a slide and slither sort of progress down hill till I reached my home. It was a threatening evening. As I entered the ravine through which Her Majesty's high road ran, the clouds gathered overhead, and seemed to shut one in. Then began a patter of rain, but the sound of a horse's hoofs was heard, and my friend, McPherson, coming up with me, told me I must come in with him. His gates were but a few yards further on, and one glance overhead at the impending storm decided the matter. In a few moments we were safely housed, when down came the torrent; the wind howled and whistled through the narrow valley. The cocoanut palms bent and swayed to the blast. Leaves were driven here and there, and the silvery foliage of the trumpet trees *(cecropia)* fluttered and flashed as they were twisted and torn by the gale. The storm was sudden, and heavy doors and shutters banged and jarred before they could be secured. Then came a sudden silence, soon broken by the sullen roar of the mountain stream which, often insufficient to turn my friend's mill wheel, was now boiling with foam and leaping over boulders and all obstacles in its hurry to reach the sea. Yes, I had a drink—perhaps there was something of a Pagan spirit that half led us to consider it a libation to the storm god, for as we took it—"it" was a cocktail compounded by McPherson's own cunning hand—we both remarked, "It's a bad night." We had dinner, and Mrs. McPherson being in town, we were alone; and pipes and whisky, with a sample of very old rum, were put on the table. Then there was a fresh down-pour, and a gust or succession of gusts that bid fair to strip every shingle off the old house, and the river roared as if trying to drown all other sounds.

"Ye can't get hame the nicht," said McPherson,

"and the wife 'll no' expect ye, so mak' yerself easy, man, and licht yer pipe."

McPherson's first statement was evidently true, and his advice was judicious. I agreed to stay and, in token thereof, exchanged my boots for a pair of slippers and my coat for one of my host's jackets. McPherson had been in the colony many years; he came as an overseer, had risen to be manager and attorney, and thence the transition to proprietor is, or was, not difficult. I don't think he had ever been home since his arrival, and his memories of his native land dated back, at least, a third of a century. He used to talk of events and people, most of us had never heard of, or if so, had forgotten. In early youth he had been a great hunter, and the tales he told of deer-stalking might have been interesting to any who had ever joined in that noble sport, but to us they had lost, indeed never possessed, any savour. But McPherson was great at personal anecdote. His memory was at times defective, but he never hesitated to break into any conversation with an account of the doings or sayings of some Scottish or West Indian worthy. He was in his glory when he found some one to whom his best stories were unknown, and on the evening in question, he had found such an one in me.

"Ye kenned auld John Christie Grant who was ance proprietor of "half of this estate, Mr. Beke?"

"No, it was before my time, I came here in 18— only———"

"Ye're richt. John Christie Grant died um——— let me see, somewhere about———ah weel, say, sax years before ye cam'; he was a wonderfu' man?"

"Indeed?"

"Aye, as shairp a man in conversation as ye'd meet in a lang day's march; and McKenzie that owned the other half of the estate—mebbe ye dinna ken McKenzie? Weel he was as guid at repairtee. Eh man, when they'd get ding donging in the verbal contest, it was a treat."

"I mind," said McPherson filling his pipe, "a remairkable instance of the power of repairtee that Grant and also McKenzie had, that occurred in this vary house. Fill yer glaiss mon—the nicht's damp. Eh! It was graun' the cool cuttin' way in which Grant gied back the word to McKenzie who felt it. It was jest like a sword thrust, clean and direct. I'll tell you aboot it. McKenzie, he was the third son of Kenneth McKenzie of the Rowans in Argyllshire, and had been Captain in the 21st—no, the 26th—Can ye say which regiment were the Cameronians? Ah weel, it makes nae maitter, but I am nearly positive it was the 26th; I should say the 21st if it was na the—but it's no maitter, weel say the 26th. Weel, McKenzie had married Grant's sister, or it would be mair correct to say his half sister, for Grant's mither had died jest after her husband (he was a Captain in the navy) had come hame from the East Indies, and he aifterwards married Dean Murray's dochter, Mary, wha bore him twa sons that died airly o' measles and whooping cough, I think it was the eldest that had the cough, but I'm no certain, and she had also a dochter ca'ed Jean, after the Dean's auld sister Jean Murray, that I meeself remember; but anyhoo she married McKenzie, and it was thocht a guid match. Weel, Sir, strange things come aboot, and McKenzie cam' out here to speer about the estate that, owing to seercumstances, hadna been makin' the lairge profits he expected; but ye ken, Mr. Beke, it's a far deeferent thing noo a days, or for a matter o' that at the time when McKenzie cam' to what it is now. Why dy'e ken that last mail I got account of sales of sugars———"

Here, I confess, I lost the thread of McPherson's discourse, but the wind had blown out one candle and its fellow had been placed where it did not shed its light on me, and so my having fallen asleep was unnoticed. When I awoke the clock shewed I had slept half an hour, and McPherson was still going on with his story, the point of which I should have been sorry to miss.

"I was saying," went on McPherson, "that in this way Grant and McKenzie met here in this vara room, and McKenzie was getting a little warm over the discussion I was telling ye of, and he said, I think, as shairp a thing as ae man could say to anither. He said, said he, 'Grant,' said he, 'Grant'—Eh! Well, well, now that's strange. What were the words he used noo? Slipped clean from me. Grant—I should say McKenzie—said; but! but! weel it's no much maitter, because, as I told ye, it was *Grant's* reply that was so guid. 'McKenzie,' said he; getting up from his chair, and his eyes bright like wi' fun and mischief; 'McKenzie,' said he; it was Grant ye understand, wha said it. 'McKenzie, I beg'—eh, noo that's wonderful—I canna at the moment ca' to mind what it was that Grant said, but, anyhoo I can assure ye it was *vera sateerical.* Mebbe, I'll recollect in the morning. Ye winna fill up your glass! ah, weel, yon's your room."

I went to bed and next morning started early. McPherson saw me off and cheered me as I left with the promise that if he minded "what were the preceese words McKenzie used to Grant—no, that Grant used to McKenzie, he would let me know."

But he never did.

A SPOILT INQUEST.

MY wife and I started one lovely morning on what we hoped would be a pleasant excursion. We were to ride over to some friends at Paul's Prospect, whence I proposed to go to hold court at Queenstown, returning to our friends for the rest of the day and then riding home by moonlight. It was in fulfilment of a long standing promise and we set off in high glee. However, on entering a village that lay midway in our journey and where there was a police barrack, I was met by a constable who informed me that an inquest had to be held on one Mingo Bacchus, an old reprobate whose setting his house on fire when he was drunk, had been reported to me some days before. He had received severe burns in the fire, and had died of the injuries early that morning.

This was a duty which could not be avoided nor indeed postponed. I arranged therefore to accompany my wife to Paul's Prospect, to ride on and hold court, and then come straight back to the inquest,—Mrs. Beke would ride over later to join me, and we would return home earlier than we had anticipated doing.

As arranged, so it was done. In no pleased frame of mind I got through my court work, dropped in at Paul's Prospect for a hasty lunch, and then cantered back to the Police barracks. On pulling up at the barrack gate, the sergeant, a fine old fellow with a head of hair that stood up and around about like crystallized soap suds, came out with a downcast air and observed:—

"I beg pardon, sah, but these negurs are too scheming—too deceitful, sah."

"What!—Where's the jury?"

"Excuse me, sah, but that fellow Mingo Barkus, sah, he fool me too bad—"

"All right" said I, thinking this had reference to some old squabble. Where's the body?"

"Body, sah? please hear me. This morning me go in Mingo house, as I go ebbery morning; he lay in he bed and me say Barkus! Barkus! but he no say nuffin, so I go and dere he be on he back, for he eye shut and mouff drop, and so me say once more time 'Mingo Barkus—in the name of de Queen is you live or is you dead?'—he no say nuffin, so me liff he hand and he let him drop, bam! den me shake um, and shake um, but he nebber 'tir, so me say Barkus dead for true, and me send call you, sah—"

"Very well, sergeant, let some one take my horse and I will swear in the jury—"

"But, sah, please hear me more. After you come and go away and me go in Barkus house, me see um sit up in he bed. "Mr. Barkus, says I, eh! eh! what dis conduck?—spose you know you has to be sat upon by his washup and de jury duly sworn strickly to enquire the cause of your de't; and Barkus, the out-lawded raskil, he begin for laff. He say, 'Me gad! sargin,' eh-berry day you come look on poor Barkus and gib' me sweet mout' and say, 'You is better to-day Barkus?' and eh-berry ebening de same ting. Sargin', you does weary me wid you quesshun and so me say me fool you, so dis morning, me———'"

"Then," I interrupted, "he is not dead?"

"No, your washup."

"Bother it," said I, "you should be more careful. I cannot ride over to Paul's Prospect, it's five miles, and I must wait here till Mrs. Beke comes." However, I lit my pipe and killed time till my wife arrived, and then we went home.

A week after, one Sunday, we saw the sergeant riding a small pony up the avenue of palms that led to our house. He dismounted, hitched up his animal, passed his fingers through his woolly hair, pulled his collar up and his tunic down, and then marched up to our porch where we were seated.

A salute in the sergeant's best manner, and "a good evening your washup" followed.

"Well! sergeant, and what brings you here?"

"Got him at last, sah, got him, sah!"

"Got whom?"

"No sham dis time, washup; he dead for true!"

"Who is dead:"

"Dat scheming outlawded fellah, Mingo Barkus, sah! me find um 'tretch out on he bed, and at first I tink he go for play he ole gáme, but he dead; howsever, for make sure, me bite he toe and he lilly fingah, and me put lighted match under he nose and me 'cratch he two eye ball, but he 'top 'till, and me say he dead and me come tell you."

"So the sergeant had some refreshment, and next day I "sat upon Mingo Bacchus."

NO TAILOR.

A GOOD many years ago there lived in Barbados a General Haynes, whose state-garb included a puce or claret-coloured coat. He was a well-known and much respected character.

A Barbadian planter went to England about that time, and, as is usual with new arrivals, desired a fresh "rig out," and with this view he took himself, when in London, to some West End tailor, the Poole of the day.

"I want ye to make a co-att."

"Certainly, sir; what style?"

"Well, look heär, ye know General Hay-uns down in St. Philip's?"

"No, sir, I can't say I have the honour of the General's custom."

"Well, I want a co-att like he own."

"What sort of a coat, sir, does the General wear?"

"It's the colour of a yam 'prout."

"I beg pardon, sir, *what* colour?"

"I tell ye, the colour of a yam 'prout."

"What colour is that, sir?"

"Well! well! me fâäther; if you doant know General Hay-uns, neither the colour of a yam 'prout, ye cannot be much of a tailor, and so I wish you good day-ah!" And the customer departed.

PAY NO OBJECT.

THE manager and I were in the gallery, we had finished breakfast and commenced our pipes. The weather was propitious, canes yielding splendidly, juice hardly wanted boiling to become sugar, attorney was satisfied, and prices had gone up with a rush.

Then there appeared a long, lanky figure walking slowly up toward the house; a stranger evidently; who could he be? The manager called for a telescope, but the boy had retired with the balance of the breakfast, and so before we could make the enemy out, the enemy was down on us.

He was tall and lean, as the medical men say, not well nourished; his hair was long and sandy, and his eyes a steel blue; his complexion was motley with a shake of the freckle castor over it; and his clothes, his boots especially, had seen better days. Off went his hat as he came up the steps.

"Morning, gentlemen!"

"Morning."

"Whilk i the twa 'll be the manager?"

"I," replied my friend (I think though, he said "me.")

"I'm in search of a situation, sir, aiblins ye ha'e a vacancy?"

"Well, as it happens, I have not."

"I'm sorry, but may be you'd tak' me on till there is ane?"

"Really, I have no work for another overseer."

"Still, ye ken, I micht be o' use as a suppernummery. I've just come ower frae St. Sinner's, whare I could na keep my health."

"I'm very sorry, but I cannot engage you."

"Ef it's the sailary ye're thinking o'——"

"My good sir," said the manager, "I have no vacancy and could not take in another overseer to pay him."

"I'd no look for pay."

"What d'ye mean? You could not do without your pay I presume."

"Indeed, yes; ef ye'll let me come on the estate I'd mak' mysel' usefu' and I'd no require ony wages."

"Why how could you?"

"Ye'll excuse me, sir, but on a big estate like o' this, there's plenty o' orra things aboot, and I'd be aye pickin' up something till ye fund it convenient to allot me a sailary!"

I protest if I had been the manager I would have hired the fellow, but my friend waxed angry, and the stranger left hurriedly, and we soon saw him stalking along with a hopeful air in the direction of the next estate.

LIQUID MEASURE.

THE chapel of St. Dunder cum Lees was built by a pious planter in the island of St. Molasses and was served (I believe that's the correct term) by one of the curates of Saint Centrifugal. There was one of the latter clergymen who was above vulgar prejudices and took his liquor not wisely but too well. It was a long up and down hill ride to St. Dunder cum Lees, and exhausted nature required to be recuperated, and so the Rev. Bibulous Absorbent arranged with an old dame who lived hard by the chapel that he might have a long drink of brandy and water at the end of his ride. The Rev. B. A. at first supplied the liquor, but he thought it went faster than it should, and finally, in defiance of excise laws, agreed to pay for his drinks as he had them.

"One Sabbath evening it had come on suddenly to rain, and the rev. gentleman was wet and weary; he alighted at Mrs. Brutus's cottage and went in.

"Eh, me fader! parson! me no tink you a come dis wet day."

"Well, Mrs. Brutus, the rain overtook me and I have got a chill, however oblige me with a little brandy."

"Reverence, me too sorry; but one wutless hog run troo de house and capsize de butler tray with all me ware, and me glass and ebberry ting 'mash up, and me no got one tumbler self."

"Never mind, I can drink from the bottle Mrs. Brutus; wet as I am, it will perhaps be best without water."

"Berry well, my reverence; look de bottle."

And his reverence drank, throwing back his head.

"Ah," said he, handing the bottle to Mrs. Brutus, "these things are given us for our good."

"Yes, me massah."

"And it is only wicked sinful men who abuse them."

"Yes, me reverence."

"Here Mrs. Brutus is the 'ten dog' (sixpence). Short reckoning makes long friends you know."

"Dat for troo, Mr. Sorbint, but it's a shillin' dis time."

"Why? Mrs. Brutus, it is only 6d. a drink you know, and I paid you last time."

"Eh, eh! massa, me no a watch dem two long ting you got nex' for you troat."

"You mean my bands?"

"Yes sah, and me watch good and me see dem band go wabble twice, so me know you a take two swaller and dat a shillin'."

And the Reverend Bibulous stumped up.

"GRASS AND RUM."

DUTY, and one of H. M. Ships on the station, once took me to St. Sangarée. We arrived there early in the morning, and as we steamed slowly under the lee of the island we saw fluttering from the signal post, the flag which informed the world of St. Sangaree that "man-o'-war 'teamer a come."

The anchor was not dropped, as H.M.S. "Leda" was bound elsewhere, and so she waited until the Harbour Master came off. Things are, or were, done in a leisurely fashion in that romantic isle, and it was half an hour before a functionary in a seedy-blue coat and battered Panama hat came alongside in a boat, which, in spite of the two-thirds of a Union Jack over its stern, looked as if its usual employment was to carry sugar barrels, instead of doing duty as Harbour Master's gig.

After the usual parley, and bidding my friends adieu, I got into this very substantial craft and reached the shore. The population of St. Sangaree was represented by three urchins and a policeman. In time I found a hospitable friend and after breakfast reported myself to the "powers that be."

A day or two after I went on business across the island, and a very delightful ride it was. A bridle path led through the woods, sometimes up sharp ridges, at others down slippery gulleys, but the varied foliage and lovely scenery which met one's view made up for any fatigue.

As I got to what were the back lands of the estates on the other side, my horse, or rather pony, got an awkward wrench of the fetlock and went dead lame. I had already walked down hill leading him, but now the animal's progress was very slow, and it seemed as if I should not reach my destination before dark. However I plodded on, and by degrees reached what had evidently once been cultivated land, although now overgrown with trees of recent growth, interspersed with tall coffee trees of considerable age; then we came to provision grounds, where no one was to be seen, and after an hour's progress I saw, welcome sight! a house before me. As I approached the gate, one half of which had became detached from the post, an old man came out and asked where I was going?

He was about sixty years old, with long white hair and a very ruddy face, due, as it struck me, less to exposure to the sun than to internal applications. His enquiry was in a polite tone, and I explained matters.

"You cannot reach P——— to-night. Allow me to offer you a shelter here. Rest your horse and continue your journey in the morning." While I was hesitating the old gentleman called "Joe" and gave my pony into his care,—telling him to rub the lame leg with "high wines" and bandage it,—and then my host led the way to his house.

It was, or rather had been, a charming residence; the lower storey was of stone, and had a raised garden round it. A mountain stream had been induced to wind its course along the front, and was spanned by a brickwork bridge covered with creepers. Some splendid cabbage palms stood as sentinels at the entrance; and here and there were well laden spice and orange trees.

I found myself in comfortable quarters; the house was, it is true, "not as it used to was," but everything showed the remains of former—I might almost say—splendour; and my host who, as I found, was of French extraction and the last of the family who first settled on the estate, was a pleasant companion. He had not left the island for fifty years, and had seen his property decline from a remunerative estate to a heavily encumbered possession on which he was now merely permitted to reside. After I had rested, we took a turn round the garden, and I listened to an account of its former beauty. Walking about, we came upon a patch of mint, and I casually enquired of my host if he was fond of julep. He did not appear to have made the acquaintance of that seductive compound, and so "Joe" was called, and a bundle of the fragrant herb carried indoors.

Our stroll ended, I compounded, as well as I could

without ice, a couple of glasses of mint julep, with which my host appeared delighted, and indeed, after dinner, he asked me to shew him how to compound another, and he repeated the experiment until he became fairly proficient.

I am sorry to say the old gentleman imbibed that evening more liquors than mint Julep, and when bed time came he had to call in the aid of "Joe." In the morning, however, he appeared as fresh as could be, and had inspected my steed, which was pronounced to be fit for the journey. In a short while, after coffee, I was on my travels again, having accepted a very pressing invitation to spend a few days whenever I could come to "Chateau Meudon."

A day or two after I left the island, and a couple of months passed before I returned. Arriving one Sunday morning, I went on to Chateau Meudon, intending to spend the day there. Dismounting at the door and seeing no one about, I shouted for "Joe," but instead of Joe a portly dame waddled up from the direction of the kitchen.

"Master in?"

"Eh! eh! massa dead?"

"Dead? what Mr. ——— ?"

"Yes sah—he dead for true."

"When did he die?"

"He died last Thursday."

"Dear me," said I, "how sad; I never heard he was ill; what did he die of?"

"Well, me massa, two months ago one wutless buckra come from de Gubnor house and he 'top here one night wid me poor ole massa and he hab berry little to do, fo' he teach de poor ole massa for drink grass and rum, and massa he drink grass and rum tēēl (till) one day he fall down and him dead. It been good if that buckra keep he grass and rum fo' heself."

I remounted and went back to my quarters a sadder if not a wiser man.

GOOD-BYE POPKINS.

WHEN I was serving as second officer on board the R.M.S.P. *Guadalquiver* we had a tremendous swell as purser. He was by no means a bad fellow, but the way in which he got himself up, and the airs he gave himself, tried our patience and our tempers a good deal. He always dressed in white, and his linen was the admiration and envy of us all. Of course we knew who his laundress was, but she respectfully but firmly declined our custom, and insinuated that as her whole time and mind were dedicated to getting up Popkins' shirts, collars, and trousers, she had no time to attend to us: so we had to put up with the inferior skill of some other practitioner.

Popkins was great with lady passengers: he could sing fairly well, and he had a quaint little instrument of the guitar tribe which he had picked up in Naples, and on a moonlight night, Popkins was safe to be found perched up in the centre of a small crowd of admiring ladies twing-twanging away an accompaniment to a lackadaisical Italian canzonetta, or notturno, or some such foolery, which he sang with upturned eyes and grimaces. And then he generally had a confounded yarn tacked on to every song. "Ah!" he would say with a deep sigh—"Ah, I first heard that sung by la Marchesa di Macaroni. Of course some of you must have heard of her! the beauty of Napoli, that is, Naples. No?—That *is* strange. Well we were great friends, poor Teresina! her fate was a sad one. What? Ah, excuse me, some other time perhaps, but not now;" and then he would go tinketty tanketty tan on the guitar, a diamond ring he wore on his little finger flashing in the light, and string out a merry dance tune to which he warbled some wordless song. Popkins was not a bad-looking fellow. He had big dark eyes and a good nose, and his well-shaped mouth was only partly hidden by a moustache. He certainly attracted the women, and was (or said he was) engaged to some fresh inamorata each trip. I need not describe his cabin. It was luxuriously furnished with all sorts of fancy work adornments, and its sides were covered with photos,—all of them of female beauties. The only portrait of a man was one representing a stern looking officer in uniform with no end of decorations, to which Popkins always referred as that of "the author of my being." We never could draw him on this subject; in fact he used to get angry if he were at all pressed, and we used to worry him by pretending that one of us thought it was the Duke of A—, and another Lord B— Others declared it resembled the King of Portugal, or the hereditary Grand Duke of Seltzerwasser; but in any case there was no doubt Popkins came of genteel, if not of distinguished parentage.

Well, one trip we had as passenger a Spanish lady, bound, I think, for Havana, who was young, handsome, and a widow, and spoke English perfectly. She very often talked of her Cuban possessions and of her family in old Spain, and being very musical sang pretty little ballads, of course accompanied by Popkins. He and she were always together. Popkins shewed her the photograph of the person who he said was responsible for his existence, and exhibited those of the English and other ladies who were his admirers, and the Señora in return brought out the portraits of her late husband and her family and views of her Spanish home, &c We used to chaff Popkins about Señora Mercedes, but he took it all quietly, and from what was gathered from the lady she evidently was rather smitten with the purser.

One night—the night before we made Barbados—Popkins and the Señora were sitting side by side in deep and earnest conversation. It was not possible to hear what they were talking about, but it was clear that the Señora's hand lay in that of Popkins, and his arm was on the top of her deck chair, and their faces so close that her lace mantilla every now and then was blown across his cheek. The next morning we were at anchor, and, of course, Popkins was very busy—too busy to be able to say much to his Mercedes who was early on deck looking at the busy scene in Carlisle Bay, and evidently amused at the appearance and talk of the Bimshire negroes. After a while, Popkins could spare a moment, and he came to her side, but on his way he was accosted by a black lady known to us as Mary Jane, but who to the outer world was Miss Pilgrim.

"Marnin' Mr. Papkin, marnin', I really glad to see you again. Eh! you look fuss-rate"—and she stuck out her hand;—this, Popkins declined and replied:—

"Good morning Miss Pilgrim—see you presently."

Mary Jane waited patiently for a while and watched Popkins as he bent over Señora Mercedes.

"Mistah Papkins!"

No reply.

"Mistah Papkins!" in a louder tone.

The purser obeyed the call, and there was a muttered whispered colloquy between him and the blanchisseuse, which gradually became louder and louder, until Popkins wheeling round, left Mary Jane and strode towards the Señora.

"Mistah Papkins"—

"D—— you" said Mr. Popkins.

"Eh! good faith! and ye cuss me—me, Mary Jane Pilgrim! Good father—you disremember how me been mo' dan mother to you—how me wash you clo'es and even make up what you want from other gentlemen's trousis and shirts and collahs and hanchifs,—and Papkins you never never pay me a cent. Aow Papkins! and now you cuss me—well, well, Papkins! I going, good-bye. If you please, when you done wear Mr. Crawford best shirt you could send 'em—Good-bye Papkins."

Poor Popkins! Señora Mercedes was convulsed with laughter behind her fan, and the purser was as red as a pepper. It was in vain he attempted to renew his conversation with the lady. As he commenced, she would go off into a fresh peal, and so at last he took his leave.

When the time came for the Señora to embark on board the other steamer, another officer escorted her over the side, but as she went she turned round for a moment, and, waving her hand to the purser, bade him farewell —"Good-bye Mr. Papkins."

D. I. O.

THE Ffysshes were an old St. Molasses family. A "Fish" had migrated from some other island in the middle of the last century, and there were dim traditions of his being the son of one of the old Buccaneers and his Carib wife. However that may be, he struck root and flourished, married into a highly genteel family, and died wealthy and respected. The fashionable wife of a descendant had brought about the change in spelling the name from "Fish" to "Ffysshe," and there was some forty or fifty years ago in St. Molasses one Frederick Ferdinand Ffysshe, whose parent had dissipated his property so that the representative of the family had been glad to accept a post in the Colonial Customs' service. The amount of salary being inadequate to meet the requirements of Mass' Fred, as he was called by the black creoles, with whom he was an especial favourite, Mass' Fred was always "hard up." Still he managed to live well—was always fashionably dressed (he had three London tailors), and being a handsome, affable young fellow with a large stock of assurance, he managed to carry on sometimes by wheedling and coaxing, at others by ignoring a stoppage of credit and coolly taking what articles he wanted out of a store, the clerks being paralysed by his audacity, or by finding a London tradesman willing to exchange his goods for Fred's promises. Mr. Ffysshe thus continued to exist in very comfortable style, and transient visitors to the island and naval officers who enjoyed his excellent hospitality carried his fame as a generous host far and wide. But of such things there is sooner or later an end. People grow rusty and impatient, and Mass' Fred's name figured as defendant in several suits. He endeavoured to appease his creditors by giving to this and to that, what he could spare of his luxurious surroundings; his pay was hypothecated, and his furniture and plate and jewellery all by degrees became absorbed, and still he was hampered. The legislators of St. Molasses, it may be mentioned, had always disapproved of bankruptcy laws, and a debtor had no opportunity of compromising his debts by surrender of his assets. At last, to Fred Ffysshe, bread and cheese, so to speak, became hard to obtain. He still preserved a respectable exterior, for his clothes were well made and he had a knack of making them look their best, but it was a matter of notoriety that Mr. Ffysshe had been compelled to occupy a room over the "Queen's Hotel" as the grubby and rather noisy Restaurant of the town was called. It was kept by an old black man, the ex-cook of departed Governors and first families of the island, and if the lodgings were not everything that could be desired, the board was excellent. None could cook turtle like Baptiste. Fish that under ordinary treatment was only eatable, was converted by him into food fit for the gods, and the same with all else that came to his hand. Mr. Fred. Ffysshe, therefore, was in clover as far as his 'provande' went; but he had to put up with humble gin and water and the disagreeableness of his home. Baptiste fully recognized "Mass' Fred" as one of a family endeared to him and his class by lavish hospitality to equals, and generous largesse to humble dependants, and he was proud to receive under his roof the impecunious Fred. He did not often see the colour of Mr. Ffysshe's money, but patiently awaited the good time which his guest always assured him was coming. Baptiste also became his confidant and this filled him with delight. When, as was often the case. Baptiste would come upon people discussing Mass' Fred and his fallen estate, Baptiste would chuckle and draw himself up and observe: "All you neegur no know nuffin 'bout de case, Mass' Fred no go trust he bidness to fellah like you—so shut you mout'" and then would strut off many inches taller. Still Baptiste was anxious about payment, and at length he ventured to remonstrate with Mass' Fred, when the latter told him he was about to leave the island, go to England and make a fresh start there. Baptiste, however, appreciated the difficulty of his lodger's getting away and hinted as much. "Chut!" said Ffysshe, "don't you know Baptiste, that every time the mail has come in for the last six months I have gone round and told every body good bye, that I was going in the mail, but they laughed and took it as a joke, and so if I say I'm going in the next steamer they will think I am still making fun."

"But," began Baptiste——

"But," continued Ffysshe, "next mail day is Sunday

and the Sheriff can't stop me. Now listen Baptiste! I owe you, but I'm going to pay you. I would have done so before but you'd have got drunk and told people I had given you money and then they would have been down on me,—now hear'ee. I'll pay you before I leave if you'll keep my secret till then." Baptiste agreed and never breathed a word. When the homeward mail came in on the Sunday, he put Mass' Fred's travelling luggage in a small canoe, and then paddled off with it to the steamer. Mass' Fred, who was supposed to be on duty, found his way easily on board and then came the parting with Baptiste.

The poor faithful old negro had tears in his eyes at thoughts of parting with his friend and patron, but with his grief there struggled a sense of fun and triumph.

"Baptiste" said Ffysshe, "here's a letter for the Controller, he has my money and this is an order to pay you the two hundred dollars I owe you. Take it to him on Monday, don't let anyone know or they may stop it—and—there goes the bell—many thanks, old man, for your kindness. I won't forget you—there—good bye"—and hastily shaking Baptiste's hand, Mass' Fred giving him a sealed envelope disappeared below. Baptiste brushed his eyelashes and slipping down the side got in his canoe and gained the beach.

Some time after, when people asked him "Where Mass' Fred?" Baptiste, with a grin, jerked his thumb seaward and remarked, "Mass' Fysh? Well buddie* he gone in de 'teamer!" And when all through that day Baptiste was besieged by anxious, angry men who asked

* brother.

"Where, where is Mr. Ffysshe?" to each and all Baptiste calmly replied with the same jerked thumb—"he gone in de 'teamer."

When the Monday came, the Controller who always went to his office early and devoted some twenty minutes to walking up and down the verandah with a pipe in his mouth, found Baptiste awaiting his arrival, and learning that he wanted to see him on pressing business invited him upstairs. When they were alone, Baptiste after looking right and left to see there were no witnesses, slowly drew out Ffysshe's envelope and handed it to the Controller who glancing the address and then at Baptiste, asked, "Mr. Ffysshe eh! where is he, Baptiste?" "Mass' Fred, sah" was the grinning reply, "he gone a 'teamer;" and the Controller opened the letter and read it, and then slowly tore the enclosure into shreds and scattered them to the wind.

"Well sah—when me come fo de ting?"

"What thing, Baptiste?"

"De money, sah,"

"What money?"

"Aow! Controller! Mass' Fred tell me sposin' me take dis lettah to Controller, Controller gib me two hundred dollah, Mass' Fred owe me."

"My good Baptiste, Mr. Ffysshe wrote nothing of the sort."

"No sah? Well wha he been write if you please, sah?"

"Well, all he wrote was 'Dear Snooks, D. I. O.'"

"D. I. O. what dat for, Controller?

"It means, Baptiste, Damme I'm Off. It was a leave taking don't you see—D. I. O."

"Aow! me Gad—he say nuffin 'bout money?"

"Nothing, and I have nothing for him."

"Well! well!" murmured Baptiste as he picked up his old hat,—"Well! well! Mass' Fred a fool me fo' true; but never mind! me boa'd† he, me feed he, and I leave he to Gad." And the old fellow raised his eyes and hands to the ceiling saying "Well! well! D. I. O.! D. I. O.," and repeating these cabalistic letters he hobbled out of sight.

It is only fair to say that 'Mass' Fred' fell on his legs in England, and before long repaid Baptiste with ample interest.

OLD BARATARIA.

THE old West Indian Governor of 1790-1830 was in every way dissimilar to him of more recent days, drawn from a different class and selected to rule a different community. The type has long since ceased to exist, while the social and other conditions of the islands have vastly changed. Every day as "oldest inhabitants" disappear, it becomes more difficult to realise West Indian political and private life in the "good old days." Let me then, repeat what I remember of some yarns about the Governors and people of "old Barataria" and other places.

Sir Charles Crosstree was a gallant sailor distinguished in several of the brilliant actions which gained renown for the British Navy in the nineties and the first fifteen years

† board.

of this century, and whose crowning exploit was the capture of a West Indian Island under circumstances which shed on him the greatest credit; and though some professional detractors hinted that gold had done more to secure victory than had iron and cold steel, Sir Charles was rewarded by a grateful Sovereign with the Government of Barataria and its dependencies where he reigned for a much longer period than the term of a Governor's command now a days. He is described as of medium stature, with what old writers term an agreeable figure,—bright searching eyes and the aquiline nose which generally marks the ruler of men.

There was an air of romance about Sir Charles's appointment, for without much private means, expensive habits had led him to outrun the Constable, and there were difficulties in the way of leaving England for the distant island he was to govern. So great were these difficulties that it is generally understood that Sir Charles travelled all the way from London to the port of embarkation in a hearse, while the Sheriff's officers were cleverly decoyed into a long-winded chase of a post chaise, supposed to contain Lady Crosstree and her maid, down the western road, under the belief that Sir Charles would call in at Falmouth to take her ladyship on board.

It was a busy time in Barataria. There was a large garrison, and ships of war were cruising round the islands, frequently calling in and making up for hardships and dangers afloat by merriment and junketing ashore. A sharp look out was kept at the Fort, the batteries which protected the different bays with which the island is indented were all manned, and at other points regulars or militia were posted. Any strange sail caused a flutter of excitement, and the troops would be on the alert, and mounted aides clattered up or down the steep road from the Garrison to Government House.

The Baratarian militia in those days consisted of three or four regiments of foot and a troop of cavalry. These had done good service at the close of the last century when the French were constantly trying to regain the island. There exists an engraving, representing the regulars and militia of the period engaged in warfare with the French and their Indian allies. To the European unaccustomed to exertion in the tropics, a jaunt up and down the thickly-wooded sides and ravines of the Baratarian hills is a serious job even when in lightest attire, and so one wonders how the gallant pigtailed warriors of that time when clad in tight coat and leathern stock, black chako, leather breeches and gaiters, and carrying a heavy musket and sixty rounds of ammunition, managed to struggle up the hills to storm the strongholds of the enemy.

The history of that island war of 1795-6 is curious reading. It tells of a Colonel employing the men of his regiment to clear and cultivate his estate, thus affording opportunity for the Indians to attack his post; of troops about to storm the encampment of the savage enemy and their French allies, being seized with sudden panic and beating hasty and ignominious retreat. Hand to hand encounters on the steep fern-clad ridges or in the thick woods that clothe the Baratarian hills were frequent. Midnight attacks were made on the enemy's posts by militia men and corps of liberated slaves who proved themselves more apt at that kind of warfare than regular troops. There were burning of planters' houses and flight to the Town and Fort or on board the vessels in the Bay. His Majesty's Ships of war strove with adverse currents and failing winds in order to land much needed, long expected reinforcements, and there were times of deep despair. But at length, four thousand troops led by some of Britain's bravest generals, among whom was Sir Ralph Abercrombie, defeated the Caribs and French, and the island had peace. Then followed general rejoicings with banquets and addresses and grateful presentations of plate or jewelled swords.

It is difficult now a days when looking at the somewhat sleepy little place, its quiet streets and dismantled fortress, with an occasional trader riding at anchor in the all but deserted bay, to picture the busy scene it must have presented in those byegone stirring times.

An old resident, who must have been nearly 100 years of age, used to talk of those days, and how she had seen the men of Colonel Soandso's regiment driven "like sheep" by the enemy who occupied the heights above the town, and had also seen the head of the Carib Chief carried in triumph through the streets.

That Chief, Chatoyer by name, had been killed in single combat by a doughty major of militia. I have an engraving of a picture taken from life, which represents Chatoyer and his five wives. He had not a very martial bearing, being short and stout, and is depicted as smoking a pipe with a most peaceful mien. His wives are not uncomely and appear to have considered that "Beauty unadorned is &c, their only garment being a short petticoat, not the queya of the Guiana "Buckeen."

They are bending under burdens carried as the Guiana Caribs of to-day bear their loads, in surianas with bands across their foreheads.

Hanging from Chatoyer's neck when he fell, was found a silver gorget like those worn by the military officers of the time, which had been given to him by Prince William Henry, afterwards King William IV when serving in the West Indies.

Perhaps Chatoyer's supremacy as Chief was due to his astuteness rather than his martial qualities, since '*Chatouer*' in creole patois means a racoon, a manicon, or iwarry.

In after years, the Baratarian militia still existed, and from some of its veterans I have learned that they were still very valiant men of war though never actually engaged. They wore black top hats, "beavers" as they were called, with a cockade stuck on one side, and armed with the brown bess of the period, they did duty manfully. Mustering on the parade ground at 6 a.m., they would march to opposite old John Peel's store where sangaree, concocted of brown sherry or Madeira, was served out—and then they proceeded to the remains of an ancient fort where they went through manual and platoon exercise, and fired at a target at 200 yards; here more liquid refreshment was dispensed, and then they were led back to the parade, where sundry manœuvres concluding with the march-past took place, and more drink was consumed. There was, of course, a dinner in the evening, and as an ex-Colonel has informed me, there were always some quarrels at night and generally one or more hostile meetings in the morning.

A militia officer was always one of the Governor's Aide-de-Camps. A dear old friend, known to many of my readers, was a Lieut.-Colonel of militia and also A.D.C. to a Governor of Barataria of later years, who, like Sir Charles, happened to be a Naval captain. Once when in London he attended the trooping of the Colours at the Horse Guards on Her Majesty's birthday. I don't think he had sufficient courage to don the uniform of the island militia, but, however, he tried to enter an enclosure reserved for military and other privileged persons, when a sentry forbade him.

"But here's my card, I am Colonel X." and at this juncture up came an officer—

"Colonel X.?" he asked looking at the not very military figure before him, "may I ask of what Corps?"

"I am A.D.C. to Captain T——."

"Ah well my good fellow," replied the officer, that *won't do*, you haven't learned your lesson. Colonels are not aides-de-Camp to Captains—shouldn't wonder if you were a swell-mob's man, so I'd advise you to make yourself scarce, or—Police!"

And our Island hero cleared out.

Since then the Baratarian militia was disembodied, to be revived at long intervals when a Governor had military proclivities or there was a scare. Once in the Island's history, when neither of these reasons existed, a President procured with great difficulty the enactment of a militia law, and officers were appointed. These paid a handsome fee for their commissions which went into the President's pocket, and the enrolment having served this purpose, the force was never, or at most only once called out.

I am reminded of another militia Colonel who was A D.C. to Sir Charles Crosstree.

At one time, there was no regular Government House and the Governor was lodged in a hired building. On one of these occasions Sir Charles gave a dance and the ball room was crowded. It must have been a brave show, for uniforms were plentiful and the Baratarian ladies then and for many years after, were the belles of the West Indies. The Governor was, I think, the originator of the idea that "any fool could govern a West Indian Colony with a fiddle and a ham," and we may be sure that where the ham was there was also plenty with which to wash it down; and so the entertainment went merrily along, up to a certain point when there was an ominous crack and scrunch, and amid the screams of the timid, the floor at one end of the room gave way, and some of the company slid down this sort of funnel into the apartment below.

The Governor's A.D.C., Colonel P. of the Militia, at the first sound of danger had fled from the room, and when order was restored and the company had assembled in a safer apartment, the Governor sent for his fugitive aide.

"Colonel P," said he in a towering rage, "I am surprised that an officer of your rank should have been the first, if not the only person, to shew signs of what I fear I must describe as cowardice; I am not sure I ought not to put you under arrest, Sir!"

"Your Excellency," said Colonel P., with an unsuccessful attempt to repress a smile, "I would advance as my excuse that I repaired to the room below so as to receive the ladies as they came through the floor."

Colonel P," rejoined His Excellency after a pause, "You're devilish sly, Sir, devilish sly. Your excuse is accepted, Sir, and you may resume duty."

The Baratarians of those days, militia men or not, were given to duelling. Once a parson, a lady of whose family had been insulted or wronged, challenged the offender, and as he reached the rendezvous exclaimed "here goes £300 a year," that being the amount of his stipend. I do not know if he "winged" his opponent, but he resigned his living, whereupon the sympathising Baratarians returned him as a member of the House of Assembly, elected him speaker and raised his salary as such to £300, and in this position, which His Honour the Revd. —— very worthily filled, he lived to the end of his days.

I remember once asking some intimate friends of mine if they would allow me to bring with me on my next visit, a gentleman who had recently come to the island to inspect the family estates. The husband at once assented in the usual hospitable way, but Mrs. M—— hesitated for a second and then asked, "Does your friend know who I am?"

"He has of course heard of you as Mrs. M——."

"I don't mean that—well—does he know that, long, long ago, my father and his fought a duel about his mother when she was Miss ——. I don't know the facts of the case nor the result, but perhaps you'd better mention it to him first as he might not like to come."

I told my friend accordingly, but he said it didn't matter; and Mrs. M—— and he often met and talked over their family histories.

The island, if report tells truly, owed to this practice of duelling one of its Chief Justices, whose brother, a naval officer, was shot by Lord C., a captain in the navy, under circumstances which were not quite in accordance with the code of honour. The relatives, however, were appeased by the appointment of a brother of the deceased officer as Chief Justice.

The following story is told of this legal magnate, who was of diminutive size and of an effeminate and finicking manner. A Johnny Newcome recently arrived in the island was bewailing his ignorance of "how to dance," and, as an entertainment to which he had been invited was close at hand, he was desirous of taking lessons. Some joker informed him that Mr. P——, who lived on the Parade Ground, was a professor of great skill, and so one morning the young man called and sent in his card. He was duly received by the Chief Justice who asked the object of his visit in the civillest and most simpering manner, which was changed to a perfect storm of bad words when His Honour found he was supposed to be a dancing master.

There was a certain amount of state kept up by the Governor in those days, and members of His Majesty's Privy Council for the island of Barataria wore the Windsor uniform at the Council Board. Military sentries were posted here and there through the town, and His Majesty's representative was usually attended by an A.D.C. In a cellar beneath the Barataria Government House there were to be seen not long ago, the remains of the Governor's state coach and a Sedan chair, in which latter the Governor's wife was conveyed to routs and balls. Of dances there appeared to be no end. Sprightly damsels would ride into town from their country homes with a long winded Mercury or Hamlet trotting behind them holding on to the ponies' tails, and carrying on their heads big Carib baskets containing the gala gear for the evening. Others would come up from the leeward side in canoes dug out of the trunks of the gommier tree, rowed by half-a-dozen stalwart negroes; and I have been told it was a pretty sight to see a string of such craft lit up with lanterns, flitting along the coast, bearing their pleasure-seeking passengers to some entertainment.

The Governor had certain privileges, a house rent free, and allowances for table &c., which, added to a liberal income, made his post a lucrative one. There were also provided suits of royal livery, scarlet and gold coats and vests and breeches for some half-dozen servants, and if an entertainment demanded more waiters—what was easier than to borrow six of the Gaol gang and to distribute between them and the regular staff the liveries aforesaid? It did not matter if half were *en règle* as regards their bodies, and their legs were encased in any oddments of breeches, or if the other division were clad in their prison shirts or even "mit noddings on," so long as their nether limbs were resplendent in gold and crimson.

This employment of convicts has had its inconveniences. In one far off colony, a penal settlement in the old days when offenders were transported there from England, a good kind-hearted Governor thought it worth while to employ an interesting young and handsome forger of great musical talent to instruct his daughters. There was a romantic consequence, about which perhaps, the least said the better; and in later years and in a nearer island, a darkie convict who, having some gift in the art of arranging flowers, was employed about the Government House table, took an opportunity to go into the Governor's dressing room and array himself in His Excellency's Sunday best, white felt hat included, and in this garb pass out at the front gate as a coloured gentleman of local distinction, getting the honour of a "present" from the sentry.

The life of a Governor in the olden days was not always a bed of roses. The legislature as a rule, fought indiscriminately against every and anything supposed to emanate from or to be recommended by the Colonial Office, and debates waxed fierce. This political antagonism at times resulted in the local patriots abstaining from acceptance of Government House hospitality; and many a colonial Hampden thanked "his God his legs had never been stretched beneath a Governor's mahogany."

Legislation was carried on in an august, not to say severe manner. There was a House Assembly of twenty-four elected members, subsequently reduced to nineteen, and in later years wiped out altogether. The Speaker and Clerk and Sergeant-at-arms were grave officials, although they did not as far as I can learn, ever effect the Court dress or gown worn by dignitaries elsewhere. One entered the hall where the solemn conclave sate with diffidence,—one's self confidence, if you happened to be the Private Secretary, not being increased by wearing evening dress like an undertaker or a waiter, and having to present and listen to the reading of a Governor's message often received with withering sarcasm or ominous silence.

There once was an awful scene, in which the Island Constitution, for which, as Thomas Tinker, M.C.P., so frequently observed, his forefathers fought and bled, was sadly outraged.

As has been said before, theatres and halls of entertainment there were none, and so concerts, dances, bazaars, and exhibitions all were held in the Legislative Halls, prophetically thrown into a Single Chamber for this occasion, by the removal of wide and ponderous folding doors.

At one time there appeared in Barataria, a Chevalier de Linski, a conjurer of renown, and he exhibited in the Rooms devoted to the Colonial Lords and Commons, the use of which was formally granted by the President and Speaker. There was a parliamentary crisis on, and the Governor was to be solemnly denounced next day, so de Linski was charged to have all his paraphernalia removed ere the House met. Somebody ought to have seen to it, but nobody did, and so when the ever punctual Speaker took the chair and the members filed in some minutes afterwards, they found His Honour with a background of gorgeous table and chairs, with mystic cups and bowls and resplendent dragons and snakes &c., &c. Other mortals would have laughed, but not so Baratarian senators. Tom Tinker called it a breach of privilege and moved the adjournment until all that d—d nonsense was removed; and then the members stalked out with their noses in the air, thoroughly, bitterly disgusted.

I have seen the Sergeant-at-arms waltzing round the

House embracing a member who had been by solemn vote expelled, but whose superior strength made it a difficult job to carry the resolution into effect. The other members retained their seats around the horseshoe table, mutely looking at the exhibition which might have been part of some mystic ceremony at which they were assisting. There were moments of excitement when one or other of the pair was forced against a window sash, which it was feared might give way, and cause precipitate descent into the Court-yard below; but, if I remember rightly, the pair made their exit at a door, and the expulsion being deemed to have been effected, the House resumed debate.

The Island press, in the earlier part of the century, was represented by a paper which, besides containing advertisements, communicated to the Islanders what news of the outer world was brought to Barataria by the "pacquet" and other irregular sailing ships. There was little said about what was going on in the place itself, and articles of local interest appear to have been confined to letters written by anonymous correspondents, more or less sarcastic, and containing allusions, the point of which is now lost to us. The one paper was conducted by a gentleman named Drass, who was editor, printer and publisher—managed a bank—and was a member of Assembly, besides being at one time a Master in Chancery. For some reason he was opposed to the Governor. Now Sir Charles Crosstree was fond of running down to a neighbouring island under his Government in a trim yacht with a few choice friends, and holding holiday there. I have heard queer yarns as to how these worthies spent their time on these occasions, but the frequent absence caused inconvenience, and worthy Mr. Drass took delight in chronicling the departure of His Excellency, adding now and then bogus intelligence from the smaller island as to the Governor's doings,—all of which greatly incensed Sir Charles. At length Mr. Drass's remarks and articles became more frequent, and then His Excellency determined that an opposition paper should be started in the Government interest: so press, plant and editor were all imported from Barbados and the strife began.

The paper warfare at this length of time seems stale, flat and unprofitable. Of course, it has lost much of its *vim* through lapse of years and unfamiliarity with the people and politics of the day, but one still can smile at the mischievous typographical error whioh led the new editor to dub his opponent always as Dr. Ass. I remember these two literary warriors. One paper had collapsed through a fire, and its owner continued to live by the sale of stationery, while the other publication struggled on as a blurred illegible print, with nothing worth reading, until the editor, printer and publisher gave up his literary career and took to hoisting and firing the evening gun.

Official correspondence in the olden times was conducted in a more punctilous manner than is the case in these days. The paper was gold edged, and the phraseology of a correspondingly extra-dignified, not to say turgid, style. There were fewer despatches from the Secretary of State and of these many were of a purely formal character.

Sir Charles Crosstree received one, however, in which

his attention was called in the most courteous terms to the fact that the returns of revenue and expenditure for the years 181—, 181—, and 181— had never been sent with a request that this omission might be repaired. What Sir Charles's answer was, is unknown to the historian, but a later despatch conveyed in politest words a request that he would explain the coincidence—if such it were—*of the figures for the three years being identically the same.* There again Sir Charles's reply and explanation are lost to us.

Governors perhaps were careless in those days. One has heard of one of them being recommended to read his despatches before he signed them, and to sign others after he had read them, and Baratarians will remember how once upon a time a Governor "in order to save trouble," used to sign blank warrants on the Island Treasury to be filled in and countersigned by a subordinate official, and how this practice led to serious complications and financial trouble.

Superior officers are often obstinate. A young Private Secretary once consulted me as to the best manner of dealing with a President administering, whose draft despatches he had to copy, and who had d—d my young friend for interfering with His Honor's views as to the etymology of the word 'which,' the President considering one 'h' unnecessary and a 't' indispensable.

One custom of the old days, the "crop over," until lately survived in Barataria. The head men of a sugar estate mounted on mules and arrayed in military garb, to which some of "massas" old militia uniform and accoutrements were contributed, rode round to the "great houses" of the other plantations, bearing banners on which were inscribed the name of their estate and the number of hogsheads made. They were accompanied by drum and triangle and there were hurrahs and complimentary speeches to the "massa and missis and de young ladies and dem." Drink was produced and healths drunk, and then the motley troop rode off to the next house followed by a small crowd of friends and admirers.

In the evening there was a dance, where quadrilles were executed with much punctilio and decorum; perhaps there was more *abandon* in the waltzes. The dark damsels were, as a rule, dressed with much taste. Some favoured ones wore frocks and jewellery given and lent by their young mistresses, and their partners wore evening dress more or less of regulation pattern. Every one was very happy and merry, and a good supper was not forgotten.

But in the Islands things now are "not as they used to was." The old time Governor has died out, and with him much of the pomp and circumstances of his day. The old time proprietor has also gone, and with him have almost ceased generous hospitality and social intercourse, while the kindly relations that then existed between employer and employed are also things of the past.

NOT SUCH A FOOL AFTER ALL.

THE Honourable Thomas Noble, a member of Her Majesty's Council in the Island of St. Molasses, was Honourable by title, but I fear Tom Noble or as some called him, Tom Nobble, had little other claim to the distinction. He had come to some Island as a supercargo, and having been left behind, obtained a place in a merchant's office, and had migrated to St. Molasses. There he had "struck oil," or "root," and flourished. Everything he put his hand to prospered. A lame horse bought by Noble became sound in a few days under his care; the reverse often happened with those he sold. If he bought a life policy of some robust but impecunious fellow, the insured was safe to break his neck, or get drowned or in some other way become a sudden and unexpected "claim." Estates ruined and branded as "sinks" "pickpockets," once they became the property of Noble, burst into profitable ventures; and at cards,—well there the Honourable Tom was always lucky. He used to express his regrets at the constant favour of the fickle goddess, because, said he "some day they'll say I cheat."

Tom used to boast that he always paid his passage and wine bill, home and out, by his cards. Night after night Tom would be seen dealing in grim silence, cards to be afterwards clutched slowly but surely and formed into a flight of step-like tricks. Whist he preferred, but any other game was welcome—and he always won. There was a foreigner one evening whom Tom cleared out at ecarté. Monsieur was suspected of not playing on the square, and we gathered round in the hope of seeing Tom conquered, even if not fairly; but we were disappointed. Tom smiled now and then, but always won and at last his opponent started to his feet, put his arms a kimbo, and told Tom:—"Monsieur—Vous êtes escroc, you are a dam cheat, you robber—tief—you scr-r-roundrel!!!"

This was rough on Tom, but he never moved a muscle.

"Mr. Noble!" said some of us, "you hear what this gentleman says. You allow such an accusation to be made? You don't resent it?"

"Well, my friends" said the Honourable Tom, putting his hands on the table, and spreading out his fingers fan wise—"I ain't a going to quarrel because my friend there has dropped his money, and lost his temper, and, I may add, his manners. Losses is always to be borne with fortitude. Besides, the gentleman is a foreigner, and as he can only be imperfectly acquainted with English, he probably don't know the value of the expressions he is using, and I give him the benefit of the doubt. I will be generous. His ignorance of the language of Shakespeare, Milton, and others, is to be pitied, not resented like." And the Hon'ble Tom betook himself to his berth.

Tom landed at Southampton, and in due course pitched his tent in London at the "Bedford." How he spent his leisure time I knew not, although I often saw him at that resort of West Indians. Afterwards, I heard he went every Saturday to Brighton, remaining there until Monday; and somehow it leaked out he had an ancient aunt, his sole relative, who kept a third or fourth-rate boarding house in "London-super-Mare."

One Saturday afternoon, he was the sole occupant of a first-class carriage on the L. & B. railway, and the starting bell had just begun its peal, when the door of the carriage was pulled open, and in jumped a young man with a small travelling bag. Hardly had he by means of his ulster and rug, arranged a corner with all the skill of a frequent traveller, than the train was in motion.

I don't know how the conversation begun or by what topics it was sustained, but Tom and his companion had a very agreeable time. Mr. Darville was deeply interested in the West Indies. Sugar was one of the things he had dabbled in. His yacht, it is true, had never yet borne him so far westward, but he was glad to learn from a person of experience all about scenery and accommodation, &c., &c., in case he did visit those gems of the ocean, the West Indian Isles, and the description of a West Indian planter's life, the cost of sugar and rum, the modes of preparation, and the best markets &c. interested him. On all these subjects Darville was as eager an enquirer as Tom was a proud and voluble authority, nor was Mr. Noble backward in telling of his estates and the balance at his merchant's. It seemed therefore only in the fitness of things that Darville should with some hesitation tell the Honourable Tom that he regretted, "if so agreeable an hour were not to be the prelude to a longer acquaintance. He, Darville, was living in Brighton and if Mr.—— he begged pardon as he glanced at Tom's card—"the Hon'ble Mr. Noble would forgive the abruptness of an invitation for which however the charm of Mr. Noble's conversation must be his excuse, and would dine with him that evening at seven sharp, at No.— Square, he would be delighted. Of course Mr. Noble would overlook the apparent liberty he, so much his junior, took in presuming," &c.—but he need not have said so much. Mr. Noble was only too happy, and at the station they parted to meet at a later hour.

Mr. Noble was punctual to the minute, and his fly drew up at the door of one of the best houses in Brighton. A soberly-clad footman opened the door, relieved our friend of his wraps, and ushered him into an elegant drawing room, where he was greeted by his young host, and by him introduced to a group of what he would have called 'swells.' Dinner was announced, and rarely, if ever, had Tom had such a 'feed.' The turtle might have been the work of a creole adept, milk punch was the right corrective; the fish, though in Tom's estimation, scarcely equal to flying fish or querriman, was first-rate, and the good things that followed, excellent. Noble had never met with such an assortment of wines; he drank of each and every kind, and wound up with a glass of Chartreuse that he openly and loudly declared "beat shrub to fits."

Dinner over, the party adjourned to the drawing room, and Mr. Darville, opening one of Erard's 'grands,' regretted his wife was from home, but, did anybody,—would anybody like a little music?—but everyone shook his head, and as a substitute for music Darville suggested a quiet rubber. Noble, as he assented, looked like the war-horse scenting battle; and in less than no time he made a fourth.

When the "terms of business" were stated to be guinea points and a fiver on the rub, the Hon'ble Tom shuddered a little, but assented in a brave tone, and rushed into the fray. He had, however, met his more than equals, and Tom lost and lost. Once or twice he was sorely tempted, as he afterwards confessed, to "shew them a thing or two;" but he dared not. He took refreshers of B. & S. to clear his brain, and screw up his nerves; but all in vain. At midnight on Saturday—in St. Molasses, we are a pious people and don't like breaking the Sabbath,—Noble rose, and, pleading that it was Sunday, declined to play any more.

"Mr. Darville," said he, "I have dropped some money, and I confess I did not come prepared to play, or we'll say, to lose so much. "Will you kindly arrange matters for me with your friends and let me be your debtor?"

Certainly, my dear Sir," said Darville, "let's have a settling. "You owe me—so much, and Captain Jinks so much—exactly—well, in all I make it £175. Is that right?"

"Yes," said Noble, "it's correct I suppose—I had no idea, but never mind, if you'll settle for me. Gentlemen, Mr. Darville will square everything, wont you, Darville?"

"Don't trouble yourself about that," said the host, and the other gentlemen gave their assent.

"And" said Noble, holding Darville by the coat, "I'll send you a bill at ninety—no, I mean an order on my merchants for what d'ye say? £175. Well, that's let me see, 480 and 360, is 840 now? Check me, Darville, let's have no mistake."

"I don't understand, Mr. Noble—840?"

"Well, that's dollars. I always work in dollars. All right, you'll have it to-morrow, but that's Sunday and I never—however I'll go now I think; I suppose my buggy, —I mean fly is at the door. Thanks for a most 'greeable evening."

"Mr. Noble," said Darville, "as we are comparatively strangers it would be as well——You would not object, I am sure, to give me an acknowledgment for the £175 I am about to pay for you."

"Give you anything, my dear fellow, a note you mean, a promissory note; of course only here you always use a stamp, don't you? In St. Molasses we've not got so far civilized as that."

"Of course" said Darville, "You're right. Without the stamp it would not be a valid instrument—but now I think of it, I believe I *have* a stamped note. Excuse me for a moment."

The cab was at the door and Noble was in his top coat, the latter conversation had taken place in the hall. Noble felt tempted to bolt, but the serious footman looked likely to stop any such game, and so, while he hesitated, his host returned with an oblong slip of stamped paper, pen and ink.

"Ah," said Noble cheerfully, "that's right, I do like to see business ways even in trifles, there" said he writing, "what's your christian name? Theodore—pretty name—and payable at what bank?—London, Joint Stock—good bank that—there—one hundred and seventy-five—and there's my name," and Noble blotted it and put it in Darville's hand, which he affectionately wrung and then went to his cab.

"Good night! Darville, many thanks—bye, bye!"

"Good night" said his host "au revoir."

Some days after, Noble was chaffed at the Bedford about his having been rooked by the "Darville Gang," and he was told how he had fallen into the hands of some of the most notorious card sharpers in England.

"Hit hard?" said one man, "I hear a thousand—eh?"

"And gave them your note of hand? Why St. Molasses will hear of it, and you will have a nice time when you go out, Noble."

"Ah, well," said the Honourable Tom, when there was a pause—I didn't do so bad—I got a good dinner and a skin full of wine, besides picking up an idea or two of what a smart chap can do with pasteboard."

"Yes," said somebody, "but dearly bought, eh?"

"I don't know that. I did not have any money with me, and gave my note of hand—it's true."

"On which they'll sue you."

"Scarcely," said the Honourable Tom, with a modest smile, scarcely, I have had some little experience of the Law, and I took the liberty of putting, instead of 'for value received,' *for money lost at play at one sitting.*' I don't think they'll sue on that."

And the Honourable Tom winked at us collectively.

FAITHFUL NEGROES.

THE Carnegies of St. Maria were an old West Indian family descended from one of Prince Charles's adherents, who, in 1741, sought an asylum in the loveliest Island of the Antilles. Here he married the daughter of an old French Count and Colonist, and so became the head of the family, of which my friend, Archie Carnegie, when I lived in St. Maria, was the representative. *Couronne d'or* for many years had been a prosperous property. In the earlier days, its mixed cultivation produced a variety of exports hardly now to be seen in the islands where a few plants growing wild, and ruined mason work are all that remain of what were once flourishing industries. Coffee, Cotton, Tobacco, (in one shop in London they tell me, is still to be seen an old time-worn notice "St. Maria tobacco sold here," though St. Maria has not exported an ounce for many years,) Annatto, Indigo—all these preceded sugar cultivation and brought in wealth to the producers; then they gave place to the Cane, and we all know the history of Sugar in the smaller islands; the crops at first so remunerative as to render each estate a gold mine sufficient to bear the extravagancies of two generations; then emancipation came, then the equalization of the sugar duties, then, to many, ruin; and in his case, Archie, who had helped his old father to struggle against the difficulties which these brought about, one day found himself alone, and the owner of a property heavily encumbered and all but valueless as a plantation.

The Carnegies had tried all manner of shifts to keep afloat; cane pieces had been given out to villagers who were to cultivate them, and the Carnegies undertook to take off the crop for a half or a third; but after the first reaping the people would not weed, and could not afford to manure the ratoons, and there resulted a return so poor as to dishearten both landlord and tenant. Then the lands were leased out, but when pay-day came rents were unpaid; some were remitted, and when recourse was had to the Magistrate's Court, the bulk of the labourers took themselves off to an adjoining estate, abandoned and unclaimed for years, where they squatted, rent free.

The works ("buildings" we should call them in British Guiana) became ruinous and over-grown with bush. The large iron water wheel, which one prosperous year tempted the Carnegies to import, was red with rust, and in its buckets grew weeds and grass. The roof had fallen in at one spot, and the tiles had been removed from another. The chimney, so tall that it was a land-mark to passing vessels, was rent, and at its top grew a fig tree, as significant as a broom at a ship's mast-head. The machinery was ruined of course, and any one who wandered through the grass-choked mill-yard ran a risk of being tripped up by old rollers, wheels, cart tires, and such like odds and ends, rusting and decaying amid the general ruin.

Nor was the "great house" or mansion in much better order. The stone wall which enclosed two sides of its garden was undermined and tottering; here and there stones had fallen out leaving gaps temporarily stopped with branches lopped from the neighbouring trees. The old roof was grey and moss-grown. Some of the windows were boarded up for lack of glass sashes. The pavement leading to the steps, the steps themselves and gallery floor, were all of marble tiles, but some were broken, some missing, and others upraised by plants struggling through the crevices, the trees and ornamental bushes once so neat and trim, had grown into huge masses of foliage that kept the place dark and damp, a few plants, roses and jasmine and allamandas, still clung to the walls like old friends faithful in adversity, and in the shattered basin of a fountain was a stone Cupid that looked most woe begone when the rain drops trickled tearlike down each side of a green and pointless nose. The interior was when I knew it, dark and dreary, the walls and floor of native wood were almost black, the furniture old-fashioned and out of repair. A couple of mildewed mirrors in tarnished frames reflected the gloomy drawing room and "hall," and the portraits of some dozen dead-and-gone Carnegies and La Tours seemed to gaze sadly on what remained of their once luxurious home. Carnegie had married, but his wife died leaving a boy four years old, whose aunts had taken to them in Scotland. Of course, it was the best for the child as Carnegie would say, but his eyes grew moist and his face the sadder whenever he spoke of his little son so far away.

"Poor little beggar, who knows, but one day he may come into the 'title!'" he would often say with a smile. This title was a peerage which had been lately revived in favour of a cousin of Carnegie's, but my friend never referred to it except in jest.

At last the crisis came. A claim held by the government had been overdue for years, and there came instructions for its recovery. There was no dispute, no litigation, and the day arrived when Carnegie had to be 'evicted.' It was thought only kind to have the formal notice served by a friend, and I as Carnegie's neighbour, was asked to undertake the task. It was not a pleasant one, and as I approached *Couronne d'or* I wished the duty had fallen on some one else, but the unpleasantness was lessened when Carnegie met me at the foot of the steps, and placing his hands in mine, said "Better, old fellow, from you than from a stranger; I know your errand. You see I don't resist, although half the village and all the old people from the negro-yard are up here half inclined to defend the house. Come in, 'tis the last time I shall have the right to say so to you."

"I hope Carnegie" said I, "you may be able before the day of sale to make some arrangements."

"You say" replied he, "what you know cannot be. I am penniless, worse than penniless, and only wonder why the men I owe have not been down on me already; but come, let us get it over, this I suppose is your authority;" and he pointed to a paper which peeped out of my breast pocket. "Out with it, and I surrender possession to you."

"All right," I replied, grasping his hand, "that's sufficient."

"I shall have to sell the old sticks," said Carnegie, smiling sadly on the contents of the room. "It would not be honest to take any of them, and these old things, these portraits on the wall that I can remember as long as I can remember myself, will have to go to people who wont value them—ah, well? *sic transit.*"

"You'll come over to me to-night, Carnegie, my wife expects you," I said.

"Thanks—yes, I will come—I wonder—"

He was standing in a doorway that led to a little boudoir off the drawing room. It had been built, he told me, for his mother and had been his wife's pet room during her short life. It had been a bright little corner, though the paper hangings now were tarnished, and the paint had lost colour. The posts at the entrance were coloured white with a little fantastic gold border running up each side, and on one of them could be seen what is common enough in old houses in the islands,—marks shewing the height of persons whose names or initials, with a date, were written against each.

"I wonder" said Carnegie, looking at this record, "if I might have this—have it taken off the post I mean, to keep."

"I dare say you can," I replied, "I'll ask for you."

"Thanks. It is the only record I have of many who were dear to me, and are now gone. See, here's my father's name, and a date, 18—, a good height, six feet one—none over-topped him—and here's my dear mother's name written by him ever so far below; that's my sister's, and that is"—but here Carnegie turned away and some tears dimmed his eyes. "Come," said he, "I must not make a fool of myself."

As he spoke, we walked out to the verandah at the rear of the house, and there were collected numbers of the people from the village and estate. As they saw me, some uncomplimentary remarks reached my ear, but Carnegie at once explained that it was a kindness I had done, that as the duty of taking possession of the estate had to be performed, it was the less painful when performed by a friend.

"Look here, Jimbo La Tour," he called out to a big, burly negro, who was shaking his head in a very unconvinced manner, "S'pose you dead, it no better for you buddy fo' shut you yie and put you in you coffin dan somebody you don't know, and don't know you and your famberly?"

Carnegie always spoke to his hands in broken English; he used to say "It's easier to learn their lingo than to teach them ours." His argument tickled Jimbo, who laughed, as did a good many others, and then arose a shout of "Dat fo' true Mass Archie!" And then Mass Archie made a great speech interrupted by ejaculations from his hearers, which showed that they were grieved at losing their "old massa." He told them that he did not know what he should do, that he should probably go home, but that he should never forgot his old friends of *Couronne d'or;* and then they swarmed up the steps to bid him goodbye and have a farewell shake of the hand. It was a touching sight.

Here in British Guiana there is not and probably never was anything of the old clan-like feeling which in the Islands bound the negroes on the estate to their employer. Even within late years, such existed in St. Maria. The old people were not ungrateful; many an act of kindness from the "missis" or the "massa—"tender care in sickness—sympathy in trouble—participation in a wedding or christening when there would be contributions of a dress ftom the "missis," a guinea or doubloon from the "massa," or substantial contribution to the feast,—all were little matters that more closely knit together employer and employed, and they never forgot what was due to each other. The Carnegies had been good masters, so that to leave them or be left by them for a new, and perhaps an unkinder, fate was a serious matter to the *Couronne d'or* negroes.

Carnegie was not unmoved, and at length he whispered "I can't stand this, I'm off to your house," and he left. When he had gone the little crowd dissolved, and only a small group remained and they came up to me.

"Massa—What we hear is true dat Mass Archie fo'ce for leave Crondor?"

"Yes, my friends, it is so."

"He no able to buy em back?" asked Mr. Jimbo.

"I fear not," said I. "You see, old Mr. Carnegie borrow money from the Queen, and now she want she money back," I continued, relapsing into the Island patois.

Then there was a consultation and several sable heads came together.

"Massa!" at length, asked Jimbo, "S'pose de Queen, and de Gubnor and dem, sell Crondor, what he go bring?"

"I cannot say. The place will not fetch near what it owes."

"Massa! me hearee Mass Archie say he no care for the estate, but he want fo' keep de house and de little French chapel and buryin' groun' where de ole buckra La Tour and Carnegie been bury, but he ho hable for buy em. You tink he hable for tro' in some?"

"Really, Jimbo, I do not think Mr. Carnegie has any money; but come, tell me what you mean."

"Well, Massa," began Jimbo La Tour, "but 'top; come here!" and he and a half dozen other old negroes led me a few yards apart.

"Massa," he continued, "you see we ole Latour and Carnegie people, we barn here, we lib here, and we look for dip in dis same Crondor. We 'member Mass Archie long ago, when he one small pickney, and he fader befo', and he moder. Eh! she been one blessed missis to a'we, and so we sorry fo true he fo'ce fo gib up de place, so

Mr. Harklees (Hercules) and Scipio, and Romeo, and Pompey say we save little bit money, 'spose Massa Archie hab little bit, we all tro' up and make big money, and we buy Crondor; den Mass Archie he keep de big house and de chutch and de buryin' groun, and de rest of a'we de estate."

I thought it a good plan and said so, and then it occurred to me that Carnegie could find perhaps his quota. I told Jimbo what I thought of the proposal, and thanked him, and mounting my horse, I left; but Jimbo running after me called to me to stop and begged me "no say nuffin to Mass. Archie till you quite sure he got de money becasin 'spose we no buy Crondor he too sorry."

A friend of Carnegie to whom I mentioned in confidence the project of Jimbo, agreed to supply Carnegie's proportion of the purchase money on very easy terms, and my friends the labourers placed in my hands a sum sufficient to buy the property. It was duly exposed for sale, and was knocked down to me for a sum even less than I had anticipated.

In small communities petty suspicions are always rife, and people who were not in the secret, made nasty remarks about my buying up my friend. Carnegie too seemed hurt, but I asked him to give me an opportunity for explanation.

Well, one fine day, I and a friend got Carnegie to revisit his old home on the pretence of installing me so as to prevent all doubt of the legality of the sale. With much reluctance he came; and in the old drawing-room round which still hung the old portraits—for friends had bought but would not remove them—I, with Jimbo and the *Couronne d'or* negroes who had helped keep the "big house" in Carnegie's hands, gave my old friend a sub-conveyance of the homestead and its chapel, &c., in trust for his infant son. Need I say that Carnegie was taken aback and was overcome, his emotion was but natural.

Blessings, like troubles, do not come singly. Shortly after, on the death of his cousin, the title and a small Scottish estate devolved on Archie. In his castle,—for he lives in a real old Border keep,—he has a long strip of white wood framed and glazed, which I recognized as the casing of the post at *Couronne d'or* he so much treasured. He came out to St. Maria not along ago with his son, now a soldier, and I had the happiness of seeing him welcomed home by old Jimbo and a few other of the *Couronne d'or* people; there was a big feast and a jollification. I lived in the house at Carnegie's request, till I left St. Maria; it is still however kept up, in memorial, as Carnegie says, of the fidelity and affection of his old servants.

PASTORAL ATTENTIONS.

A neatly made, neatly dressed little man, not at all likely to blossom into a Rector, still less into a Dean or other dignitary. His black curly hair was parted precisely in the centre, and his moustache and beard were trim, his hands long and white; his eyes were dark and lustrous, but they usually were down-cast in a manner which some said was shy, and others described as sly. But the Revd. Simon Chasuble was welcome to us in a remote parish in St. Maria, where we had borne for some months with the Revd.——, but never mind him.

Chasuble had come out from home and we all were gratified at having a curate who, apparently, would have been an ornament to any English parish. We wondered why he came, until he told us he felt it his duty, and that his lungs were not strong, and English winters all but fatal to him.

One night when he had been with us a few months, I met him at dinner at Charlie Anson's. Anson was a magistrate and a wonderfully cool hand. He always impressed on other fellows that it was bad style to make a fuss, "kick up a row" in short, over any matter capable of quiet settlement. Still more did he always deprecate any scandal about one's women-kind, and he used to tell with great gusto, how once in England at a County ball, a stranger observed to him what a capital dancer Mrs. Anson, "that little woman in pink," was, and how awfully pretty too, and then what a pity it was she was such a flirt; and how he informed the stranger that Mrs. Anson *did* dance well, and *was* pretty, and that she was a flirt before he married her, and he didn't object to it; did the stranger?

Anson would say, "I admire that fellow in Balzac's novel, who when he had reason to believe another fellow was secreted in a cupboard in his wife's *boudoir*, though she declared he was not, coolly ordered in a mason and and had the chap bricked in, d'ye see, and smoked a cigar all the time, while Madame got whiter and whiter. The man died of course, but there was no beastly row about it."

On the night I refer to, I sat on Mrs. Anson's right and the new Curate on her left. He was awfully attentive and kept on mumbling something to her and she changed colour from time to time. Poor I had no chance of speaking to the lady, and so had to listen to a wonderful discourse on rainfall from my neighbour, a thin old planter, who was great on meteorology.

Presently Mrs. Anson made a movement, she had dropped a ring, and in a moment Chasuble was on his knees searching for it. Just before he re-appeared above the table, Mrs. Anston started, and a vexed look flitted across her face; however, she thanked Chasuble and all went on smoothly after. Dinner over, the ladies and gentlemen rose together and we men adjourned to the verandah.

Mrs. Anson said a whispered word or two to her husband, and he sauntered up to Chasuble who was near me, and we three wandered to the end of the gallery. "Have a cigar, Chasuble? Try one; I think you'll say it is first rate;" and we all lit up.

"Awfully glad to see you, Chasuble" said Anson. "So good of an English fellow like you, to leave your books and come up to enliven us. You must find all us Colonials so wanting in much of which London men are full; hope you'll come again."

"Thanks, very much," said Chasuble. "I have spent a very pleasant evening, and I have to thank you and Mrs. Anson——"

"Ah, that reminds me," interrupted Charlie; "Mrs. Anson is rather peculiar you know, of course I don't mind telling *you* she has different tastes and fancies to the women you've mixed with. Out here, one's wife doesn't have advantages and so doesn't fall in with the ways of a more fashionable world. But Mrs. Anson,—you won't mind my saying so—does not quite like, (as for me I don't mind a button you know,) but she doesn't like a fellow making eyes at her, and, if she drops her ring or handkerchief, taking the opportunity to kiss her hand; and now there's your pony, but have a B. & S. before you go. No? Well, good night."

The Revd. Chasuble left rather suddenly but silently, and we rarely saw him again, till, the climate disagreeing with him, he went home.

A ROMANCE OF BARATARIA.

THE Lieut.-Governor of Barataria whose health had begun to suffer from a prolonged residence of twenty-six months and five days in the tropics, went to England on leave. There were people who said he hurried home so as to apply in person for the government of some larger colony which afforded better pay, but however this might be, the day of his departure arrived. The steamer's boat lay waiting with the mails, and His Excellency, accompanied by a small knot of officials in their Sunday clothes, walked down towards the place of embarkation. The twenty-four policemen whose pleasing duty it was to guard the island from foes domestic or foreign, were there drawn up in line, entrusted on this occasion with muskets and fixed bayonets. They also wore boots, and had donned the tunics served out three years before, and which, with the boots, were only worn on solemn or festive days. The Inspector General's scabbard clinked and clanked as he passed up and down before his men. The drummer (there was much more drum than drummer) and the bugler, who was so tall that when he blew his bugle, it was always some seconds before the wind found its way up from its reservoir to the mouth-piece, were painfully on the alert. The crowd—it was a serious draft on the population of Barataria's metropolis to make a crowd—was calm but evidently impressed with the spectacle. At last at a signal from a ragged boy at the corner of the street, the Inspector waving his sword shouted "'Shun!" so very suddenly and vigorously, that No. 3—he was from a remote country district and nervous—dropped his firelock with a clatter; but this accident was repaired before the word to "shuller rums" was given, and cautiously and deliberately obeyed. A few minutes more, and the Governor appeared on the scene, and as he nearly reached the right hand man—"'Sent rums" shouted the "General," and up and down went the glittering bayonets in a way that would have dismayed an enemy; indeed, on approaching No. 3, the Governor promptly took ground to his right, for that warrior appeared about to "resist cavalry." The drummer and bugler—I had nearly forgotten them—beat and blew a wild melody that nowadays might have been mistaken for a bit of "Lohengrin," while the crowd cheered with excitement and the Police "shullered rums" once more.

At Barataria there are or were, on the crest of the hill that formed a background to the town, some old decaying fortifications from which a dozen or two guns of great size but doubtful strength poked their mouths. Old Sergt. Flinders, who had been at Waterloo in the artillery, and whose duty it was to hoist signals, had routed out some powder from the stores and having dried it, had loaded the most trustworthy of the pieces, so that to add to the delirium of the populace there was a salute, not perfection perhaps, for as the guns had been loaded over night, and the damp had affected some charges, so there were gaps and intervals; still the half-dozen bangs out of the regulation thirteen were uproariously received, and Flinders was declared to have done very well "considering."

But the parting at last came, there was a great shaking of hands and a small chorus of sincere wishes for better health. "Hope to see you back again," "Sorry to lose you, Sir," said the by-standers as the Lieut.-Governor stepped into the boat with a general wave of the hand and a jocose warning to one prominent personage to "take care of Barataria, Mr. President, till I return." This so completely conquered Mr. President Brown, that although he had lately been a stern political opponent of the Governor in the matter of an additional tax on salt-fish in which article Mr. Brown principally dealt, the Honourable Benjamin took off his hat once more, and in return called out, "Thank you, Sir; God bless you," and then wiped his face, and his eyes too, with a large old-fashioned bandanna.

The boat made its way to the steamer with the Lieut.-

Governor, who, as if he were an extraditioned offender, was accompanied by the Inspector; and then there was a consultation among the officials, in which Mr. Brown, standing apart and flopping his handkerchief at minute intervals towards the receding boat, took no part. Presently, after much whispering and glances at Mr. Brown, the conclave broke up, and one of the party, a shriveled old gentleman in a coat of bye-gone fashion, with a big shirt frill, and a huge wisp of muslin for cravat, approached the worthy president, who appeared to be most intent on waving his handkerchief gracefully.

"Your Honour!" said Mr. Sneezley, who was Colonial Secretary, Registrar of the Courts, Notary Public, and a host of other things, besides the holder of a Colonel's Commission in a defunct, or at least dormant, militia, "Your Honour!"

"Mr. Colonial Secretary!" replied Mr. Brown, lifting his hat as Mr. Sneezley removed his.

"Your Honour," continued Mr. Sneezley, "I venture to approach you in order that I may learn Your Honour's commands as to the hour and place at which you will be sworn in," and Mr. Sneezley drew himself up and paused for a reply.

"Any time that may be agreeable to yourself and the other Honourable members of the Council will suit me, Mr. Secretary."

"Then I am commissioned to suggest the Court House at 12 to-morrow."

"I shall not fail to be there. Good afternoon, Mr. Colonial Secretary," and the President's bow was most gracious.

"Your Honour's obedient servant," said Mr. Sneezley, and he bent like a mandarin, and slowly withdrew.

There was a queer look in Mr. Sneezley's eyes, and he bit his lip, while the President buried his features in his handkerchief, for they felt very much like what Thackeray supposed modern Heralds must feel when they meet. They both no doubt considered that there was a certain amount of humbug in all this deference and hauteur between two old cronies, who that very morning had slapped each other on the back, exchanged snuff-boxes, and stood sangarees to each other; but still etiquette was not to be disregarded, certainly not in those good old times.

Mr. Sneezley rejoined his companions and the Inspector General having landed, sent his men home under charge of a sergeant and then hitched up his sword. The others looked at one another and winked, and then with one accord they all made for the hotel, a shabby wooden edifice crowned by a rickety staff from which was hoisted a red ensign. Miss Fan, as the old mulatto lady who presided over the establishment was called, happened to be at the door as they entered. President Brown followed, but at a distance, in the same direction. A shade, several shades, of care were on his brow, and he lent heavily on his closed umbrella as he plodded along. Once or twice he returned the salute of passing friends, and as he neared the hotel he made a step towards its door, but happily restrained himself in time, as he reflected that what was possible to Ben Brown, would, in a President, be *infra dig.* It was still warm, and after the exciting events of the day, a sangaree would have been excusable under other circumstances, but

"No" said the President to himself, as summoning his resolution, he continued his solemn walk towards his house, "No! position has its drawbacks, and here's one of them." He however cast his eyes surreptitiously to the window and detected Sneezley and the others peeping out at him. "Ben Brown," they would have asked to join them, but His Honour President Brown,—it could not be thought of. Indeed, as it was, their glances met those of their now superior, and half ashamed at being detected, they retreated to their table, while His Honour sighing, strode homewards.

Nothing further occurred, save that a hireling negro boy, employed in a recently started opposition store, rudely yelled out, "Hi! wha dis', dey make ole sa' fish, Gubnor! hi! wha' next?" but Mr. Brown was not discomposed, and in a few moments he entered his door which was opened by Mrs. Brown, who, flinging her arms around her husband's neck, to the disarrangement of his hat, saluted him with a warm kiss and a hearty "Welcome! Mr. President, welcome! my dear Ben," and His Honour did not think it derogatory to return the salute, with a hearty "Bless you, my Bess."

Old Benjamin Brown had come to Barataria some years before the time of which we speak, in a humble position, and by degrees had improved his fortunes, until at length he had set up in business as general merchant. Being active and of good repute, he soon found correspondents, and was in a very flourishing condition; in fact, Ben Brown was reported to be "warm"—"worth a plum," &c.

He had married at the outset of his career, a young

creole whose face, together with an affectionate heart and a store of good common sense, was her only fortune. Ben Brown and Bessie, his wife, had gone through the world hand in hand, and the one owed much of his success to the other's shrewdness. There was, however, one, shall we say—weak—point in the wife's character, and that was an implicit belief in Ben's superiority to all his friends and fellows, and a tendency to assert this on all occasions.

They had one child, a daughter of eighteen, whose charms had turned the heads of the young male Baratarians. Whenever Norah Brown, clad in a well fitting habit, with a saucy little hat, from beneath which her brown curls always would escape in a most enchanting fashion, rode down the bay where all the stores were, business was suspended; clerks perched on the top of piles of lumber, stood spell-bound with foot rule in hand; clerks in their shirt sleeves, up to that moment most eloquent on the qualities of the herrings or cod-fish they were inducing some customer to buy, were suddenly dumb; young Osnaburg, the Adonis of the retail dry goods store (just started to the prejudice of the peddling interest, until then the only means of purveying such wares to the public and gentry,) on one such occasion, being lost in admiration, nearly poked out a customer's eye with his yard stick; clerks, stuck as it were, midway up long ladders of figures, lost their heads, and had to begin at the foot again; in short, Norah Brown's presence was always a serious, if only a temporary interruption to business. There was some excuse for it, for although pretty faces were not scarce in Barataria, Norah's eclipsed them all. Her dark blue eyes and winsome features were not to be matched, and she was known to be as honest and good as she was fair.

Mrs. Brown had for some days known of the honour that awaited her husband, and indeed, from the day when his being nominated a member of His Majesty's Legislative Council of the island of Barataria gave her precedence over a good many dames of the landed aristocracy, who had turned up their noses at Mrs. Brown's social position as the wife of a mere merchant,—from that day, she had looked forward to the occasion when her Ben would be at the top of the tree, and she, of course, perched beside him.

And this was very pardonable, for Barataria was her native place, and her home which she had never quitted, and in those days with a resident gentry, some of whom whether planters or merchants, had sprung from good old families over the water, while others were descended from creole ancestors so comparatively remote as to be quite as good as the FFs of Virginia, Barataria was considered to be an aristocratic island, a very Belgravia among colonies and by no means to be despised. It was therefore something to be, if only for a while, the constitutional head of such a community. Besides, the constitution of which Ben Brown was, next to His Sovereign, the apex, was it not an exact counterpart of that of Great Britain?

In those days Barataria had a Privy Council—not a sort of hob and nob conference held any how, which a Governor's advisers could attend in cut-a-way coats and trousers of garish hue and billy-cock hats, but a solemn assembly, convened with much form and ceremony, at which His Majesty's representative wore a uniform that, with many buttons, epaulettes, sash and sword, and a most warlike cocked hat, was a thing to gaze at; and the Honourable members, as was to be expected in so well ordered an island as Barataria, wore a garb hardly less gorgeous. To them were denied indeed the epaulettes, and sword, but their dark blue coats with scarlet and gold collars and cuffs were simply splendid—if a little heavy. Then were not the minutes taken down in a masterful way, following the fashion in the mother country and writing only the first and final letters of a name, so that B—n B—n and J—n S—h became to the uninitiated, crptographs, and defied detection as Benjamin Brown and John Smith?

There was a Legislative Council then. A House of Lords in fact, which was the Privy Council minus the Governor, but under presidency of the Senior member, and which would open its proceedings with prayer,—not read in a perfunctory way by a clerk,—who in those days when Church and State were closely knit together, would clearly be ineligible to pray in public, but by a Chaplain, paid and robed as such, and who if it happened to be Jack Fairfax, Rural Dean, &c., the best whist player in the island, and related to at least half the Council, would be kicking his heels and using strong words in the ante-room. Besides the Chaplain there was a Sergeant-at-arms, a tall bent greyheaded old gentleman who had seen better days and who, seated by the door, nodded and took snuff all through the most exciting debates, it is true; but was ready, as far as his feeble powers would allow, to remove the burliest Councillor if disorderly. Old Mr. Greypole had been unfortunate, and so had been his many creditors, but he was uncle to a Councillor and father of at least two members of Assembly, and so he had had been made Sergeant at a comfortable salary.

The third estate was the Commons, the House of Assembly consisting of a score of members whose proceedings were conducted on British principles. It is true that out of the whole population of Barataria only a few were eligible as voters, and of those few, but a handful exercised their privilege; so that very often two members would be returned by their own votes and that of some odd man who happened to be present, but in this they were not very different from the unreformed English House. The Assembly met under a Speaker who sate robed in solemn state, in a large carved chair on a dais; and there were clerk and usher, besides a big mace which some patriotic and generous occupant of the chair had contributed to the greater glory of the House. On the walls were pictures of His Majesty George III. and his Consort, the work of the Court Painter, and costing some good sum. There were also portraits of later sovereigns, so that the hall had an appearance of some splendour. Measures were introduced and passed through three stages and in and out of Committee, in strict and decorous fashion, even though they affected the smallest matters conceivable; and some members were eloquent, and delivered themselves of speeches manufactured and committed to memory for the occasion, bristling with quotations, (always however in English, for to quote Latin was not considered quite fair play,) and sparkling with impromptus that had cost some slight study.

Such was the constitution over which our friend Benjamin Brown was called on to preside, and of which few, if any, examples now exist, less cumbrous machinery supplying its place, but of course, there are still some old fogies *laudatores temporis acti* who shake their heads and sigh for the days that are gone.

We left Mrs. Brown in the arms of her beloved Ben, and he had in turn to embrace Norah, whose satisfaction at her father's freshly acquired dignity, was due entirely to her love for him. These congratulations and expressions over, it became necessary to arrange for the morrow, and the President's Windsor uniform was brushed and fresh lustre given to its lace and buttons by Mrs. Brown's deft fingers; then the good lady took out of the book case some neglected volumes, and after dinner, Norah read out aloud several elegant extracts from the speeches of byegone statesmen, with a view to her father gathering therefrom what might be appropriate for him to say on the occasion of his being sworn in, and to which he, pipe in mouth, listened for some time attentively.

"Norah," at last said he, laying down his pipe, "Norah, my dear, read no more. I don't believe in warming up those cold bits of eloquence for present use. No hash is ever so good as the original boiled or roast."

"I don't know that, dear," interrupted Mrs. Brown; "with a dash of that Demerara stuff, what d'ye call it? —casareepe, or a little roucou and some cives and tickle thyme."

"I expect," continued her husband with a wave of the hand that silenced her, "that Sneezley and those other fellows at the Council would rather have some few words, plain-spoken words, coming from my heart in my own fashion, than a page of borrowed stuff, so shut up your books, my dear, thank'ye; and mix me a little brandy and water. As for quoting things other fellows have said, bless you! it doesn't follow that the man who does that believes in 'em, and may be he only does it to brag and show off his learning;—and some of the fools that hear him, think he has the brains of him that wrote the book, as if a man that stole a board off a house owned the whole building,"—and Mr. Brown puffed at his long clay in silence.

"Ben" said his wife after a pause, "we must give some sort of entertainment you know, a dinner or a dance."

"Of course Bess, of course, one or both of them, let's say both; the dinner will suit us old fogies, and the dance the young ones like our Norah here; eh! little one? Who knows but that you may bring to book some of the fellows that have been flitting round you like Jack Spaniards round a molasses cask; not that I see any of them worthy of you, my pet, but 'mountain dove can't cross sea fo' look odder dove', as the niggers say." As the worthy old gentleman said this, he raised his glass to his lips, while his wife, stealing a glance at Norah whose eyes became somewhat dimmed, put her hand on his arm and whispered, "hush!"

Mr. Brown looked up with an enquiring glance, then nodded as if he remembered something, and forgetting that he had already commenced a draught, took down the rest of the contents of his tumbler.

"Shall we make the dance select or general?" asked Mrs. Brown.

"What do you mean, Bess?"

"Well, dear, shall we ask every one we know, or considering our, I mean your, present position shall we only ask the—well—what we may call the fashionable people, our equals as it were?"

"How, now Bess!" said the President, tapping his spouse's rosy cheek, "that's not like you, you wouldn't have us forget the old friends of along ago, that when we were working our way up never turned a cold shoulder to us, but often gave us a helping hand, would you? No! no! we'll have our old chums who have kept themselves decent, and we'll have the aristocracy as well."

"My dear Ben, don't be foolish, the mixture won't answer."

"Why not?"

"Don't you see you'll have the cream a-top and at the bottom the milk——"

"From which the cream has risen, eh?" said her husband concluding the sentence. "My dear Bess, we are going to try it; if it fails, the blame won't lie at our door, nor with our former friends, and as for what you may call the aristocracy, the Macduffs and Sneezleys and Greypoles and La Roches and all that lot, why they're bound to come. I'm not especially proud of it, as you know, but I am as good as Governor and Her Majesty's representative, and so, if they do cock their noses in the air at Ben Brown, and snigger at the store, et cetera, they must respect his office; besides, my love, well, it's vulgar perhaps to allude to it, but a precious lot of 'em remember that Ben Brown has in his safe, slips of paper with their aristocratic names of them, that they prefer to let slumber there; and mind you, Bess, there's generally a lot of civility to be got out of a man when you can't get your money out of him, sometimes it's all you *can* get," and Mr. Brown peeped into his tumbler from which likewise nothing more could be got.

"Well, Ben, so be it; you know, dear"—and here Mrs. Brown kissed her husband's brow—"you know you always have your own way."

Then the couple settled down with Norah to make out lists of guests; a long proceeding, for Ben Brown's memory would often, at the mention of a name, recall some anecdote or occurrence of bygone years, and again time would occasionally be consumed in debating whether this or that person had not rather passed even the line which the President had liberally and generously drawn in the matter of invitations.

It was a long list when done, and Norah promised to send out early and get all the cards she could on which to write the invitations in the style of those usually issued from Government House. There was a newspaper in the island, the history and vicissitudes of which would require columns to narrate, but at this period the staff,—editor, reporter, London correspondent, compositor, devil, pressman and publisher—was centred in one man, who had a financial difficulty with Ben Brown and could not be asked to print the cards; indeed their completion would have been as uncertain as the date of issue of the *Banner* of Barataria usually was.

Norah, however, had no difficulty in getting her cards neatly written by some of the young fellows in the town, whose hearts as well as their hands were hers for the asking.

The ceremony of installation went off very well. The police formed as excellent a guard of honour as when the Lieut. Governor left. Flinders having only a smaller number of guns to fire, acquitted himself capitally. The Chief Justice administered the oaths in an impressive manner and the President said a few sensible words in a sensible way. His old friends shook hands with him, and altogether it was a sort of quiet friendly affair. The crowd shouted and cheered, greatly encouraged thereto by knowing that Ben Brown had given orders for liquor to be freely dispensed; and in half an hour all was over.

Mrs. Brown was only at the commencement of her labours and anxieties; no ball or dance is complete without a supper, and she, good woman, was determined there should be no falling off, no cause of complaint on that head. The dance was to be at Government House, an ugly building with no great accommodation other than a large huge room devoted to purposes of entertainment. It was difficult of illumination, for the only means were only old-fashioned bronze oil lamps very difficult to coax into a good temper, and still harder to keep going. The musical arrangements lay between a sorcophagus-like grand piano of Tomkinson or some other pre-adamite maker, and the local band; but the floor was good, and the galleries afforded ample space for promenade and the tea tables. The room dressed with foliage of which there was practically no end, and brightened up with flags, promised to be a pretty sight when filled with lovely faces and fresh dresses.

But as the days passed by and replies to invitations came in, there came also signs of trouble. There were many notes declining the honour; some with excuses probably false, and as Norah put a big, big D against the names in the list they mounted up to a large majority as as far as the landed aristocraey were concerned. In a short while the reason was known. Folks of blue blood did not object to the Browns, but then the friends of the Browns were some of them so very queer—some of them certainly proper—but people not met in the best circles of Barataria. As the list continued to shew more D's, so Mrs. Brown struck off a turkey or a pair of fowls, reduced a cake and cut short a trifle or a custard, from the evening's menu. Sometimes the colour in her cheeks would be heightened, and she would bite her lip; but Ben her good man only bade her keep heart, all would go well, and he never once descended to a "Told you so."

At the time of which we speak, there were no troops quartered at Barataria, and H.M. ships rarely visited the island. All this was very different to the old times when there was a tolerably strong garrison at the Fort, and scarcely a week passed without a visit from a vessel of war. A few months, however, before the Lieut. Governor went on furlough, H.M.S. *Arethusa*, about the last of those 32-gun frigates of which none now remain, but which were the most beautiful craft the English navy has ever known, had run into Barataria, to the great delight of the inhabitants. Dinners, picnics, and dances were hastily got up, and the week or so of the *Arethusa's* stay was one long revel. The Baratarians declared they never had met such charming officers; the washer-women and fruit-sellers loudly declared that "the buckra sailors were real gentlemen, fo true" while the ship's company voted Barataria to be a real western Paradise, its male inhabitants 'bricks,' its women Peris and angels.

Now Miss Norah Brown, the belle of the island, did little but ride and dance all day and all night through that eventful week, and when she was quite alone by herself, used to confess that of all the *Arethusas* there was none so handsome or so nice as a certain Lieut. Trevor; and Lieut. Trevor, who did little else but ride about and dance with Miss Brown, thought, and (to a few chosen friends) openly avowed that of all the Baratarian demoiselles, none came within a cable's length of Norah. I am afraid that at that farewell hop on board the frigate, when Mr. and Mrs. Brown insisted on Norah's leaving, although it was only 3.45 a.m., and Lieut. Trevor put Norah's shawl over her shoulders, there was a sly squeeze of the hand and a still more sly glance that meant a very great deal between these young people. And when the *Arethusa* sailed, Norah watched her till the ship was hull-down, when her eyes became very red, and she was altogether out of sorts for many days after. One mail brought her a letter from Trevor, written in the most proper terms, enclosing some little nic-nac he asked her to accept as a souvenir, and after the receipt of this, her health revived, and one would have believed the little Naples coral ornament had proved a "charm" indeed. Trevor, in the course of one long romantic ride, had told Norah he was poor, and had only his profession to look forward to: and as they had grown rather confidential, he added some other information about himself, while Norah described her life in Barataria since her childhood, and they took quite an extraordinary interest in each other.

The President's ball would be the first dance in the island after that on board the frigate, and Norah naturally drew comparisons between the pleasures of the one, and the uncertain success of the other. She was worried too at doubts of her ever seeing Trevor again, and old Phœbe, her nurse, 'who had eyes to see,' drove her half wild with recounting her own love experiences, and how bitterly she repented having encouraged one Apollo Hector, the captain of a sloop, who proved faithless, having one wife in Barbados, and several sweethearts in sundry other islands; Phœbe not neglecting to observe that "in lub buckra same as neegur, you no hable to judge from he 'kin, if cat be tief or no;" and that "sailor man like doctor bird,* he find sweet flower on mo' tree than one."

However the eventful evening drew near, and the preparations were more or less complete. Mrs. Brown had made all her arrangements betimes, and, being a good general, had at length some leisure on Monday (the ball being fixed for Thursday,) and Norah looking towards the Fort, saw the Union Jack run up at the signal mast. She flew to her mother who was her sole confidante, and who was seated at her writing table with a heap of household accounts before her, reckoning with her fingers, for all the world as if playing on an invisible piano.

"Oh mother!" cried Norah, "a man o' war!"

"A man o' what, love?" enquired the old lady, con-

* Humming bird.

tinuing her occupation, and keeping time with her head.

"It it should be the *Arethusa!*"

"What does she say; has she accepted?"

"Dear, dear mother! do, just listen one moment; there's a man o'war signalled."

"Never, Norah! Well, we must send them invitations; here, sit down and write."

"We'd better wait till the ship arrives; come into the gallery, and look if we can see her," suggested her daughter.

No ship could be seen, and there was considerable doubt as to whether the vessel signalled was the *Arethusa*, and as to its destination, and Norah passed a considerable part of the day in anxious wonderings. It was late in the afternoon before her patience was rewarded by the sight of a frigate, with the lines and trim that Norah in a few days had learned to know almost better than she did those of her father's coasters, standing into the bay. By and bye she heard her father's voice, and hastened down from her room to which she had retired to put on a fresh dress, and pay some little attention to her hair. There was a stranger with her father as she could hear, and when she entered the drawing-room she was terribly disappointed at finding only Captain Clinton whom she greeted with a rather cast-down air.

"What stay can you make, Captain Clinton?" Mrs. Brown was asking rather eagerly. "I hope until the end of the week, for we have a dance on Thursday and you will all be so welcome."

"Well," said the Captain, "I dare say we can manage that, and get away on Friday morning at daybreak; no doubt we can count on a breeze than at this time of the year."

"And have you brought back all our old friends, or any new ones?"

"There have been some changes, or rather I should say, one; Lieut. Trevor's name is no longer borne on our books——"

Poor Norah's eyes filled, and turning away she bent over some flowers in the window.

"Nothing wrong, I hope——"

"Oh no; he's a lucky fellow and has got promotion unexpectedly."

Old Benjamin Brown's face grew very red and he looked at his daughter with a peculiar expression in his face—"Has he left the *Arethusa* then?" he burst out.

"Our second lieutenant" began the Captain "is now ——Miss Norah I am afraid you are unwell."

Mrs. Brown at these words turned round, and saw that her daughter was much agitated, so putting her arm around her waist she escorted her from the room.

"Captain Clinton" said Mr. Brown as the two men resumed their seats, "our poor Norah there, allowed herself to listen too long to your Lieutenant Trevor, and I confess I didn't care to interfere, especially as Mrs. Brown undertook to keep an eye on the two of them; but I must say, I did not expect to see the *Arethusa* back without Mr. Trevor, or at least a letter from him. If he merely thought proper to amuse himself, when he was here, with our girl, who's as good as gold, and then chucks her aside like a banana skin, all I can say is, that as old as I am, it won't be a pleasant afternoon for Mr. T. when he and I meet. Forgive my haste, I conclude you have no letter from him."

"No," hesitated the captain "I have no letter—nor any message."

"Then begging your pardon, he's a rascal."

"Well! well!" said Clinton, "he may yet explain, but I must be off now. I suppose Mrs. Brown won't object to as many dancers as the *Arethusa* can supply; you'll want some bunting for your rooms, and I'll send and have it fixed for you, and I'll find the music;" and then shaking hands he left the house, while the President went up stairs to see Norah.

Hardly had he left the room before Mrs. Brown entered with some visiting cards in her hand, and as she did so she was joined by a gaunt lady, followed by two smaller, or at all events, younger editions of herself.

"My dear Mrs. Brown," said the eldest lady, rushing up and shaking hands, while the younger ones presented their cheeks for a salute, "my dear Mrs. Brown, I do hope you won't think me odd, but I thought it best to call myself and explain that when I wrote declining dear Mr. Brown's and your kind invitation to the ball, I made such a silly mistake; I find it is Friday not Thursday we expect our friend, and so if you don't mind, we shall be so glad to come; you will let us, won't you? You understand how important it is for young girls like Edith and Rosina to lose no chance of meeting eligible people; and at *your* dance we know that they will have every opportunity."

"Really, Mrs. Mt. Fitchit," replied Mrs. Brown, "the President and I only looked to have the company of our friends, and you know what sort of people are met at dances."

"Oh, but Mrs. Brown," broke in Miss Edith Mt. Fitchit, with an amount of candour that made her mother frown and wink as if she were unwell, "you know the *Arethusa* is in and they are all sure to come, besides there's a swell on board."

"A what, my dear?"

"A swell, I beg pardon, mamma, some big wig, he's travelling as the Captain's guest."

"Well, Mrs. Brown, it is so, and if he does come to the ball I want you to promise me one thing."

"And that is?"

"To let my Edith and Rosina dance with him; he's a titled personage my dear Mrs. Brown, what title I don't know, but in poor little Barataria since we had Sir—you know—Sir Thingumy—who was a baronet, for a Governor, we have not seen anyone of consequence. I know he's somebody of great importance and there is a mystery about it all."

"A lettah, ma'am!" and Rachel, a small protegée of the establishment, brought in a rather crumpled and muddy envelope. "The boy"—and here the damsel giggled—"the boy all over mud, ma'am, and begs an excuse as the letter all dirty up, but for he mule bad mule and he throw he and that make so. He say you must be so kind as gib he anseah now."

"You'll excuse me" said Mrs. Brown to her visitors, and opening the note—"Ah? it's from Mrs. Macduff, oh! I'm so glad, it turns out not to be measles her second boy had; he was only over heated."

"*Over eaten* himself no doubt," suggested the second Miss Mt. Fitchit.

"And she now finds she can come to the dance. Of course I must tell her to come."

"De bearer say," observed Rachel, as she re-entered the room, "he ready for go, but he fraid he catch cold; besides he swallow some of de mud and he tummick—"

"Silence, Rachel!" interrupted her mistress, "give him some rum and tell him to wait."

However, the Mt. Fitchit trio rose to take their departure.

"Mind, dear Mrs. Brown, remember our dances with the——"

"Well, well," was the reply, "remember I dont know who the personage is, and I really can't promise."

"Ah! but we know you will; good bye," and away went the mother and her two young ones.

It seemed as if the arrival of the *Arethusa* was to undo all that cruel Fate had brought about in preventing so many of the President's subjects from accepting the invitations to the Ball. More notes arrived in the course of that and the subsequent day, and as much ingenuity was displayed in framing excuses for coming, as had been shewn in explaining why it was impossible to be present. Some people, as the Mt. Fitchits had done, thought it better to call, and although good Mrs. Brown was not in the least deceived by the flimsy pretences now made, she thought it politic to accept them all as if they were Gospel, and to look pleasant; and to some extent she was repaid by the amusement afforded her by the very awkward fibs and devices of her friends.

There was, however, a matter that worried her a good deal, and prevented her dwelling too much on what some women would have resented as an insult. She was very anxious about her Norah;—she knew of her daughter's *penchant* for Lieut. Trevor, and mother-like, she wished to see her child happily married and settled. To the Browns, money was no object; Norah's dowry would be very handsome, and indeed for some years past, her father had continued the business, less from love of gain, than from love of occupation. Oft times he and his Bess would plan what they would do when Norah left them; to close the business, and travel, so as to see something of the world, of which they had heard so much, and knew so little, was the chief item in the programme.

Norah kept her room for the rest of the day on which Capt. Clinton had called. She was annoyed with herself for having attached such value to Trevor's honeyed words, —angry with him for having made a fool of her. Ashamed, and dreading the condolences and covert sneers of her female friends who had observed, and envied her, the marked attention of the faithless sailor, the poor girl was in a fair way of making herself really ill. Her father's caresses, alternated with smothered denunciations of Trevor, and her mother's hopes that all might yet be well, and rather contradictory advice to think no more about the fellow, all helped to agitate her. The result was that Norah was very wretched.

The next day her father had, in his official capacity, to return the formal visit which the Captain of the Frigate had paid at Government House, and our old friend attired in his Windsor uniform, and attended by a half dozen high officials, went on board the *Arethusa*. Seated in the Police boat which carrried a big flag, and was well down in the stern, the party looked resplendent. The *Arethusa's* yards were manned, and there was a guard to receive them as they ascended the ladder, which was rather a perilous affair, for the Inspector, whose sword got in the way, nearly came a cropper, and threatened a general capsize to the rest of the party. There was the usual bowing all round with some introductions and then an adjournment to the Captain's cabin where a capital lunch was spread. The formal duty being over, swords were laid aside and one or two buttons of the heavy uniform loosened. The company broke up into little knots and some went round and renewed acquaintance with the good ship and her officers.

Captain Clinton however, took the President under his wing and carried him off to a quiet corner of the cabin, and the two had an earnest conversation. The effect on Mr. Brown was evidently very startling, for his eyes dilated, his mouth opened, and his old face became puckered up into an expression of the greatest surprise, then came a sudden smile that rapidly changed into a saddened disappointed look as he slowly shook his head.

"I doubt if it will succeed, Clinton. I do indeed—however it is only fair to do as you suggest"—and the pair rose from their seat.

The Captain ringing his bell, gave some directions to the quartermaster, who in a few minutes returned with a "Will be glad to see you, Sir."

Following Capt. Clinton, the President found himself at the door of an officer's cabin and in the presence of its occupant, lying in his cot whose hand he grasped, not without some hesitation.

"I am very sorry you're ill, though I confess I am glad that your non-appearance at my house is due to no other cause than your not being well. I must congratulate you however—"

"My dear Mr. Brown," interrupted the officer, raising himself into a sitting posture, "you may be sure I should at once have come to you, but the doctor forbids my leaving my cabin for another day. He's a good soul is Dr. Narcott, but I fancy he's more nervous about me than is quite necessary, and I wanted to be the first to acquaint you with my altered circumstances, and so begged the Captain to tell you."

"Well, that wasn't a fib exactly, but—I kept your secret very well," said Captain Clinton.

"Yes," added the President "and I was completely deceived; however, you'll be able to land to-morrow. Good bye for the present."

The Captain and President turned to leave the cabin, when the latter was detained by the grasp of the officer, and Clinton taking the hint, left the two together.

What passed between them is unknown. One thing is certain, that the President came out of the cabin somewhat agitated, and had not regained his equanimity when he joined the Captain, whom he found engaged with some of his visitors. Then luncheon was announced, and though he was placed at the Captain's right,—so eagerly did every one fall to, that amid the clash of knife and fork and ring of glasses and the buzz of a general conversation he could only find opportunity to inform

Clinton in a whisper, that somebody was "a first-rate fellow."

The repast over and a cigar smoked, the Island party took their leave with the usual ceremonies, and got safely to shore.

There the President at once sought out his wife, and the pair had a long and serious conversation.

"There's no doubt," said Mr. Brown, "that he loves her, and we know only too well that she returns his affection. Well, Bess, my dear, there is enough money to make her comfortable even as his wife, and he although by no means well off, has what money can't buy. He'll make her happy I do believe, and so we mustn't say no. The only thing is, old lady, we'll have to put up the shutters. B. Brown & Co. will have to disappear; there never was a Co—and you and I must take as well as we may to London folks and London fashions. Well! it's a queer world."

"But Ben,—you don't explain why he wanted to play us such a trick?"

"Well, my dear, when he got news of his uncle and his only cousin, being killed in a railway collision, he says he wasn't quite sure if Norah really cared for him, and then he was afraid that in spite of what had happened, we should think him too poor; then he got a slight attack of fever and begged every one—Clinton and all—to keep his arrival a secret till he could see you and me."

"Of course, you told him what we knew about Norah's feelings."

"Yes I did, and it seemed precious queer to be

shaking hands with the fellow whose head I only yesterday had wanted to punch. He has begged, and I have promised to let him be the first to tell Norah. So not a word to her."

The President's Ball came off in due time, and was a perfect success. Space does not allow of a description of the decorations, the company, and of the wonderful toilettes that graced the scene. The room was crowded; people came from the remotest ends of the Island. Ben Brown's old friends mustered in great force and devoted themselves rather to refreshments and mild whist than to dancing, and those who did dance, preferred quadrilles which were executed by them with every detail and precision; a few of the more giddy ones venturing on a polka which as compared with the romps of now-a-days, was done at a funeral pace. But besides these, there were quick footed agile damsels who were whirled here, there and everywhere, by the *Arethusas* and the more accomplished Baratarian youths. The supper was excellent, thanks to Mrs. Brown, and the music capital; in short, the whole thing was, as the *Banner* several weeks later remarked, a Terpsichorean Triumph; and dear old Mr. and Mrs. Brown sat side by side looking on with delight and some not unpardonable pride.

Mrs. Mt. Fitchit and her daughters were there,—the latter were dancing their best, and their mother seated next Mrs. Brown was watching them and their partners in blue and gold. Presently an officer passed the group with Norah Brown on his arm.

"Dear, dear!" whispered Mrs. Mt. Fitchit in Mrs. Brown's ear, "I'm so glad to see dear Norah is bearing up so well, such a disappointment as it must have been!"

"I don't understand, quite," said Mrs. Brown.

"Why, about that Trevor. We were told he had thrown her over, and after all his attentions. Well! well! but she seems consoled. Who is that with her?"

"That's a lieutenant of the *Arethusa*."

"Why, my dear Mrs. Brown, so I imagine, but who is he?"

"I don't suppose" said Mrs. Brown, "there need be any further concealment: that is Norah's future husband, please God!"

"Her future husband! She's engaged? Why you don't say so? When was it all arranged? That can't be Lieut. Trevor."

"Well, dear Mrs. Mt. Fitchit, it is, and it is not. Since the *Arethusa* was last here, Lieut. Trevor has unexpectedly succeeded to the title and is now Lord Killbarry."

Mrs. Mt. Fitchit "thought a lot" but confined herself to the expressive remark "Well, I never!"

Yes; so it was. Trevor who was supposed to be faithless, had turned up, but under a different name, and as a Peer and a poor one as Peers go, but his affection for Norah was unaltered, and the interview with her father had given him encouragement. An hour or two before the ball began, therefore, he had come ashore, had met Norah's father and mother and Norah herself, and explained all; and so in due time Norah Brown became Viscountess Killbarry. Her father and mother followed her home, and took kindly to their new life, and for many years their house was a rendezvous for their West Indian friends.

A RUN-AWAY.

ONCE upon a time there was a grave official scandal in St. Maria. The—well never mind what he was, but we all called him Portman—Cavendish Portman—early one morning walked through the streets of the capital of that island, and accosting men of business, planters, and professional men, quietly asked them each and all for the loan of £300, which, in St. Maria, in those days, was a large sum. Portman had the reputation of being a wag, and as he appeared to be quite sober—which was not always the case—the good people were inclined to consider that Portman was "poking fun," especially when he coolly added that he was short in his money that amount. And so they dismissed him with a "nonsense! you're joking" or some such remark, and passed on.

When ten o'clock came, Portman was seated in his office with his legs on the table, evidently watching for the arrival of someone, who soon appeared in the person of Governor Fairfax, accompanied by the Colonial Secretary.

Portman jumped off his chair to receive him.

"I have your letter, Mr. Portman," said His Excellency "and am deeply pained at the contents. I did not expect this."

"Well," said Portman with a smile, "I confess I did. I expected though, to make it all right, and even up to this morning I was trying to raise the money."

He did not mention that he had about him some £50 which he had scraped together.

"Three hundred pounds?" enquired the Colonial Secretary, whose name was Scott.

"Well, that's a covering amount. The actual deficit is £293 15s. 4d. up to date. Of course I am very sorry and all that, and I confess I don't see my way to replacing it. You see, Scott, it would take such a deuced long time to pay it by stoppages out of my salary, wouldn't it?"

"That," said the Governor, "is entirely out of the question. I am very sorry, but of course you are suspended, and on a charge of embezzlement."

"Oh! hang it! I beg Your Excellency's pardon—but not embezzlement. I assure you I have put in my I O U for every sixpence of the money, so that I have been above aboard;—no one can deny that."

His Excellency shook his head and saying, "Mr. Scott, you will put Mr. Jennings in charge of the office forthwith," strode away towards the Attorney General's office.

"I say, Scott," said Mr. Portman as he returned from the door whence he had seen the Governor go into the Court house, "the old man isn't going to do anything rash, is he?"

"Anything rash?"

"Well, I mean any d—d law work over this stupid affair, because he's gone into Codicil's chambers."

"I don't know I am sure," replied Mr. Scott.

"Which means, old fellow, that you are perfectly sure. Well, I'll go home to my diggings. Suppose I shall hear from some of you later on. Ta-ta!" And Mr. Portman put on his hat, as usual a little one side, rolled up his umbrella into the slimmest proportions, and walked jauntily towards his house.

The result of the Governor's interview with his Attorney General was the framing of an information and the issue of a warrant against Cavendish Portman for that he, &c., &c.

This was not done in haste. There was a search into books of law and into Portman's books and the Treasurer's books, and an Executive Council was held, and the Police authorities consulted, so that it was quite late in the day before the Senior Officer of Police armed with a warrant proceeded to Mr. Portman's residence. That gentleman was not at home, no one seemed to know where he had gone; but there was nothing to indicate that he had fled, indeed the cook was preparing dinner. Then there was a search through the town; people had seen Mr. Portman walking about, so he did every day; his friends were interrogated, but without result. Messengers were sent post haste into the country districts, but St. Maria saw Mr. Portman no more.

Now the nearest island to St. Maria is St. Molasses, not many miles distant, and the St. Maria boatmen were first-class oarsmen, so that it was an easy matter for a four-oared canoe to cross the narrow channel in fine weather. The Corporal of Police at Point-á-Mire in St. Molasses, therefore was not at all surprised when at day-break on the morning after Portman's disappearance, he saw a boat run up on the beach just below the station. Speculating as to whether it was "rum" or "cattle," smuggling or larceny, that caused the visit of the strangers, he went down to where the canoe was being hauled up and challenged the party in *patois*.

There was no reply, but a gentleman, who was the only passenger, came up to him,—enquired if the Corporal knew who he was, and on the Corporal's answering in the negative he confided to that officer that he was the Chief of Poliçe in St. Maria,—that an official had escaped from that island and was wanted for robbing the Treasury. Had the Corporal seen any other vessel cross from St. Maria?

The Corporal had not.

Then followed enquiries as to how long it would take to reach the chief town, and in the end, his boat-hands being liberally paid, and some instructions given them which they readily promised to obey, the stranger after a cup of coffee and something to eat, and provided with a mule lent from the neighbouring estate on the written request of the Chief of Police of St. Maria, started for town with a policeman as guide.

The ground only permitted a slow pace, which however, enabled the policeman who carried his boots and the traveller's carpet-bag on a stick across his shoulder, to keep up with the mule. It was a fine morning and cool. The mountain which in that part of the island leaves but a bridle path between it and the sea, was covered with mist that occasionally lifting, disclosed the ravines with which the hill side was indented, and against which tiny streamlets stood out like silver threads on a green ground. On the other hand, the white cedar and grape trees formed a screen through which could be seen the grey sea flinging itself with a sob on the shingled beach. Now and then a little settlement was passed, a group of reed-thatched houses, sun-burnt to dark brown, within bamboo fences half hidden in rich foliage, varied here and there with the dark-red dragon-blood planted as a boundary mark, while overhead waved cocoa-nut palms or well-laden trees of bread-fruit. By and bye, the travellers came to an estate where the manager was interviewed, and the mule exchanged for a gig which the policeman undertook to drive; and later on, there were halts at a place where a late breakfast was obtained, and at others where a fresh horse was borrowed, until ultimately the hill overlooking the town was reached, just as the signal for the steamer was hoisted at the Fort, and the warning gun fired.

The policeman who had been kept in ignorance of the position of the gentleman in his care and of his errand, was here dismissed with a liberal tip, and strict orders to drive the gig by easy stages to where it had come from, and the traveller, transferring his bag to the head of a small boy, walked into town. People stared and looked after him, and questioned one another, and audibly made all sorts of guesses, but he took no notice, and continued his journey until he reached the door of the one hotel of St. Molasses.

In a few minutes he came out, looking all the fresher for a hasty rub-down and a change of clothes, and strolled down towards the store of Mr. Thomas Tinker, already mentioned in these yarns, where that worthy was found in his shirt sleeves leaning against his door-post smoking a big and strong cigar.

Now Governor Fairfax had at one time acted as Governor of St. Molasses, and had created no little trouble by the introduction into the local legislature of certain measures, exciting thereby the opposition and anger of Mr. Tinker, who radical in all else, was very conservative when any one tried to interfere with the duties payable on the goods he sold.

When Mr. Tinker saw a well-dressed stranger step up to his door, he at once concluded that he wanted to take his passage by the steamer for which he was agent, and his conclusion was correct. But there was to be some preliminary talk, and the stranger began "Mr. Tinker I presume——"

"Right you are, sir" replied the Honourable Thomas.

"I have heard of you, Mr. Tinker, from—I cannot say a mutual friend—rather the reverse," and the speaker smiling, added "I believe you know Governor Fairfax."

"Know Governor Fairfax? Rather! No one better. He is one of—"

"Precisely," interrupted the other.

"Now Mr. Tinker, I am about to confide in you, and I feel I can safely do so,"

"If it's anything about Governor Fairfax you can confide or you can blow it off on the housetop which ever you darned please." (Mr. Tinker perhaps from dealing in American goods had picked up not a few Yankee expressions and a slight accent). "You can trust me, stranger."

"Well, my name is Portman. I have just come from St. Maria—crossed over in an open boat at the risk of my life, and come overland. I am on my way to England, sir, to denounce Governor Fairfax and his tyrannous ways. I am his victim."

"Allow me to shake hands, Mr. Portman. Any man that's oppressed and down-trodden by Governor Fairfax, has a claim to my sympathy. He acted—mind only acted—as Governor here for six months, and a nice mess he'd a made of it, but we were firm and re—sisted. Take a chair, sir," and Mr. Tinker flicked some flour off a rocker with his straw hat. "Be seated."

I forget what wonderful things they were which Portman invented, thereby rousing the indignation of Mr. Tinker, who responded with a recapitulation of Mr. Fairfax's misdeeds in St. Molasses.

"Would you believe it, sir! He wanted to upset everything—wanted to introduce what he called a more liberal scheme of edication, as if what we have taught the little niggers for the last twenty years wouldn't do for the next fifty. Then there was some tomfoolery about improving the harbour, as if that there bay that's held ever so many tons of shipping, wanted improvement now that our im-imports and exports are gone down. Wanted to join in telegraphic communication! Damme! it makes me laugh to think of that. Here's Thomas Tinker that's made his pile without telegraphs. Telegraphs be blowed!"

"Telegraphs!" echoed Mr. Portman, who, thinking of his own fortunes at this crisis was quite justified in adding, "I believe if we had a cable running to the island, to some of us it would simply mean ruin!"

"A truer word you never said, sir," and Mr. Tinker, in the exuberance of his delight, slapped Mr. Portman on the knee. "And then," he resumed, "the changes—reforms he called 'em—he wanted to introduce. Why sir! he wanted to sooperannyate my own father-in-law that's been in the Customs here since he was a boy, and he's 75 if he's a day. It's true his sight had failed, and he may be rayther hard o'hearing, but he's got what money won't buy, Mr. Portman, and that's experience; and simply because the poor old gentleman made a trifling error or two and couldn't come to office for a fortnight, he wanted to chuck him over."

"Shame!" murmured Mr. Portman.

"Any useful measure such as disestablishment of the Church, disbanding the police, abolishing paid magistrates—Fairfax opposed; why he actually argued that an employer of labour couldn't decide a question of labour law as well as a lawyer fellow fresh from home, who'd never seen a cane field in his life. But the worst of all, sir, was a barefaced attempt to raise the duty on salt fish. That man—Fairfax—actually wanted to put the duty at three dollars a quintal—mark that! three dollars. Why sir, it was robbery. I'm not sure if it didn't come near sacrilege. He had a design on our pockets, sir! that's what he had—he wanted to support a set of bloated over-fed officials at the expense of men like me,"—and Mr. Tinker beat his breast with indignation.

Conversation of this kind and the consumption of a bottle of champagne made the time pass rapidly until the near approach of the steamer rendered it necessary to talk of business. My pen cannot describe the smooth, oily way in which Portman improved on the impression which his own wrongs and his sympathy with those of of Mr. Tinker had made on that gentleman's heart, so that it was not a very difficult matter for Portman to hint that his exchequer was low, that the underhand conduct of the Governor prevented his drawing his pay, and finally that £25 was wanted and that for that sum he could draw a bill on his father, Lord Piccadilly.

Mr. Tinker, in all his commercial transactions, had never cashed a bill drawn on a live lord; and besides that, he was quite won over by Portman, so in exchange for the bit of paper which Mr. Tinker regarded with a degree of reverence, he handed Mr. Portman twenty-five sovereigns.

"Not that I would have done it for any one else" he remarked, "as it's not strictly business, but I look on you as a victim to oppression and down-trodden by that Fairfax."

Mr. Portman made no objection to the transaction on this ground, and in due time having got his carpet bag he stepped on board the *Eider*, was commended to the purser's care by Mr. Tinker, with whom he had a parting Soda and B, and took up his quarters in his cabin. In due time the steamer started, and as it did not call at St. Maria our friend was very easy in his mind.

Of his subsequent adventures I know little, except that he came utterly to grief; his poor mother "to save his honour" as she pathetically put it, paid up his deficiences, and the last I heard of him was that his death was advertised. Subsequently to that, however, a friend who had been a lieutenant on board H.M.S. *Iris*, and had become acquainted with Portman in St. Maria, was visited one night in London, by a wretched broken-down creature whom he recognised as Portman, and to whom he gave refreshments and alms; and that is the last I heard of Cavendish Portman of St. Maria.

That £25 bill held by Mr. Tinker, however, was never honoured, and it was not prudent to refer to it in the hearing of Mr. Tinker, who not long ago, passed away.

A ZOOLOGICAL SPECIMEN.

OLD Punshon, the Honourable Jabez Punshon, of St. Maria, was very fond of natural history, and at one time eager on forming a menagerie, to which end he rather pestered his neighbours and friends for specimens. Like a good many collectors he was fond of using scientific terms, and rarely called an animal by its common name, a bit of pedantry which greatly amused his friends.

Once there was a vacancy on his staff, and he was difficult to please. A good many applicants had presented themselves without success, when, one afternoon as he was half dozing in his gallery, a tall and rather woe-begone young man, who evidently was "seeing hard times," came up the steps. The butler-boy met him and conveyed the letter he had brought to his master, who hastily read it.

"Eh, what," he said—"a specimen! Where is it?"—and Mr. Punshon jumped off his chair—"Where is it?"

The stranger observed that Mr. Fitzwagg, of Boodles, the next estate, had given him the letter.

Mr. Punshon therefore re-read the missive and turned very red. "Confound his impudence," he called out, and the next moment burst into a fit of uncontrollable laughter.

The poor visitor murmured "a good afternoon, sir," and turned to go away.

"Stop, my man! wait a bit," said Mr. Punshon, who was a little ashamed of having laughed at the lad and also touched at his evident distress—"Let me hear where you have been working."

A conversation ensued, and the visitor's face brightened a good deal as he went away "an engaged party."

"Confound that fellow Fitzwagg's impudence, what does he say?" Mr. Punshon inquired of himself, and for an answer referred to the letter:—

My Dear Mr. PUNSHON,

I send you on approval a very decent specimen of the "episcopus campestris," quite tame, which, I think, you will like. If you do not, just turn him loose and he will find his way home all right. Yours truly,

A. FITZWAGG.

"Episcopus campestris!" that's poking fun at me,—of course it is a sort of bogus scientific name for field overseer. I'll be even with you some day, Fitzwagg, and as for your specimen, I hope the poor devil will suit me and the place suit him. Boy! a sangaree!"

AN IMPORTANT CRISIS.

BATHSHEBA is an unsanctified Island. I mean it does not bear the name, as so many of them do, of a calendared Saint; but, by way of recompense, it has—or had—an Ice-house where cool drinks and dainty refections could be obtained all the day long. The drinking saloon was well provided with tables and cosy chairs, and there was a bar, behind which the civilest bar-men dispensed delicious decoctions. A misguided and military friend of mine one day undertook to drink through the list of liquors whose appellations shone in enamelled glass from a series of frames hung across and round the room. Ill-fated youth! He began with Siegert's bitters, followed by brandy, sherry, Bass's beer, champagne—and then he faltered. Guiness's stout was the next on the list, and he took some, but with disastrous results that necessitated his being conveyed to his quarters without delay.

The arrival of the ice ship with its welcome cargo, in which were imbedded choice meat and oysters, fish, partridges, grouse, pheasants, &c., was an event! Gourmets hurried to the well-known store and selected what they wanted, and for days after they would compare notes with one another as to the flavour of this, and the tenderness of that, until their eyes glistened and their mouths watered. Bathsheba was not an eventful place, and could afford to be stirred to its inmost—well we'll say—heart by the advent of these luxuries. It was the one thing expected, enjoyed and remembered until the next vessel came.

H.M.S. *Lily* had her steam up, and the Governor was to go in her to a distant island on matters of importance. The Legislature was reported to be ready to change the constitution—all had been prepared by the Lieutenant Governor. The opposition had been won over; the press (one paper which appeared at most unexpected times) was propitious; all that was wanted was the presence of the Governor-in-Chief to—as it was forcibly put—clinch the nail. This change of constitution was a nail "the

Office" had been hammering at for some time, and Governors, great and small, had done their best to drive it home. It was therefore a case of "now or never," and the Governor made arrangements accordingly. Matters of importance to Bathsheba yielded to the affairs of St. Molasses. A big supply of official paper was laid in, uniforms packed up, and memoranda as to local affairs dictated to the Private Secretary and his clerks, and everything was in a state of hurry-skurry; in the midst of which a venerable and conscientious official demanded audience. The Governor looked at his watch, there was hardly time,—but poor old Mr. Jakes had come up all the way from town, and so he was admitted.

Now there are officials who never worry a Governor unless there is reason. Such men will plod away in their offices and never dream of wishing "to see His Excellency." While there are others who have always something to suggest, something to fuss and worry about, and who would despair of their official salvation were they to omit seeing the Governor four days out of six, and all about nothing; but old Jakes was not one of these latter.

The Governor explained how pressed he was for time, and Mr. Jakes occupied a good deal of that time in apologising for his intrusion, but his business was important, still if His Excellency was occupied he would come again.

But the Governor preferred having it over; and as Mr. Jakes's business was merely to express doubts as to the steadiness of a junior clerk, no great time was consumed. Still he sate on, in that dreadful way in which some men when they have said their say and done what they come to do, will linger on; but there came an interruption. The Governor's servant brought a message that the luggage was on board and the Captain waiting.

Now Captains R.N. are mighty men, and, as a rule, dislike carrying Governors about, and so His Excellency jumped up and told Mr. Jakes he must really run away. "On his return,"—

"On your return, Your Excellency! may I ask where are you going?"

"Going, Mr. Jakes? Well, I am going to St. Molasses in the Lily, and it is time I was on board—"

"St. Molasses!" said Mr. Jakes in a thin piping voice; "St. Molasses!" and here he began to cough in a most distressing way.

You can't well leave a visitor—even an official visitor—black in the face with a sudden cough, but His Excellency grew very impatient.

As Mr. Jakes recovered himself, he gasped, "Going to leave Bathsheba at this crisis?"

"Crisis!" asked the Governor, "What d'ye mean by crisis, Mr. Jakes?"

"Yes, Your Excellency, I may call it crisis"—

"Why, what's the matter?"

"Well, Sir, are you are aware that the——" and here his cough recommenced.

The Governor's face was a study. "Aware of what, Mr. Jakes?" he thundered out. "What is this crisis?"

"Why—Your Ex—Excellency THE ICE SHIP IS SIGNALLED!!"

Now the Governor was a good pious man, but he said a naughty word with a big D— as he strode from the room, leaving Mr. Jakes struggling with the last notes of his troublesome cough.

COLLECTIONS.

SOME years ago, in a snake-infested West Indian island, the Legislature voted the means of paying a reward of a shilling for every head of the deadly reptile brought to the authorities. Then a London savant, who wished to analyse the poison, requested that the heads be sent to him, and to this end strong rum was forwarded to the several police stations, so that the heads collected might be preserved therein.

The heat of the climate presumably caused such an extraordinary degree of evaporation of the spirit that the supplies had to be frequently renewed, and the waste was not checked until evaporation was retarded, if not prevented, by the admixture of a strong dose of carbolic acid with the rum.

The collection went on capitally. The supply of serpent heads was plentiful, and there seemed a prospect of the island being rid of these pests. Time passed and still there came these snake heads, until it was found that the wily creoles were importing them from a neighbouring island, whereupon the premium was reduced to a penny and the supply ceased.

This reminds me of a planter in Barataria whose cane fields were ravaged by mole-crickets*,—an insect which with its formidable mandibles bites off the young cane

* Eryllotalpa.

shoots. My friend set all the small people on his estate to collect these 'varmint,' and promised a 'tampee or penny a tumbler full. He soon got plenty of them. Every morning there would be a small mob of creole children, each with his collection, for which the promised reward was given for the insects destroyed. There seemed however no diminution in the catch. Week after week the mole-crickets poured in, and the outlay became rather serious. So one morning the "maninger" informed his small hearers that "he no able fo' gie tampee, dese ting too easy fo' catch, so he give ha'penny for a tumbler full after to-day."

There was a howl of remonstrance from the little darkies, one of whom called out "Maninger we hab to "fetch dese ting all de way from Richmond Park."

Now Richmond Park belonged to another man with whom our friend's relations were the reverse of friendly, and he learned too late that he had been paying to clear his enemy's fields of mole-crickets.

The rat-catcher is an important person on some island estates. Followed by a couple of mongrel curs, he saunters through the estate and makes his "bag," which is duly produced to the overseer who certifies the number killed.

There is so little confidence between man and man that the tails of the captured are cut off lest an animal be produced a second time and secure a double premium.

In Barataria, one manager used to set down on his pay-list the names of four rat-catchers: Bill, Jack, Bob, &c., as earning a pound a month each, and who were never absent from work. It is true they were his own terriers, but this was a fact not generally known, not even to the proprietor.

Collectors are not appreciated by the humbler class of creoles. One day, a geologist who had made a weary tramp from the northern end of the island, halted at my house where he was an expected guest. He was at once ushered within doors, and handed over to the care and attention of the hostess, while I attended to the disposal of his luggage. 'Peter,' one of the most rascally of the town porters, bore a Gladstone bag in one hand, while over his shoulder was a carpet ditto slung to the end of a stout stick and apparently somewhat heavy to carry.

"Aow, me Gad!" said Peter as he lowered the last named bag to the ground, "wha nex buckra do? He go pick up pick up stone all along and go fill dis bag till me back mos' bruck. Massa! you think it harm s'pose me go empty dis bag and fill up when me get nearer town?"

I rather discouraged this idea of Peter's, and having secured the specimens, warned my friend as to Peter's probable dodge.

SHAKESPERE IN THE TROPICS.

I have met two very worthy men, instances of love of Chess and intimate knowledge and appreciation of Shakspere being united in the same person.

In St. Maria. there was a Mr. Paul, an official, whose leisure was spent over the chess board, or the "Divine William." To him life seemed to have no other aim than to work out and follow openings and gambits, or discover fresh beauties in his only author. He was a tall gaunt man with a singularly gentle manner, he wore his hair rather long, and the pallor of his face contrasted with weak pink-rimmed eyes and a red nose, which latter, as Paul had been from childhood a strict abstainer, was due to chronic dyspepsia. His appearance and manner however had obtained for him the unkind and undeserved sobriquets of "Stiggins," and "The Shepherd." The only times that Paul shewed signs of temper were when his idolized author was misquoted or in any way disparaged; then, he really was no longer himself, his eyes would fill with tears, or his contorted features would show the difficulty he had in repressing his anger.

Our friend worked on qufetly and patiently, never seeking promotion or change; but one day, a vacancy occurred in St Molasses, where it was deemed advisable to import new blood, and so to Paul's surprise he was offered advancement to a well paid post in that island.

The creoles of St. Molasses, who were jealous of intruders, and had an idea that St. Molasses was for the St. Molassians and none others, might well have been those of whom Marryat wrote that they were the proudest people on earth exeept fan-tailed pigeons. They prided themselves on their country and all appertaining to it; even on their peculiar mode of speech, for the St. Molasses folk suffered from a chronic diæresis which converted their canes into cayüns and their roads into roäds. So peculiar were the St. Molassians that Paul's friends who had vouched for his efficiency and steadiness were pleased to find that he, after a few days, had been well received in his new home. He soon proved his ability; he was intelligent and prompt as well as polite to the public, who at first were a little startled at Shakesperian quotations being mixed with official communications; but that was Paul's way.

Every one who knew him, therefore, was horrified to hear that he had on an evening some months after his arrival, misconducted himself in public, had been intoxicated, and had narrowly escaped being locked up; and this report, of course, had been carried to the Governor as evidence of the natural result of bringing strangers into the St. Molasses' official circle. It was very sad to find that the scene of the escapade was in River Road, the most disreputable quarter of the town, and at Poll Flanagan's, the least respectable house in it, where there was a large room usually the scene of dignities and objectionable orgies.

As soon as I heard of this, I sought "The Shepherd" in his office, and found him as meek and mild as usual, attending to his work, and certainly shewing no signs of any "ruction." As delicately as was possible, the story of his misdoing was introduced. "The Shepherd" blushed and stammered out an admission that the report was in some respects correct, but he would explain.

It turned out that my friend had been attracted by a notice that the Rivertown Amateurs would give a representation of Shakspere's Richard the 3rd; and finding his way to Poll Flanagan's whose *salon de danse* had been converted into a temporary theatre, he obtained a front seat. The arrangements were simple; the footlights a row of candles protected from the wind by shades of all sorts and shapes, while the curtain was composed of flags. The audience consisted almost entirely of the lower orders; and among them Poll's female friends mustered strongly.

Any one but a simple creature like Paul would have hesitated at assisting at a performance in such company, but he had but one idea, one desire, viz., to see his beloved author's work on the stage. To him it would be a novelty, since of theatricals there were none in St. Maria, and so he sate on, unmindful of the heat and odours that oppressed him, and deaf to the 'orchestra,' a horn, and drum, which discoursed discordant music.

When the curtain rose and Gloster appeared, Paul was much moved, for he was not prepared to recognize as Gloster, a tall weedy man, whose black face frowned and scowled from beneath a red cap with three white feathers, his dress being an artillery man's tunic, bound round the waist with a sash of red cloth from which hung a cavalry sabre, white duck trousers rolled up above the knee, shining leather leggings and white canvas shoes with spurs attached.

As the actor strode up and down awaiting the conclusion of 'Cheer boys, Cheer,' by the band, Paul's excitement increased; he half rose from his seat and convulsively clutched his umbrella, and when the Island Roscius burst forth in the St. Molasses' tongue with "Now is the wintur of our discontent maäde glorious "by the sun of Yo-ork," poor Paul could restrain himself no longer; with a yell he dashed across the footlights smashing two of them, and rushing at the affrighted Gloster, smote him to the ground with his umbrella. The rest of the corps dramatique and some of the audience came to the rescue, but "The Shepherd" cleared a way with his gingham and escaped at an open door; then followed a chase down River Road, in which the police were distanced by the fleeter Paul.

In the early morning, the sable Gloster received a visit, apologies and pecuniary compensation, and so the matter ended. Paul, admonished by the Executive, promised never again to attend Shaksperian performances in St. Molasses, where he remained for some years, a very deserving and useful official.

CAPTAIN HEEPS, U.S.N.

CAPTAIN Hiram T. Heeps, U.S.N., commanded the corvette, Scudder, in West Indian waters, in the year 18—. He had just looked in at a good many parts, but had stayed at others, and at length we in St. Maria were honoured with a visit.

The Captain and officers mounted on horses or mules, explored the vicinity ot the town the first day of their arrival, and were hospitably received.

At 7 p.m., Captain Heeps was due at Government House, but he was late,—a hardly pardonable sin in those days, and the company sate down without him.

The party comprised the Commanding Royal Engineer, a very stately officer, who was a great stickler for etiquette, H.M. Attorney General, a white-headed dear old man with massive gold spectacles and a gentle manner, the U.S. Consul, who had been a naval officer and other things before he represented his country, and dispensed rope, tar, yarn and spars to the needy mariners, who called him fellow country man, a Planter, who cultivated canes, race horses, and unlimited loo, and a Surgeon Major. There were, of course, the Governor and his Secretary.

Soup had hardly been got through when Captain Heeps appeared with an unsteady gait and many apologies. He tried the *bisque*, but could not manage it, however he tossed off a glass of sherry, and began to talk.

"Excellency! you hev' been in the U-nited States, I believe."

The Governor nodded assent.

"You may have become acquainted with Admiral James Porter of our service."

His Excellency said 'No,' he had not that honour.

"Wall! he was called King James on account of the austerity of his manners."

The other guests stared, but in politeness said "Indeed."

"Yes, *Sir!* Admiral James Porter of our service was called King James on account of the austerity of his manners, and I am about with your permission, to tell you an anecdote of Admiral James Porter, who, I may observe, was called King James on account of the austerity of his manners, which has never yet appeared in print—"

The company was all attention.

"I was going to remark that Admiral James Porter, who was called King James on account of the ——"

"Yes," politely said the Attorney General,—

"Austerity of his manners (continued the Captain) commanded on the Potomac. You will recollect that the Admiral was a man, who, on account of his austere—"

"You were about to tell us of what he did on the *Potomac*, I presume," said the Governor.

"Excellency! right you air. I was about to tell you an anecdote never yet appearing in print about my old friend Admiral James Porter of our service, who—"

"He commanded on the *Potomac*, I think you said."

"He did so, Sir! I am glad you are aware of that fact, I may also add that on account of the austerity—"

Well, you know the politest of Governors and Governors' guests could not stand this, and so one took wine with the Captain, and the others all began to talk, but still ever and anon through the hum of voices and clatter of knife and fork would come the nasal tones of Captain Heeps insisting on the fact of Admiral James Porter being called King James on account, &c., &c.

Dinner was finished, and it being the evening on which there was a card and billiard party, the wine and dessert were got over rather rapidly, and the guests prepared to go, some upstairs to cards, others down to billiards.

"Captain Heeps!" said His Excellency "you will join in a rubber, won't you? But we do not play long whist as I remember so many do in the States, but short, still I hope—"

"Excellency! Short or long it's all the same to me, whichever Your Excellency darn pleases."

This mixture of politeness and slang upset the Governor so that the Secretary interposed.

"I thought Captain Heeps, you would prefer billiards, and that you would come with me."

"Secretary!" assented the Captain, "you bet! that'll suit me down to the ground;" and taking the Secretary's arm off he went.

Arrived in the billiard room, Captain Heeps carefully removed his uniform coat, unfastened his braces and twisted them round his waist, rolled his shirt sleeves up to the elbows and selected a cue.

"What's that?" he asked pointing to the balls. "Guess I play the four ball game."

The Secretary, whose billiard education was defective, regretted he did not know it, and the Captain resignedly commenced to play the English game.

From some reason, perhaps the advent of a man servant in gorgeous livery with a tray of glasses, and wherewithal to fill them, the Captain did not succeed in hitting a ball, or anything indeed except the cloth, so at last he grounded his cue, and said, "Secretary! Guess I shouldn't make five cents out of you at this, if I was to play all night. No! *Sir!*"

Presently came in the Consul and other guests, and the party engaged in conversation rather than billiards until Captain Heeps, seizing a cue and arranging some balls on the table, offered to bet the Consul (Counsel he called him) ten dollars he would make this stroke.

The Consul declined; he never betted money.

"Wall, then" remarked the Captain "let it be drinks, —drinks for the company."

Everyone was of course startled at this, and still more so when the gallant mariner having missed the ball, called out to the bewildered domestic—

"Bhoy, take the gentlemen's orders."

Josephus did not move.

"Now, be smart; gentlemen, name your drinks."

There was only one out way of it, so the Secretary said he would take brandy and soda.

His politeness was rewarded by a heavy slap on the back from Captain Heeps, who remarked—

"Secretary, I esteem a man whatever his nationality, who has his mind ready made up as to drinks. Gentlemen, will you order if you please."

Some of the guests complied with the request of the Captain, who then addressed the astonished Josephus thus—

"Now, Bhoy, you chalk up that to me, Hiram T. Heeps, d'ye see, and you take partickler darned care I don't leave the bar without payin'. It's a bad trick I've got, but——"

The door had opened, and His Excellency was on the threshold, looking anything but satisfied.

After a while, Captain Heeps was conducted home by the Consul, declaring as he was slowly moving away that he should use his influence at the White House to get his friend, the Secretary, nominated as 'Counsel' for St. Maria; and that the Governor reminded him of Admiral James Porter, who on account of the austerity of his manners, was called ——

SNAKES.

I ONCE was calling at a certain Government House and found there a minister and his wife who had lately arrived from St. Sinners. The Governor's wife was evidently doing her best to engage her visitors in conversation, but they were both very shy. At length however she asked:—"I believe the snakes in St. Sinners are very numerous?"

"Oh! very."

"And their bite is fatal?"

"Oh yes! most fatal. If you get bitten, you die immediately."

"Sometimes sooner than that, William," added the lady visitor by way of helping on the conversation.

"And what is the name of your most poisonous snake?"

"Ah well, my lady, I confess I never studied the *botanical* names of the snakes."

Then the talk languished, and soon faded out.

A RETURN HOME.

IT was a calm moonlight night in July. The R.M.S. *Niger* was going at rather more than contract rate, and her passengers were speculating on arriving at Plymouth in something like 60 hours. There was a good many on board, but the ship was not overcrowded, and there was space on deck for a promenade without risk of a collision with other people's chairs or a stumble over their outstretched legs. Several couples were pacing up and down, some more leisurely than others, stopping occasionally to listen to a Spaniard who, gifted with a tenor voice of no ordinary quality, was singing to his own accompaniment on the guitar before an admiring audience. Others were chatting in little groups, and from one or other of these, every now and then there would come a loud boisterous laugh that drowned the singer's voice. In the saloon were a few solemn silent whist players with some lookers-on at their game, while round a table forward was gathered a large party engaged in monte. All nations were represented there. One silly English boy with a cigar in his mouth,—a lieutenant going home on sick leave, was winning silver and losing gold. There were flabby-faced Hamburg Jews whose fingers looked all the dirtier for the many rings on them,—men on whom varying fortune appeared to have no effect, save when a grunt that might have been an oath, escaped their lips. There were lean brown men with quick furtive eyes, hailing from South American republics where life is rarely safe, men who watched the banker's hands and cards suspiciously. One tall white-faced Danish Official from St. Thomas with oddly-shaped cap and golden badge, peered through his great round spectacles, and seemed to risk and often to lose large sums that spoke well for the liberality of his government. There was a young Scotchman, a coffee planter from Costa Rica, lounging against his cabin door, who between puffs at his cigarette, threw down his stakes with a *nonchalant* air, and lazily stretching forward, lifted his winnings which were frequent and considerable. On the table were exposed larger or smaller heaps of coin, and these melted or were swollen as the chances of the game varied. The scene was a strange one and with the glare and heat and the atmosphere thick with tobacco smoke, and heavy with a mixture of odours, some of them not the pleasantest in the world, it contrasted strangely with that on deck, where the night air was cool and fresh, and the silvery moonbeams the only light.

There was one gamester whom we have not as yet

noticed,—a tall young Englishman with features that would have been handsome, but for an expression of anxiety and anger that sate upon them. He was pale, and the nervous twitching of his lips shewed that for him the game had a more than painful interest. The money before him had disappeared by degrees, as had the coins with which he continued his stakes, till at length, one unlucky card appeared, and he pushed all the money before him to the centre of the table. Thrusting back his chair, with a muttered oath, he strode from the saloon through the crowd of gamblers.

"Hard hit!" observed the lieutenant with a heartless laugh as he took his cigar from his lips.

"Pobre diablo!" muttered a Chilian, sweeping into his pocket a pile of glittering gold pieces.

Robert—the Honourable Robert Rossdale,—for so was the Englishman called, paid no heed to their remarks, beyond casting a defiant glance at the group as he mounted the companion. Then threading his way towards the stern, presently found himself near a lady and gentleman, who seated in deck chairs, were conversing in a tone sufficiently loud to be heard by Rossdale, who sauntering behind them, quietly sank into a chair he found there.

The lady was about twenty-five, a little somewhat below the medium stature, with a figure the graceful outlines of which would have displeased the æsthete of now a days, so far was it removed from any thing angular and unwholesome. Her features was not very striking. Some people called hers a baby face; it perhaps had no claim to any higher style of beauty, being rather round than oval, with a mouth which was perfect in its way, only a little too apt to disclose teeth which were white and regular. The face was set in a frame of golden hair, left much to its natural mode of growth, that is, not frizzed and fuzzed out in a wad over the forehead, but rippling round a pair of shell-like ears, and caught up in a big knot that to some appeared untidy, but which was very fair to behold. Reclining in her chair, amid the folds of an overcoat of a rather masculine cut, which allowed two dainty feet to be seen, and crowned with a soft crushable hat, that was perhaps more suitable for a man, Mary Grenville, widow, would have made a pretty picture.

Her companion was tall and powerfully built with features that recalled those of some hero of Greek sculpture ; a rather sad face when in repose as that of one who had been disappointed in life, but capable of brightening up with a flashing eye, and a mouth almost as eloquent in silence as in speech ; for there is a dumb language ot which some lips have the gift. On the occasion of which we speak, John Lancaster's face wore a rather amused look, as with hat drawn over his brow he sate back in his chair with appreciative eye and listening with attentive ear to his neighbour.

"Not been home for years?" said the lady, "why how changed you will find everthing and every one too!"

"No! Mrs. Grenville, I shall find no change in people. I shall be spared that, simply because I shall know no one, and no one will know me."

"You strange creature! what do you mean?"

"What I say. When I left London thirty years ago, I was a penniless, friendless lad, I have since picked up some pennies it is true, but as for friends—" and the speaker shrugged his shoulders.

"You mean I suppose that you do not care to renew the friendships,—the associations of bye gone days."

"Forgive me, but you are quite wrong there; you do not know how I should welcome one friend, one companion of my boyhood, but mine was a queer hard life, and I was little more than a child when I came to the West Indies."

"Some day, you must tell me your history Mr. Lancaster."

"Some day! well then, it must be now, for in two days we part, and I dare not hope we shall meet again."

"You wish then that our parting at Southampton may not be final?"

"Mrs. Grenville!"

"Mr. Lancaster!"

"You are laughing at me."

"Indeed no, why should I? We have made ourselves, I suppose I may say, very agreeable to each other on the voyage—I'm sure you have, and I hope I have—so why on earth should you think I laughed at the idea of the acquaintance continuing? You say you don't intend returning to the West Indies, and I have settled all my affairs there and don't propose ever going back; you tell me you have picked up pennies, meaning, I conclude, dollars, and Charles—that is my poor husband—was well off and generous enough to leave me all he had; so no doubt I shall settle down and live in the same style, as you will; we shall often meet, and it will be very pleasant;—likest thou the picture?" she added after a pause, quoting Claude Melnotte.

"I would like it better if you were serious."

"I am."

"It is hard for me to shew you why such a prospect is very tempting to me, and why I fear to hope that I may realize it."

"Of course, if Mr. Lancaster talks riddles, and rates people for not being serious, and looks very gloomy, and glum and ghost-like in the moonlight, one can only wait until he pleases to make himself intelligible. I am all attention;" and Mrs. Grenville wrapped her light ulster more closely around her, and leaning her head on the side of the chair nearest her companion looked at him out of her great blue eyes, while a rather saucy smile played about the corners of her mouth.

"Now then," said she, "begin."

"Mary"—said Mr. Lancaster.

"Why, that is my name!" said the widow, and then, after a pause and in a half whisper, she added, "Yes, John!"

Their eyes met, and John Lancaster laid his open hand on the elbow of his chair, and some little fingers that shyly stole into it, were gently imprisoned.

"Mary," said Lancaster after a long pause, "I cannot begin my history as you call it."

"Why, can't you do as the story books do?—'Once upon a time'—or, 'I was born of humble though respectable parents'?"

"I cannot begin so."

"If your parents were not respectable you need not say so,—I want to know about *you*. If they were not humble but were somebodies, so much the better, you know."

"I don't know who they were; that's all."

"What?"

"I was a foundling. God only knows who my parents were. I was bred in a workhouse—a sort of Oliver Twist, and then I ran away, shipped as a cabin boy, got more licks than ha'pence as the saying is, was taken on as a house boy by a planter in St. Molasses, became in time an overseer, then manager—bought an estate—lost it—resumed the life of an overseer, emigrated to Demerara—then went to the Main—worked in one gold mine—discovered another; and then came success and wealth. That's my story."

"It's rather an eventful one, somewhat romantic too, but you must tell me all. You know no romance is perfect without a love story in it."

"Love story!" and Mr. Lancaster laughed. "I have none to tell."

"None at all?"

"None, save that I love you," said Lancaster in a changed and eager tone, "and that if, now you know the story of my life, you are content to make what may remain of it to me, a recompense for all I have before suffered, I shall be very proud,—very happy."

Mrs. Grenville made no reply.

"Well; is it 'yes,' or 'no,' Mary?"

"It is not 'No,' John."

And then the two faces approached each other with a not uncommon result.

"I want you to promise me one thing" said Mrs. Grenville after some moments.

"And that is?"

"I don't like your friend, Mr. Rossdale. Are you so linked to each other that you cannot drop him?"

"Why do you not like him, Mary? You have only known him during this voyage."

"Because he's no good: he is a rascal, and a mean one into the bargain."

"My dear Mary! these are strong words"

"Not too strong though. He has been as good as dismissed from his appointment, and even the money you gave him——"

"I gave him!"

"Yes, I saw this afternoon the way in which he was wheedling you, and my eyes and ears were sharp enough to detect you giving him the means to visit the monte table."

"What I lent him wont hurt me."

"I don't say it will—give as much as you like—lend as much as you like, but not to a fellow like that; he looks sometimes as if he could stab you. I half believe he has the 'evil eye' a Neapolitan friend once told me of."

"I think, dearest, you are a little hard on poor Rossdale. He's well connected—good family you know, and——"

"And has thrown away what advantages that gave him, his good family has enabled him to supplant better men, and has saved him from what has been dealt out to men less culpable, whose names do not appear in Burke or Debrett."

"Why, you are a democrat, Mary! I did not know a sprig of nobility would have made you so angry."

"I am angry, because I am *not* a democrat, and

because I hate to see old names, old families, dragged into the dirt by fellows like that."

As Mrs. Greville spoke, her companion marked how her soft 'baby face' lit up and the almost fierce light of her blue eyes which in repose seemed like cloudless skies; and to him her features under the influence of her angry emotion appeared all the more beautiful.

Robert Rossdale was, as Lancaster had said, of good family—good that is, in the sense of being ancient, and of frequent mention in byegone and stirring times. The Rossdales had been crusaders, had shed their blood in many a fight. Their name was to be found in old records of pageants, plots, and parliaments; but of late they had been noted chiefly for their aptitude for getting rid of their money, and encumbering their old castle home and the remaining lands, so that at this time the younger sons had to work for a living. Robert had tried soldiering, and had passed an examination with tolerable ease, for he was in some respects no fool; but he had never acquired the art of making both ends meet, and so a shabby bill transaction that found its way into the papers ended his military career. Then he was sent to St. Maria, but the work was uncongenial, and amusement there was none. It was impossible to win more than a dollar a day from the fools who played with him at billiards, or any of the card games of which he seemed to know no end, and there his salary, as a larger one would have done, fell short of his requirements; then a deficiency in his cash deprived the Government of that favoured island of Mr. Rossdale's services, and so he had shipped in the *Niger*. Every one wondered how he got off, and his creditors were angry to see he had flown, but Rossdale had observed the Sabbath for once, and knowing that bailiffs were powerless on that day, he waited till he was lucky enough to find the steamer's arrival and departure happen on that day of rest and sanctuary. He had heard of Mrs. Grenville, and was glad of the luck that had thrown her in his way, for he thought it would be rather a good business to captivate her and secure her fortune; but although he laid his plans cleverly, and made his advances cautiously, the widow gave him no encouragement, until on one occasion, when he became bolder in his attack, she repulsed him in a way that taught him the game was up in that quarter. As he sate there in the shade, watching Lancaster and Mrs. Grenville, he had heard much of what had passed. The widow's denunciation of him called up an ugly smile, and although he was not exactly jealous of Lancaster, Mrs. Grenville's rejection of his proferred attentions was neither forgotten nor forgiven. He was ready to frame and work out any plan by which he could gain profit at Lancaster's expense, and pleasure in avenging himself on his fair companion. At length, after a minute or two, he rose slowly and silently, like some wary animal, and then making his way round by the other side of the deck, sauntered towards the pair of friends as if he had just come from below.

"I hope I do not interrupt you" he said, as raising his hat, he fell into a vacant chair.

"Um—no—not at all" said Lancaster in a tone which implied the contrary.

"In a few hours, Mrs. Grenville, we shall be in the

old country—ah! well there's no place like home—is there?"

"No" was the reply, "except to those who have made home too hot for them."

"I beg your pardon, I did not quite catch what you said, Mrs. Grenville."

"I thought you did. 'Home' to some, means a place hallowed by old associations, old ties, to others it is an Eden from which their vices have driven them, and they revisit it to find it a hell of remorse and regret."

"Mrs. Grenville is pleased to speak in parables" said Rossdale with a sneer.

"I think Mr. Rossdale you can read the riddle," she replied.

"Lancaster" asked Rossdale after a somewhat awkward pause, "what do you intend to do with yourself when you land? But first, where *do* you land, Plymouth or Southampton?"

"At Southampton."

"And thence you of course go to the 'little village.' If Mrs. Grenville will excuse me, there is no place like London. It must be some years since you were there. Can I be of use in recommending you an hotel? I need not say I shall be delighted to serve you in any way."

"Thanks" said Lancaster, "but I have my arrangements. I go to Southampton, thence to London where I have to perform a vow."

"A vow?" said Mrs. Grenville in a low tone, "a vow?"

"My dear Lancaster" asked Rossdale as he lit his cigar "a vow?"

"Yes, it is no matter my telling you, you both already know I left home a poor lad."

"Yes" said Rossdale, "I recollect the yarn you told me."

"Well then, the night I ran away, my head full of my plan of taking to the sea, I found my way down to an inn, a public house, at the waterside at Wapping, and there I crept in foot-sore, hungry and weary; the landlord and the woman who passed for his wife took me in, made me welcome. She begged me to go back to my mother and home, and when I told her I knew neither, she took pity on me, and helped me to get a cabin boy's berth. My kit, slender as it was, she furnished, her husband pressed some shillings in my hand, and she, as I stepped into the boat, blessed me and kissed me. It was the first blessing, the first caress I had ever known, and as I left them I promised that whenever I came home their's should be the first roof to shelter me."

"My dear John! Mr. Lancaster I mean" said Mrs. Grenville "you don't mean you intend to carry out this—forgive me—quixotic idea."

"A promise is a promise."

"And where is this tavern?" enquired Mr. Rossdale.

"The Blue Anchor inn"—but before he could finish the sentence, Mrs. Grenville had warned him by a sudden grasp of the arm to be silent.

"Well," said Rossdale, "after the Blue Anchor you will of course, take some more agreeable quarters, where I hope I may be allowed to look you up; and you, Mrs. Grenville, may I enquire where I may pay my respects to you?"

"Mr. Rossdale, our acquaintance ends where it began, —on board this steamer."

Rossdale made a low bow and then turned away.

"Mary" said Lancaster "you are a rash woman to 'rile' that man."

"I don't fear him for myself, but I do hope you will not continue the acquaintanceship. Tell me where will you send your luggage. Can I take any for you? I am afraid the Blue Anchor is not a very safe lodging for your goods and chattels."

Lancaster laughed.

"I have but a small portmanteau" said he, and I carry my valuables on me—Bank of England notes and sovereigns. I never trust bills or drafts. A miner's belt is my Bank, little woman."

Mrs. Grenville shook her head.

One afternoon some five days afterwards, Mrs. Grenville was seated in her room at the——Hotel. A table was covered with papers,—newspapers, telegrams and letters, while a tray with refreshment on it had remained untouched for some hours. The widow was walking up and down the room, stopping every now and then to gaze out of the window, or to listen at the door. There was an anxious expression on her face, and her somewhat disordered hair and careless toilette shewed she was troubled. Presently she threw herself into a lounging chair, and resting her cheek on her hand, became for some minutes absorbed in deep thought. Then, hastily rising, she went to the table and eagerly read a telegram, and while thus engaged, a knock sounded at the door.

"Come in" she said, throwing down the paper.

A short stout man with a red whiskerless face and dressed in black, entered, making a low bow to Mrs. Grenville.

"Well, what news?"

"I regret, Ma'am——"

"Then you have none"—interrupted the widow.

The man slowly wiped his bald head with a large red cotton handkerchief, for it was rather warm weather, and he was heated.

"I was about to say, madam, that from information received, I find that on the day in question, namely the —— the ——" and here he fumbled in his breast for a greasy pocket book and took out some papers which he leisurely consulted, while Mrs Grenville's foot tapped the floor with impatience.

"Ah!" he resumed, "on the 5th May a gentleman dressed in wide-awake, blue serge suit, with dark hair and eyes, moustache and beard, no luggage, left the Waterloo Station at 7.25 p.m. in a cab, four-wheeler, No. 112, owner, Podgers of Grays Inn Lane, driver No. 211, Swiffkins, of——"

"Never mind these absurd details," cried Mrs. Grenville.

"These are the links, Ma'am, important links."

"Go on, then" said Mrs. Grenville, as she resumed her chair.

"Driver, No. 211 Swiffkins, of Clarendon Mews," continued the man, "on leaving the station, the gentleman shook hands with a lady, yellow hair, round face, blue eyes, no particular marks on teeth or otherwise, short and —and—cannot make out the word."

"Never mind Mr. Peters, I know the lady, these details are worrying."

"Ah" said Mr. Peters, "I've got it——and scrumptious."

"What?"

"Beg pardon, Ma'am, what the people that write novels call exquisitely moulded;" and Mr. Peters with his outstretched pudgy hands made some passes in the air as if modelling a statue. "Swiffkins heard the lady say 'Remember then to-morrow, take care of yourself, dear John.'"

"Well" said Mrs. Grenville "and after that?"

"Swiffkins says he drove the gentleman as far as Tower Hill where he got out, and paid Swiffkins a sovereign as the fare, and then walked away eastward. That's all the information obtained from the cabman. The Blue Anchor——"

"I know" interrupted the widow "no longer exists."

"Right, you are Ma'am, it was pulled down six years ago."

"You can find no trace of Mr. Lancaster after he left the cab."

"None."

"The portmanteau left at the station has never been claimed; it is so strange, so terrible, this uncertainty, The Scotland Yard people tell me they suspect——"

"Um!" said Mr. Peters "they rarely get beyond that point at Scotland Yard. For worming out a matter that requires patience, perseverance, tact (he called it tack) give me your Private Enquiry man. For coarse work the peelers may do, but for delicate investigations—Lor' bless you!" and Mr. Peters looked up at the ceiling with a self-satisfied smile.

"Thank you, Mr. Peters, you have nothing more?"

"No! Ma'am, except that Swiffkins says when he had

dropped the gentleman and turned to go home. he saw a Hansom going before him; he could not see the number, but he suspects it had come on behind him."

"Yes" said Mrs. Grenville "and when he set down Mr. Lancaster, the Hansom turned back, is that what you mean?"

"Well, yes, it does look like that."

"No hope of finding that Hansom?"

"There's no saying what mayn't be done with tack, patience and—"

"Oh yes, I know" interrupted the widow, "see here, Mr. Peters. It seems that we do not get on much further in this matter; much of the information you give has already been furnished by others; after to-day we will make this bargain if you like,—when you satisfy me as to Mr. Lancaster's fate you shall have £100; till then—nothing."

"Very well Ma'am," said Mr. Peters after a few moments consideration, with his head cocked on one side "very well" and he scribbled a note in his book. Thrusting his handkerchief into the crown of a rather seedy hat he turned to go, but first bowing he observed "Thank ye Ma'am—the labourer is worthy of his hire of course; but professional pride in a pursuit which demands patience and perseverance makes up for anything short or skimpy in the pay, and when as in this case, it is our duty to aid, if I may say so, Beauty in distress——"

But Mrs. Grenville had turned away at the commencement of Peter's oration, and seated on her chair was giving way to a flood of tears, and the Private Enquiry man observing this, jerked his hat on to his head, and uttering the one word 'spoony' betook himself down the stairs.

Mary Grenville's search for Lancaster went on for weeks and months. She left no stone unturned in her endeavour to find him, but all in vain. Of one thing she had felt assured from the first, that Lancaster was kept from her by some untoward circumstances. She was shrewd enough to read his character aright, and knew that he was a man to keep his promise, and so the hope of finding him grew fainter and fainter until it faded out. She came to the conclusion that he was dead, and had died a violent death. She had gone in a half crazy, desperate hope of finding some clue to where the Blue Anchor formerly stood, and wandered about the squalid streets and dirty alleys, as if she expected Lancaster to be spell bound in some maze from which she alone could guide him. Her frequent visits and enquiries wore out the patience of the police-officers whose aid she sought, and at length she gave up all hope of ever again seeing the object of her love.

There was one suspicion Mrs. Grenville had entertained from the first,—that Rossdale had some hand in the disappearance of Lancaster, but she could discover nothing to warrant her acting on this idea. She had found out every movement of Rossdale's after he left the station on arriving from Southampton, with one very important omission; he could not be traced from that point to the next morning, when he drove up to his old lodgings in Jermyn Street. Thereafter he had been watchod by the widow. He was evidently well provided with money, a circumstance which to Mary Grenville was very suggestive; but the coins and notes which Lancaster had about him could not be traced. His portmanteau contained no papers, and if Rossdale had possessed himself of Lancaster's money, to identify it was all but impossible. Mrs. Grenville, however, had attempted this, but much correspondence was first necessary to ascertain where Lancaster had been living in South America, for he had never mentioned, or she had forgotten the place, and in the meantime Rossdale had left for the continent.

And then Mary Grenville having given up all hope of ever again seeing Lancaster, formed some idea of hunting down the man to whom she attributed his disappearance. He should not be permitted to enjoy his ill-gotten wealth; and so, she was soon on Rossdale's track. She possessed Mr. Peter's three requisites, patience, perseverance and tact, and in addition, her pretty face and pretty ways won for her success that, in their absence might sometimes have been denied her. Every one was ready when appealed to, to assist 'la belle Anglaise' and so she cheated herself into the belief that her errand was a righteous one, and was specially favoured by Providence.

Wherever Rossdale went, she followed. Were the company he frequented high or low, he always found this woman dogging him. They rarely, if ever, spoke, but as Mary perceived on the first occasion of their meeting, her presence was a threat, and he not knowing how much or how little she knew, feared that the secret he carried within his breast might any day be disclosed. And Rossdale was nothing more than a sneak and a coward.

So things became burdensome. At every banquet—at

every dance—at the theatre—at M. Blanc's table at Monaco, at smaller and more private houses where Rossdale courted fortune, he was sure to meet Mrs. Grenville. His wine turned sour, and the choicest *plats* were robbed of their savour, music became discord, and luck!—why, once, when on the point of breaking the bank, and when all the habitués of the place gathered round so as not to miss the *coup*, the little widow appeared at his elbow, and Rossdale's and her eyes met. He went on the wrong colour, and his rouleaux disappeared, and were raked in. Fresh supplies followed their fate, and Rossdale was for the time beggared. Mrs. Grenville rose, and was leaving the room, when Rossdale beside himself with rage, strode up to her. "That is your doing, Madam," he said, looking at her with a most unamiable expression.

"I fancy it was an aroused conscience that spoilt your game, Mr. Rossdale," and the widow returned his stare with a provoking smile.

"What do you mean?" said Rossdale, "and why do you follow me as you have done for weeks past?"

"Why do you ask? You know my reason."

"I do not. Why don't you—have you deserted that fellow——"

But before he could utter the name, his lips trembled.

"Ah!" said Mrs. Grenville, "see! you cannot, you dare not pronounce his name. You know when and how he ceased to live."

"You are mad! do you mean to say I—I murdered him?"

"Robert Rossdale," said Mrs. Grenville very slowly

and in solemn accents, "*I know you did.*" There was a pause for a second, and Rossdale looked as if about to fall, then recovering himself, he came one step closer to the widow, and raising his hand struck her.

"Liar!" he shouted, "Liar and——"

The word, whatever it was, was drowned in the noise that arose from the by-standers at this cowardly act. Rossdale was held at once by half a dozen men; but there was no fear of his repeating the outrage. A few women gathered round Mary Grenville and proffered their aid.

The attendants had hurried to the spot and were inducing the crowd to leave the saloon when a Frenchman (he was a captain in the . . Lancers and a chivalric squire of dames), came up and respectfully enquired of Mary Grenville if she had any friend present.

"No, Monsieur, else I should have been spared this violence."

"This gentleman is no relation?"

"None, thank God!"

Then the officer went up to Rossdale, a few words passed, cards were exchanged, and the crowd dispersed.

The next morning there was an 'event,'—a scandal; the Honourable Robert Rossdale had been run through the heart, and his friends had been wired for, and there was of course a hubbub, but not for long. These occurrences are soon forgotten, and duels are, or were, not uncommon at such places in those days.

Mrs. Grenville was soon after enabled to trace some of the notes which Lancaster had obtained in South America, to Rossdale, and so she felt confirmed in her suspicions.

The last time I saw her she was a member of some charitable guild, and was working in London among the poor, by whom she was idolised.

A WIDE AWAKE PATRIOT.

TINKER on his legs in the Legislative Hall, was a thing to see and hear. He ruthlessly cut down votes—denounced expenditure necessary or otherwise—had a power of talk beyond any other two members, and *more suo* was an eloquent statesman. Tinker's sharp eyes detected any error in the estimates (we were careful about our estimates in St. Molasses where a deficit of fifty pounds created a financial crisis). He opposed all additional taxation, and thought that one man (say Thomas Tinker) could manage St. Molasses on half the Governor's salary, and find an official staff out of it.

But there came a time when it was deemed expedient that St. Molasses should have a militia of about 300 strong. The youth of St. Molasses was in ecstacies, and at least fifty made sure of a commission each; but Tinker and his party were of course opposed to it. The House of Assembly was dissolved, and by dint of immense efforts and great tact, a new one elected, of which the majority were in favour of the scheme which in due course came on for discussion. Tinker was angry and furious, as the clerk read out the clauses of the bill, he moved its being read that day six months,—he proposed that such and such clauses be cut out, be declared the whole thing to be a sham. Then he called the supporters of the measure, Esaus, who had sold their birth rights for a mess of "porridge" (this the Tinkerites considered a flight of withering sarcasm since the Scottish element was strong in the house); and he also ridiculed his opponents, delicately touching on the personal defects of some who, like old Groggins, was lame, and Pyebald who could not see without glasses; and triumphantly asking what sort of Milishy officers they'd make.

But the bill went on. A rather imposing list of officers, Colonel, Majors, Captains, Ensigns was passed, though by the lowest of majorities and then came other provisions.

One clause was to the effect that in case of invasion or domestic tumult, an alarm should be given by hoisting the Union Jack half-mast at the Garrison (empty barracks in those days), and firing three cannons, whereupon all members of the militia were to repair to the market place, there to form a "general nucleus."

"There! there!" yelled Tinker as he sprung to his feet, "I told you so; this bill, this iniquitous measure is but a series of snares and pitfalls; we have had, I should have thought, officers enough, and now comes in another by a side wind—a by-blow—who's General Newclus? I say, who is he? Is he some pampered—but there I've done, I cannot remain to see the people's rights———"

And Thomas Tinker got up and left the House, waving an umbrella to Heaven as if appealing against the misdeeds of the Legislature of St. Molasses.

AN ELECTION.

I RECEIVED on one occasion a very pressing request from our Governor (I don't mean my father) to stand as a candidate for a parish in St. Montejus at the election of a new House of Assembly. His Excellency had grown weary of attempting to get measures passed when there was a big majority against government. Some half-a-dozen planters sat in a row, headed by an old merchant named Lovat, to whom they were bound by that closest of all ties, hopeless indebtedness, and voted as he bade; another party so far independent that the greater number of them usually ratted at the last moment, together with three or four officials who voted for "bread and cheese," made up the House, and after the rejection of one pet measure, out came a proclamation and the Provost Marshal's drummer.

I felt more than half inclined to ask the Governor to excuse me. I lived some miles from the town, which could only be reached by a long pull through sometimes very rough water, or by a wearing ride over not the best roads in the world, and I did not care to be absent from home for one or two days in each alternate week. Besides the worry and fatigue, these journeys would involve considerable expense, and above all, I never was an orator. On the other hand, it seemed to be one's duty to assist the Governor in his difficulty, and there was a sort of hope that such service would be remembered when a vacancy occurred in some post better paid than mine was; and so after some argument with my Chancellor of the Exchequer who pointed out that while the désagremens were certain, the advantages were problematical, I said, yes, to His Excellency's proposal.

My colleague was a Mr. Moss, who, like myself, held a small government appointment, and he and I agreed that it would save us a lot of trouble, and probably secure our success, if we employed some one to canvass and conduct our tactics. We therefore availed ourselves of a most energetic carpenter, who for some reason which I forget, was a very pronounced "government man." Mr. Shavins not only promised his best efforts, but prophesied our success.

The constituency by the exertions of both sides had been swelled to 20. I may explain that anyone could register as a voter, only, when he came to the poll, if the enquiry were demanded by a candidate, the voter's qualifications were examined into, and admitted or rejected; but, in general, elections were uncontested, and the voter qualified or not, was allowed to poll.

At our election, however, things were different. We were opposed by two planters,—one a manager and the other a proprietor, who counted on their influence with their friends of the landed interest, and on the small villagers whom they employed. Moss and I, from the first, had little hope of winning the day; we could reckon on one employé of the government, a couple of parsons, perhaps the doctor, and a friend who was a member of Council; but when we looked down the list we shook our heads. Mr. Shavins, however, rubbed his hands, while a sly smile stole over his sharp brown features.

"Gentlemen," said he, "trust me, I know the people.

I will not mislead you. When Shavins undertakes a thing, he is bound to win. I have my fingers on the pulse of the electors, and every man's heart beats true for Beke and Moss—for Moss and Beke."

"Very well," we said.

"Now, gentlemen," he added, "luncheon will be required;—it will serve to celebrate your triumph, or if not, it will soothe your defeat; not that you *will* be defeated. You will entrust that to Shavins?"

Our friend always spoke of himself in the third person, and we assented.

"Shall we say a couple of fowls, tongue, round of beef, salad, &c., &c.? Ah! exactly, and liquors—assorted I presume? some of a superior quaiity for your personal friends, and some for those who will carry you in triumph to the head of the poll. Gentlemen, your confidence shall not be abused."

"Well," said Moss "there mustn't be any bribery you know, or you'll spoil all."

"Bribery!" said Mr. Shavins, "I would not descend to it. No, sir! Purity of election is my motto, as it is yours."

Shavins worked well for us, he interviewed every elector,—strove to make them feel that the safety of the colony depended on Moss and myself being returned. He selected the materials for the lunch with taste and skill, and selected the liquors with the judgment of a connoisseur; and in short worked as if he had worked at nothing else all his life. At length the important day arrived and I set off in my boat,—a dug-out tree 'raised upon' with white pine boards and pulled by three sturdy fellows—

for the little town or village, where the election was to be held.

Ah me! How the remembrance of that day comes back to me across many long years; I recollect the pull over the still blue water, below the surface of which we could see the corals and waving gorgonias, with brilliant-hued fish flashing through and between them, the listless water rising an inch or two, and as it were lazily kissing the weed-clad feet of the many-coloured cliff that rose above, the little bays that we passed with strips of silver sand and lines of cocoa nut trees; the fields of canes, the miniature buildings or works as we call them there, the well known houses of friends, picturesquely perched on the side of hills that closed in the lovely valleys; all these come before me, and I seem to see them once again, though with eyes that grow dim at the recollection of bygone days, and of dear friends that are now no more.

The little town which was once the capital of St. Montejus shews like too many other settlements, only traces of its former position. Onaballie, for the place retained its ancient Carib name, consisted of a few rows of more or less dilapidated houses, parallel to the sea. There was the usual beach of sand with scattered cocoa palms and two or three splendid tamarind trees and an almond or two; a boat house here and there and a few rude sheds where either cassava was baked, or arrowroot was ground. A mass of masonry shewed the site of barracks occupied some fifty years before, by a company or two of King's troops, while a few rusty old cannon half buried in the sand, were all that remained of the battery's armament; another heap of brick work was the remains of a rectory destroyed in the hurricane of 1780 and here and there old stone walls marked where had been the houses of the former wealthy colonists.

There was a long white building enclosed by tolerably lofty walls, the lower story of which consisted in part, of cells some five feet square and a couple of feet higher, in which slaves used to be placed when taken down from the tread wheel, which in former days occupied a large arched recess; and above these was the court room where the election was to be held.

As my boat touched the beach, I was welcomed by Moss and the indefatigable Shavins, and we went up to the court room. There, at the table where the magistrate usually sate, was the Marshal, and beside him our two opponents and two or three others. We were all very good friends and our greetings were hearty. Of course there was some chaff at the hopelessness of our case, and I found that while we had 3 votes, Duncan and Alexander had 6. We sate and chatted until our friend the Executive Councillor rode into the yard on a long-legged mare, and then sauntered into the room. There was again a good deal of hand shaking before he voted for us.

"Wonderful" said Duncan, "how havin' Honorable tacked on your name blinds a man to a sense of duty."

"Ye forget Mr. Hope" added Alexander, "that we represent the agricultural pairty and oor interests are the same, and we looked on ye as a man who'd rescue the puir planters from the tyranny of Government."

Hope screwed his face into a queer smile as he replied, "Humph!" and sate down. With Hope had come three of his tradesmen, small house-holders; they were got up in their Sunday best and came forward bobbing and bowing, and ushered by Shavins.

"Your name?" said the Marshal to the first.

"Peter Othello."

"Now, Mr. Othello" said Duncan, putting his elbows on the table and resting his chin on his hands "I'd like to see your qualifications."

Othello dived down into his coat pocket and produced a folded paper, which the Marshal took from him.

"Not recorded in the Registrar's office," said the official, "and therefore not qualified."

Othello received back his deed with a "thank'ye me massa" and went away, while we looked glum at the loss of a vote. However, the other men had their papers in order, and having voted, were led away by Shavins to an adjoining room whence a sound as of drawing corks and clinking of glasses proceeded.

The business went on in an intermittent dreary way, and we all began to yawn, when a happy thought struck the Marshal who proposed to mix us some "topets." A simpler drink than the topet which had then lately been introduced from a neighbouring island, does not exist. It is merely a spoonful of syrup, or a couple of lumps of sugar dissolved in no more than sufficient water, and then the wine glass filled up with spirits. It is therefore easily made, and as easily swallowed. Three or four taken at short intervals promote conversation; but it is as well to stop here.

I don't think either Moss or I appreciated such short and strong libations, but our hardier friends did, and it was perhaps lucky that the arrival of the two voters recalled the Marshal to his post.

The two new comers voted for our opponents and so they were two ahead, much to their delight. Moss and I had got sick of the whole affair and we went down into the Court yard to stretch our legs. In a few minutes however, we were recalled by the sound of angry altercation upstairs, and we found our friend Shavins and Mr. Alexander slanging each other in fine style. Mr. Alexander had apparently so far got the worse of it that he was driven to make an uncomplimentary allusion to Shavin's complexion, and to express a doubt as to the respectability of his mother, when he was silenced by his antagonist reminding him that people could recollect when he (Alexander) was "imported." It was true that he had come out as an apprenticed tradesman to an estate, but had raised himself to a position of worth.

We all interfered and stopped the quarrel, and I, taking Shavins aside, expressed doubts as to our success.

"Sir," said he, "never despair; in twenty minutes the poll will be closed, but in that twenty minutes Shavins brings up his reserve; let me suggest your asking Mr. Alexander and Mr. Duncan to join you and Mr. Moss in a friendly glass. It will remove any little feeling after the late squabble."

I did so, and we were about to be followed by the returning Officer when Shavins stopped him, and the others retired to the refreshment room. We were there some ten minutes, Moss and I taking in good part the way in which Duncan and Alexander who made sure of their victory, chaffed us; and we two felt I confess, rather pleased at the prospect of defeat relieving us from an irksome duty.

Then we all returned to the Court room, and the Marshal proceeded to declare the result of the poll. To the amazement of Moss and myself and the disgust of Duncan and Alexander, we found ourselves returned by a majority of four. I looked at Shavins who placed one finger at the side of his nose and winked.

"But" said Alexander "these last six men, when did they vote?"

"They came in" said the Marshal, "when you were having a drink ot reconciliation."

Of course there was no help for it, and our opponents accepted the position not ungracefully. Luncheon followed and we parted very good friends. Moss was going to town, and I got into my boat. Before I did so, however, I thanked Shavins for his assistance.

"Why did you bring in those voters at that time and in that mysterious fashion?" I asked.

"Sir! Shavins knows a thing or two. Those devoted adherents of yours were technically unqualified, they had their deeds, but had not recorded them. Hence Shavins took the opportunity of the absence of the opposing candidates to lead them to the poll."

"But Shavins, you have made me a party to rather a trick."

"You were innocent, Sir."

"Yes; but I thought purity of election was your motto."

"Dear Sir, it is; but all things are fair in war."

And so I became a Member of Assembly.

AN OFFICIAL INVESTIGATION.

THE Colonial Secretary of St. Sangaree was a man of good family, who had won distinction at his University, and for a long while filled his official and social position satisfactorily, but for some time he had given way to bad habits and become what teetotallers called a "votary of Bacchus." Much inconvenience and much scandal was the result, but still there was nothing so flagrant as to warrant a direct charge being made with a view to Halson's dismissal until an official—I forget what he was—died, as now and then happened in St. Sangaree, and there was a funeral attended with some pomp.

In these small islands there is not often much to break the monotony of existence, and in St. Sangaree, beyond the arrival and departure of the Steamer, people had little to interest them; and so it happened that grief at the loss of a friend was frequently tempered by satisfaction that it wasn't 'our turn,' and by the excitement of a well-ordered funeral.

There was on the occasion referred to, a big "turn out," and heading the body of officials who followed the mourners of the family, was the Colonial Secretary, then acting as Lieutenant-Governor, who, to shew his official sympathy, had donned the blue and scarlet Windsor uniform which was then worn by colonial officers of a certain rank.

Mr. Halson having taken the place assigned to him the cortége set out, while from the lines of people between which the procession passed, there issued mingled regrets for the loss of the deceased, sympathy for his family, and admiration of the Colonial Secretary and his uniform, the gold of which glittered and sparkled in the sun. And so the long line of sable clad people—black being the prevailing hue—accentuated by the bright but erratic spot of colour contributed by the Secretary's uniform, moved slowly and solemnly towards the cemetery over the cobble stone pavement, which even to people accustomed to it was anything but comfortable walking ground.

Some said it was grief—some said otherwise—but at one point the Colonial Secretary, who had evidently become unequal to further progress of a dignified character, on the advice of some of his friends, "fell out" but, grasping the arm of one of them, stood gazing with the smile that is sometimes begot of nervousness, until the last mourner had passed. In due time the procession, minus the sad burden which had preceded it, retraced its steps,—for in St. Sangaree it was the custom to return to the house which had called the departed one 'master,' in order to take refreshment that should revive the saddened hearts of the survivors; and as the mourners wound down the hill and through the street, there stood the unhappy Secretary, still in his uniform, but mounted on a flight of steps before a house not his own, laughing, waving his cocked hat, and saluting the procession with his dress sword. The St. Sangareans were scandalized. The Secretary evidently was drunk. He was taken home, and in some quarters the incident—painful, disgraceful as it was—was hailed as the means of removing a scandal from the service. The Governor, who was in a neighbouring island, came to St. Sangaree with some officials to try the offender, and often as Halson had managed to escape before, every one looked upon him now as a doomed man, and the store-keepers began to make out their accounts, and junior officials to speculate as to the promotion the expected vacancy would bring to them.

But the Colonial Secretary was married. Mrs. Halson —Hetty Halson as her friends called her—who was clever as she was handsome, had won the hearts of all the men in St. Sangaree. The Garrison had gone wild about her, and from Limber, the red-faced Major in command, to young Spoone, the junior Ensign, (there were Ensigns in those days) all the officers were "hard hit." Mattins, our curate, used to stop short and lose his place when reading the lessons, if he chanced to catch Mrs. Halson's eye. There were reports that Halson when in his cups, ill-treated her, and there were times when a whispered story, half sighs, half sobs, with a few pearly tears, led the favoured confidant to call the Secretary confoundedly hard names, and the ill-used wife very tender ones.

Hetty Halson knew however, that loss of place meant to her the loss of an otherwise comfortable home, and to her husband loss of pay and position ; and so he must be saved anyhow.

The Governor had begun life in a humble way and eventually became a great politician in another colony, where his extreme views on certain public questions had brought down on him the thunder of the Government, and his liberty, if not more, had been in peril; but he saw the error of his ways—ratted—and was rewarded, as was due to one that repenteth, by being made governor over St. Sangaree and some other islands, while a good many of the faithful were left out in the cold.

Governor ——— on his arrival ought to have been lodged at Government House, and Halson had made arrangements to turn out, but the big man, who was determined to appear polite and considerate, would not hear of it, as it would inconvenience Mrs. Halson; and he and his suite were glad to accept the invitation of Major Limber and the Officers of the Garrison for the few days His Excellency would remain in St. Sangaree.

Halson had been furnished with a copy of the charge and was very miserable. He knew he was guilty, and that there was a score of witnesses against him. It was no use, after former escapes and unofficial warnings, to appeal to the Governor's mercy; and the Governor had a most deserving and efficient, if altogether inexperienced nephew whom Halson's billet would exactly suit. So there was nothing but disgrace and ruin before the poor Secretary, as he paced up and down his verandah with his hands in his pockets, and chewing an unlit cigar. It was a bad look-out for him, and not being an entirely selfish man, his thoughts turned to his wife and the misery his misconduct would bring on her. He was very fond of her in spite of her flirtations which made him uneasy and jealous, and something like tears stole into his eyes as he pictured her in the future, reduced to poverty. So impressed was he with this apprehension on his wife's account that her appearance at the end of the avenue, riding between Major Limber and Surgeon-

Major Steele, both of whom were laughing heartily, did not disturb him. He smiled sadly and shook his head, and continued his walk to and fro.

"You won't come in, Major?" he heard his wife say, "Harry will be glad to see you."

"No! no! my dear lady, excuse me, I should never keep my countenance and Halson wouldn't understand. No thank you, I'll wait for Steele at the end of the avenue. Bye-bye! *au revoir!*" and the Major turned back.

Dr. Steele, however, helped Mrs. Halson from her horse and accompanied her indoors, where they met the Secretary.

"Halson," said the doctor, "I want to see you for a minute in private."

"What for, Steele?"

"Never mind!"

"Yes, Harry, do go, and ask no questions," and Mrs. Halson, who was a wee woman, stood on tiptoe and patted his cheek.

Halson and the doctor retired, and after a while, rejoined Mrs. Halson.

"My dear," said the Secretary, "it won't do, it is too absurd."

"It's our only chance, Harry."

"Well, I'll do you as you advise. There's paper and pen, Steele, make out the certificate,—but really—"

Steele having written something on a sheet of official paper, and promised to attend the enquiry, which was to be at 11 o'clock the next day, rode away.

Well, that night the garrison mess was *en fête*. The

Governor and his party numbered half a dozen and there were about as many civilians, so that the guests were about as numerous as their Officer hosts. The dinner was first-rate, and the wine went round rapidly, and afterwards there was a little speech from Limber and the Governor responded, and the party adjourned. Cards and brandies and soda were introduced, and the Governor was rejoiced at spending what he called so friendly an evening. Limber was most attentive and refilled His Excellency's tumbler over and over again. The fun grew fast and furious, and one can hardly believe the stories that were afterwards told of the high jinks that went on, and the active part taken in them by the Governor, who at an early period of the morning was conducted (carried, some say) to his bed.

Early next morning Mrs. Halson was at Fort St. Joseph, requesting an interview with the Governor, who at first demurred, but eventually gave in, and the two met in the anteroom. The exact nature of the conference will never be known but when they parted there was a bothered look on the Governor's face, and a slight smile on that of the lady, as she was lifted into her saddle by Major Limber, to whom she nodded as she rode away.

The Council met; Halson appeared much concerned, but was relieved when His Excellency who looked as if the proverbially bad climate of St. Sangaree had already begun to tell on him, said he was glad to say there would be no enquiry. Mr. Halson's conduct was to be attributed to over-pent feelings of regret at the loss of a brother official to whom he was much attached, and as to the unsteadiness of gait, which had been chiefly relied on as evidence of his being under the influence of liquor, Surgeon-Major Steele, a medical officer of much experience, had certified that Mr. Halson was a martyr to those painful excrescences, corns; and to those, and the uneven pavement were the symptoms to be referred. And so the Council broke up. The Governor remained quietly at Government House till the steamer took him away, and Halson retained his post, at all events, for some years.

Soon afterwards, the Governor died, and then it was openly stated that His Excellency had been led into dissipation as part of a scheme concocted by Mrs. Halson, who, the next morning had coolly told the Governor that she knew of his intoxication and undignified behaviour, and that if he pressed the charge against her husband she would expose him.

Such at all events, was the story told me; but it happened long, long ago, and it was not always easy to give full credence to all the yarns one hears of the people of that by-gone period of the island's history.

A DOCTOR'S YARN.

"CAP'EN say he ready sah!"

I was leaning out of the verandah of the 'hotel' in St. Maria, and although I had been waiting an hour or so for this summons, I was loth to stir. It was a lovely night. The moon was full, and lit up the scenery of the bay. Through and under the latge almond trees that lined the shore I could see the gently rippling waves, flashing and breaking into a thousand fragments of silvery sheen as they ran up the pebbly beach. The tall, scarped hills stood out sharply against the sky, and in the mountain behind the little town the ravines seemed all the darker and more gloomy because its crown and ridges were bathed in light. Every thing seaward was as visible as in the daytime : the very ropes in the couple of barques that lay at anchor could be discerned, and I could see the cap'en on board the *Gem*, a little sloop I had chartered, making ready for a start.

So I had to be off; and giving Peter a bundle of wraps to carry, I followed that imperfectly-clad imp to the beach where a small dingy was waiting, in charge of the man, who with Peter, composed the crew of the *Gem*. With a struggle, a stumble and a bump, I deposited myself and my belongings in the bow, and with the help of some good-natured idlers we shoved off. A few strokes of Peter's primitive paddles brought us alongside the sloop, then, aided, by a grasp of the cap'en's hand, I scrambled on board. The *Gem* was not indeed a roomy craft, for a hop and skip, without the jump, would have cleared her, so narrow was she; and what with a boat on deck, and some barrels and other lumber, she looked not a little crowded. However, the crew and passenger managed to haul the dingy on board, and when the foresail was set and the anchor raised, the *Gem* turned her head slowly away from the shore. A few pulls, and up went the mainsail, and then we heard the welcome ripple and swish that told us we were under weigh. The water in St. Maria—that is, in the bay which we were leaving—is bold enough, and it was only necessary to keep a look out for a fishing-boat or for a drogher that might pop round the corner—as they usually did—at a swinging pace. The crew, who was called Jimbo, steered with the tiller under his arm while he lighted his pipe. Peter, who was only rated as boy, employed himself in raising a fire out of some of the embers in a galley formed out of an iron coal-pot fixed in a cut down barrel filled with sand; and the cap'en was busy in putting things tidy: so that as the crew appeared confident of his safety, so was I.

Cap'en Barrington was a tall, burly negro of about forty, with a good-natured, frank countenance. He was innocent of boots, and his hat, an old felt wide-awake, would have been useless for baling purposes. His nether garments were partly of blue-serge, much faded and stained, with a patch of different colours on the knees and seat, but his 'bamboo' shirt was apparently a more recent purchase.

"A fine night Doctah," said Captain Barrington squatting near me—

I assented.

"I beg you, sah, for a leetle bit baccey. I forget for buy some a' store."

I had experienced instances of the forgetfulness of other cap'ens in this matter before, and had provided acccordingly.

"T'ank you, doctah."

Perhaps I had better here explain that I was a district doctor in St. Maria; that my work lay in a mountainous part which I had to traverse two or three days a week on a wretched, weedy pony, that barely managed to carry one up and down the roads and stony paths, which, after rain,—and it was almost always raining in St. Maria—were as slippery as frozen ointment; that my salary was small and my family large, so that I jumped at an offer to run down to the adjacent island of Petit Sangaree and vaccinate every man, woman, and child at so much per head or rather arm. And so, as I have said, I chartered the sloop *Gem*.

The cap'en lit his pipe and then began to question Peter as to certain commissions with which they had been entrusted :—

"Peter, you 'member dem boots for Miss Flora? and she hat and de oder ting from Miss Phœbe, she dress-maker?"

"Yes, cap'en."

"You know she well partickler and she have for marry to-morrow, please God. She is a nice nyoung lady that."

"Cap'en! I hope you put de cake from Mammy Betsy where he no get bruck. He fuss'rate, man—all ober sugar and sweeties!"

"All right, Peter, me put 'em in for me bunk."

"Aow! Me Gad, cap'en, no forget to take 'em out if you does turn in, else he got mashiate in trut'!"

And so they went on discussing the approaching wedding, and retailing the little scraps of gossip, chronicles of very small beer, which each had picked up on shore. As for me, I simply lay down on my rugs gazing up into the bright sky, or watching the phosphorescent waves as they danced by, and thinking of things past and things to come,—thoughts that come chiefly, if not only, at such times.

The *Gem* tripped along, and we were out of the bay, and Jimbo steered her for a dark mass, that rising out of the sea some twenty miles off, was Petit Sangaree, and in due time we were under the tall cliffs that shut in the bay for which we were bound, and then the breeze died away.

The *Gem* was bearable when making way, for she only pitched and shook herself if a big wave met her; but drifting she was a very uncomfortable craft. She rolled with a short jerk and bobbed about, while her boom had a most unmusical squeak and grunt as it swung against the mast. And then the exigencies of trade having caused the *Gem* to be a carrier of all sorts of unsavoury goods, such as sugar and molasses, saltfish, guano, &c., &c., these left behind them odours which were most obtrusive when the *Gem* was becalmed and her rolling set her bilge-water in agitation.

However, there was nothing for it but to wait; and so I lay, watching the mast head as it wobbled and jerked as if trying to poke out one of the many stars above us.

Petit Sangaree from the sea, looks barren. Its hills are covered with low shrub, and though in some places the white cedar, so useful to boatbuilders, raises its head above the surrounding trees, they generally present a somewhat depressing appearance, which moonlight intensifies. And I got impatient at the slow progress which in spite of the cap'en's long sweep we made towards the village which lies at the bottom of the bay.

There was something weird and uncanny in thus stealing into the moonlit bay. All the little world had apparently gone to rest. Not a light was to be seen; not a sound heard save the lapping of the waves against the rocks, or the moaning of the palm trees as their heavy foliage was swept by the night wind. The white-washed buildings stood out clear and sharp, while across the water were broad bands of silvery light, broken by boats at anchor, or by the buoys marking where nets were set.

As we stole nearer and nearer the landing-place, I saw standing out from a background of dark mango trees some yards from the beach, a white stone mansion, or rather its remains, that I felt must have a ghost, or at least be the scene of a jumbie story.

"Dat! my massa? Dat McFarlane house. Black McFarlane—no but wha' he been buckra but he heart been black. Me fader! dat man! Wha' God A'mighty do for make sich a man me no know. Wha' God been a do wid um now he dead me no sabe. Brimstone and fiah too good for like of him. Me massa, you believe dat man tie poor negur to de tail ob he mill all troo de day, and let water go drop from one calabash pon he head, drip, drop, drip, drop, teel he dead. Den he no go flog one woman, and becasin' she big and no hable for lie comfortable on she tummick he make 'em dig hole in de sand fo' receive she. Aow! dey tell too many ting pon McFarlane. But good so; de debbil carry him away. Yes, massa, dat fo' true. Le'me tell you. McFarlane had one big, big black horse dat he ride all ober de island—day, night, moonshine, dark, all de same to McFarlane—and de horse, me 'member dey call de horse Miss Tofeles tho' he no been mare. Well! doctah! One night big storm come; thunder and rain and lightning too, and in de marning dey give alarm. When de sarvin' gal go take McFarlane coffee he no in he chamber, he no up'tairs—he no down'tairs—and de front-door open. Den dey look in de horse-'table, but de horse no dey. So dey get frikened; dey send all round and round. De parson a come, de magistrate, all de buckra and 'sponsible people a come, and den dey find de track of de horse fresh in de dirtie all de way from de 'table, but dey 'top, dey no come so near dat de horse been hable for jump in de sea, and so ebberyone say it a bery 'strange ting. People nebber see McFarlane again nor he horse, and den de talk come dat de debbil go take 'um; and massa, believe me! I tink dat 'tory true."

As the cap'en told this legend we were close in shore—so close I expected to feel the sloop run aground, but she went ahead slowly till her cutwater touched the white sand-beach and then the boy leapt overboard with a line, and in a few seconds we were made fast to a stout almond tree. Presently, there were opened one or two doors in the village, and quaint figures in white peeped out. Then light appeared, and by degrees the inhabitants came down to the beach and spoke as follows:—

"Eh! Eh! de *Gem* fo' true."

"Cap'en Barrington?"

"Yes ma'am?"

"You come safe now! Tank the Lord!—you bring de parcel and ting fo' me?"

"Yes Miss Flora, me beg excuse, but me no catch you v'ice. Ebbrything come!"

"Good so!"

Whereupon they all clustered together till the cap'en got ashore, and Peter followed with all Miss Flora's wedding gear; and up went the jabbering group till they reached Miss Flora's cottage, at the door of which they all sate down and cross-examined Peter about the valuables he bought for the expectant bride, and a score of other commissions. I, who landed and stood up near by, wondered how the lad remembered all he had had to do, and had managed as he seemed to have done, to content his exacting employers.

After a while, I strolled towards the ruined house of Black McFarlane that stood a few hundred yards off. It had been built of stone, and in the end of the two large rooms on the ground floor, there were three sided bays with large apertures for windows, the sashes of which had disappeared. Over-head were half decaying beams and the walls of the upper rooms were shattered and in ruins. The house had evidently been pulled to pieces for building material, and its dark recesses and door-ways were in strong contrast to those parts which were lit up by the bright rays of the moon. I did not care to make any close inspection of the place at such an hour, but at the entrance door I fell in with an old horse that was mumbling at the short grass that grew there. Going up to it I patted it, and then a slight noise inside the ruined house attracted my attention, and I turned round, and as I did so the moon's beams fell on the horse and me.

Suddenly there was a yell of "Oh me God, "Look McFarlane and Miss Tofeles ! !" and three men rushed out through a window and fled as if indeed they had seen a ghost. I walked on to where they had been and found some kegs and boxes, with a shovel and a recently dug hole.

It was no business of mine, so I walked back to the sloop and thence to the police station where the one constable, on learning who I was, gave me quarters for the night.

Next day, I found out that a few days before a sugar-laden ship from Tobago had been stranded on the reef near Petit Sangaree, and some people of the island who had wrecked her cargo were concealing their plunder in old McFarlane's house, when they were disturbed by two figures which they believed to be apparitions of the long lost McFarlane and his horse, Mephistopheles.

A JURY.

IN the good old days, with Sugar at £50 a hhd., and merchants willing to give unlimited credit, Barataria flourished, at all events when Sir Gregory Graplin ruled it. He had done gallant deeds in the Peninsula and was rewarded with a Government. He had little trouble, his word was law, and if there was any friction between the Executive and the Legislature a dinner or a dance cured the evil.

So with good prices and plenty of money in circulation, a somewhat large garrison, a tolerably frequent visit of a frigate, and the prettiest girls in all the West Indies, Barataria was as jolly a place as could be.

Then Sir Gregory died, and other Governors came who went in for high politics, despised dances and dinners and so made more or less a muddle of affairs. The visits of ships of war became scarce, and the garrison was withdrawn, and Barataria from being joyous and gay drooped into a slow, dull colony. But once upon a time, a squadron arrived, and there was considerable excitement. The usual landing of the Admiral under salutes, the display of local forces, militia and police, dinners on shore and on board, delightful picnics and excursions to the various natural beauties of the island, impromptu 'hops,' liberal leave to "Jack" who took unstinted advantage of it—almost upset the place; and steady-going traders unblushing deferred the conclusion of any business till the squadron was gone. Even the Bank manager (who had a couple of pretty daughters) acquiesced.

Of course there was a big ball. A committee was formed to carry it through. Dunshunner, one of its members, undertook the supper arrangements. Dunshunner's enemies said that by judicious patronage he wiped out some of his own old scores, or at all events warded off a pressing demand or two. The officers from the garrison decorated the rooms most tastefully. Tootle and Bellows, the leading local musicians, superintended the militia band, and the Admiral lent his. Others issued the invitations, men who knew where to draw the line, being acquainted with the history of every family in the colony; and so the affair was a success. All enjoyed themselves. The supper was excellent. Half-a-dozen happy girls parted with gloves, or ribbons, or rosebuds to gallant partners who vowed and declared they would never, never forget them. The Admiral was eloquent in his acknowledgment of the compliment paid him, and the squadron he had the honour to command, praised the island and its Governor, flattered the ladies, buttered (if I may so say) the men, and was voted chorally a jolly good fellow. No end of tiffs and quarrels were made up that evening. Men shook hands and agreed to let "that matter drop;" women who declared *no power on earth* should ever make them speak to each other, literally kissed and made friends; and really it appeared that West Indian prosperity and happiness could always be brought about by the visit of one or more ships of war.

In one respect the Admiral's visit was inopportune. The Criminal Court was in session.

Now in Barataria the building where laws are made and enforced is a grim two-storied erection of no architectural beauty. The ground floor of the main building was used as a Court of Justice. Two rooms above it were the halls in which the Legislative Council (or House of Lords) and the House of Assembly (or Commons) sate and deliberated, and smaller ones were the private rooms of the Judges, President and Speaker.

In Barataria there was no town hall or other building available for public balls, and so the upper storey of the Court house was used for the purpose, while the Court itself below served as a supper-room.

When the squadron came and the ball was determined on, the Chief Justice was induced to suspend the sitting of the Court for one day, to allow of the necessary arrangements, on the understanding that all signs of revelry would be removed, and the hall *in statu quo ante* when the Court reassembled. And so it was. When the last reveller had gone—and it seemed as if some would never go—the tables were removed, and the place swept and washed, and all made ready for the administration of justice.

The Inspector of Police had, it is true, omitted to remove the fire brigade ladder which he had placed against one of the upper windows of the building in case of need, but the hose and engine had been wheeled away early in the morning, and no one could have told that there had been any festivity over night.

I don't say that Judges, Juries, Barristers and Officials are not more than human, but the proceedings of the next day went languidly. The Chief Justice was evidently thirsty, and a bailiff was despatched at intervals for something which may have been water, probably was, but a false delicacy in wrapping the tumbler in a napkin so as to conceal its contents instead of bringing it on a waiter, led to several uncharitable remarks. The Marshal too was noticed to cry "Silence" more often than was his wont, and then to rush out of Court in pursuit of an imaginary offender, and had he not invariably wiped his moustache on his return, people would not have indulged in doubtless wrong suspicions. The Jury also were thirsty, but there is no reason to suspect that they were supplied with aught but pure water; altogether there was an arid look about the whole company, and the work went on but slowly. The case was one of larceny, and must have presented some difficulty, for the Jury retired to deliberate, and according to custom were conducted upstairs into the vast Legislative Hall in charge of a venerable old negro constable, whose white head and massive staff, to say nothing of evening dress clothes, were evidence of incorruptible respectability. Here they remained until morning. People who had been up late the previous night, as they turned in, pitied those poor devils of jurymen, and lazily speculated as to what were the points of difficulty, and who the obstinate minority.

When the next morning came, and it struck ten, and the Court was opened, it was evident that something had occurred. The Marshal was seen in anxious, nervous conversation with his subordinates. The Inspector of Police, who was a bit of a wag, was on the broad grin. The Judge looked perplexed, and the Attorney General was turning over the leaves of half-a-dozen law books.

"Better call in the Jury," said His Honour.

The white-haired constable grasped his rod of office, and trotted out. Presently he returned at the head of as queer a set of jurymen as ever were seen. They could not walk steadily, their dress was disarranged, their hair all brushed the wrong way. Paler faces, more downcast features, fishier eyes could not be. As their names were called, each replied in a whisper from parched lips, and they slunk into their seats more like criminals than jurors.

The Attorney General then rose and said that he had to bring to the notice of the Court a painful, and he believed, unprecedented occurrence. His Honour was probably aware that two evenings ago an entertainment had been given in that building.

His Honour made a note as if he had only then heard of it.

Some wine—the Attorney General believed he was correct in describing it as Champagne—to the extent of three or four cases had remained unopened and had been placed in one of the rooms above. The Jury now in Court had retired to consider their verdict. Enquiry had been made at a late hour, but it was found that they were not likely to agree, and they were locked up for the night. He regretted to say that those jurymen had abused the confidence placed in them, and instead of considering the evidence in that case, had broken open a case (no levity was meant) of that wine. The constable in charge of the jury very properly had the wine at once removed to his own quarters in the Court yard—but he, the Attorney General, regretted to say that the jurymen got out of their room—out of that building indeed, by means of a ladder left by the police—broke open the door of the constable's quarters—took the three or four dozen wine, and drank it either there or in the jury room on their return, or in both places, but that was immaterial. The result was—but he could only point to the appearance of those jurymen, and leave the case in His Honour's hands.

Then there was a long pause—

"Gentlemen! have you considered your verdict," asked the Judge.

The jury shook their twelve heads.

"Mr. Foreman, you have heard the Attorney General's statement."

"Yesh, Y'r Honour," replied the foreman standing up, but grasping the rail of the jurybox, "can only shay—feel position placed in by conduck of Shury—puffickly 'graceful—tried reshtrain Shury from drinking shampagne—Shury wouldn't listen—wanted fight—gave it up—

pufficklу 'graceful." And the foreman sate down and buried his face in a very grimy handkerchief.

"Your Honour," said a juryman, jumping up, "What our respected fo'man says is all lies, he was as bad as the rest—more so."

And then a third got up. And so on till each of the twelve had his say, each protesting he was sober, but their speech betrayed them.

"Mr. Attorney," said the Judge, "this is most sad. I doubt if I am not called on to mark the sense of the indignity passed upon the Court, and the—the heinousness of the offence committed by these unhappy men—"

"Mercy! mercy!" murmured the foreman.

"By," continued the Judge, "incarceration, that is, imprisonment."

"Oh Lord" said one man, "and I am going to make sugar on Monday."

"Mos' happy to pay for wine Your Honour, don't want to be incarcer—hic—arcerated"—said another.

"Silence" said the Marshal so gruffly that the Jury one and all burst into tears.

"Do my Honour—do, I beg, take money—don't send us to jail. I've got wife and family" said another juryman.

"As you show some signs of contrition"—said the Judge after a whispered conference with the Attorney General—"I shall not inflict so severe a punishment, much as you may deserve it—bnt you will observe that you are guilty of contempt—of larceny—of breaking and entering—however you each will pay £5."

The fines were paid on the spot, and the jurymen

looked relieved, and one of them to shew his willingness to make amends by performing his duty, asked the Judge if he would like them to go back and consider their verdict, but His Honour thundered out "No, you are discharged—begone!" and the jurors sneaked out of the Court.

The prisoner looked up from the dock and meekly asked, "Please Your Honour, you could let me go becasin' me no tief half so bad as dem jury."

The Attorney General caught the Judge's eye, and moved a *nol pros.*, and so the affair ended.

COINCIDENCES—STRANGE BUT TRUE.

CROSSLEY, the Doctor, Inspector Vann, and I, the Coroner, were seated in the verandah of my house in St. Molasses, looking out across a deep dark ravine of bamboos, palms and ferns, and a wooded hill to where the sea sparkled in the moonlight. We had had a long ride and a somewhat exciting day, and having dined, we were smoking our pipes, repairing waste of tissue, and at peace with all the world. At Paul's Trust (a sugar estate not far off) there had been a death under suspicious circumstances, and we three officials had assisted, as the French say, at the inquest.

Phœbe McCurious—into which queer surname a Scotch planter had twisted the classic name Mercurius, borne by some slave ancestor of Phœbe's—was engaged to be married to Bill Othello, and, until the wedding day arrived,

Phœbe had taken up her residence with Bill, and owing to several causes this had gone on for about eighteen months, when one day Bill became jealous, and having signified his displeasure by smashing everything breakable in the house, and slashing the bed, table and benches into bits, turned Phœbe out on the world with a bundle of clothes and anything but his blessing. But Phœbe who was *philosophe en jupon* accepted the situation and obtained a shelter elsewhere, and though the former friendly relations were never restored between her and Bill, after a while they exchanged "Howd'ye" when they met, as if they had never quarrelled. A few months passed and Phœbe found favour in the sight of Joe Adonis, the head stock-keeper, and as Adonis was comfortably off, there was no need for delay, and the banns were read for the time. Bill Othello's mind was somewhat disturbed at this, and he gave vent to some mysterious remarks which might or might not be taken as threats.

On the Wednesday after the publication of the banns he met Teresa Jacobs, who was Phœbe's sister on the mother's side, and by her sent a message to Phœbe to the effect that if she went to the cattle pen next morning, there would be a bottle of milk for her, which she was to take for her own use and not to give any of it to anyone. Phœbe, on receipt of the milk, boiled and drank about half of it. A few minutes after, she was seized with agonizing pains, and, in spite of the hundred and one remedies applied by her excited friends and neighbours, died before the doctor could be fetched.

The Sergeant of Police was informed of the occurrence, and at once arrested Othello, who was placed in the lock-up whither he was escorted by a small crowd who loudly denounced him as the murderer of poor Phœbe. Of course, there was an inquest, and the overseer's house was thronged. Othello was present in custody, and his face wore an anxious dazed look, but he continually protested he was innocent. The public opinion was that he was guilty; effect had never so quickly and naturally followed on cause, as death, in this case, had followed on the drinking of the poisoned milk.

The circumstances were clearly stated by the witnesses of whom Othello asked no questions, and things looked very black for the prisoner. But Crossley who had gone on with his post mortem examination while the depositions were being taken, came across from the cottage, and declared that he had discovered the cause of death to be the bursting of an internal tumour. The milk had had no ill effect on two children who had drank it, and so of course there was no poisoning, and the jury brought in a verdict of death from natural causes, and Othello was released. We had some fear as to how he might be treated by the people on the estate, but their faith in Crossley was great, so they agreed in the verdict, and Othello was left unmolested.

We were talking over the affair and the strange coincidence of Othello's giving the girl the milk and her dying as she drank it, and then we began to mention other cases of curious coincidences.

"One of the oddest things I ever knew," said Crossley, "happened in this way. When I had passed my examination, I had no more idea of coming out to the West Indies than of visiting the North Pole, and in fact was thinking of buying a country practice at home. I was however engaged on some work which took me every day for a couple of months, to the College of Surgeons, and I was there as a rule, punctually at 10, and returned about 4. My lodgings were out Bayswater way, and I always walked when the weather permitted. I noticed after a while that an elderly gentleman took the same route, and at the same hours, and we met with each other so regularly, that at last we walked in company and conversed on the topics of the day.

"Although a well informed and agreeable companion, he was somewhat stuck up and immensely proud of his family and name which was—we'll say Howard; he was an official of high standing at Somerset house, and, as he told me, owed his advancement to his aristocratic relations, and he used at times to rather bore me with his swell friends and the big houses he visited. His wife too, he told me, was of an excellent old Scottish family, the MacAdams of Glen Eden.

"In due course, I spent a couple of evenings with the Howards; they lived in good style, and the wife who was several years her husband's junior, was a quiet but agreeable person. She had been perhaps good looking as a girl, but was evidently delicate, and her sallow colourless, complexion contrasted with her jet black hair which she wore in wavy bands over her forehead. She had no family and apparently no accomplishments, but was much interested in Missionary work.

"Well one day came the news of the death of a distant relative, whom I had never seen, and who, why I can't tell, left me Mount Megass; and so you see I came out here.

Before I sailed I took leave of Mr. and Mrs. Howard. They were good enough to express regret at my going away, knew nothing as it appeared, of the West Indies, and I left loaded with their good wishes for my success, and a bundle of tracts for distribution among the poor dear black people of the Island.

"As you fellows know, very soon after coming here I became engaged to my wife, and as Mount Molasses is not very far from her father's place, I was often there. On one of my visits we were all at breakfast, Mr. and Mrs. Sinclair and the girls and a couple of men, the Magistrate and another, and in the course of conversation I mentioned my acquaintances, the Howards, and described how we met, and in short, just what I have been telling you. Evidently I had touched on an awkward subject. Mrs. Sinclair grew crimson, the old man looked half amused, half perplexed; and Archbold, the magistrate who was an old friend of the family, frowned at me. Of course I stopped, and was thankful when we all rose from table. I felt very awkward, but old Sinclair, after a while, said 'Crossley, if Margaret will spare you, we'll take a ride round the estate,' and a few minutes after, we were mounted. Several times I was tempted to ask Mr. Sinclair the meaning of the sensation I had caused by mentioning the Howards, but I waited and waited until we came to a newly cut cane piece, in the centre of which was a railed space with several tombs in the enclosure, and outside of it one of brick. Mr. Sinclair pulled up and pointing to them said: 'There, Crossley, is the burial ground of the MacAdams, Mrs. Sinclair's family. There are three generations of them there, and in yon tomb that's outside the rails rest the remains of your friend Mrs. Howard's mother.'

'Good Heavens!' I said 'how extraordinary, Are you quite sure? because when I mentioned I was coming here, Mrs. Howard never said she had even heard of the place.'

'As likely as not, my boy. Ye see, my wife's uncle, Sandie MacAdam was never married, and so he left the estate to her—but—well he had a house keeper, it was in the old slavery times—and—and so—well I leave you to guess the rest;—but my agents pay your friend Mrs. Howard an annuity of £300 a year that her father charged on the estate.'

"That's a queer story," said Vann, and I assented, and we for a while talked of the odd chance that made Crossley as it were a link belween Mrs. Howard and his future wife's family.

Then I was asked If I knew of no odd coincidence, and told my friends as follows:—

Years ago when I had just left college, I made the acquaintance of an old London Solicitor whose clients were West End people, and he had an office in Savile Row in a fine old house, in the upper part of which he lived. He was a widower with a widowed daughter who kept his house; and with them lived his ward, a young lady of about twenty-five. She had an English name, Rose Murray, but there was a half-foreign look about her, owing perhaps to her wearing her hair in a fashion quite uncommon then, but afterwards brought into vogue by the Empress Eugénie. She was of rather a queer disposition, and given to undue merriment on very small provocation. I know I often made remarks in which I could see nothing to warrant the laughter with which she greeted them, and I didn't like her manners nor did I like her. I understood she was an orphan, that her father who held some appointment abroad, had left her a small income, and had consigned her to Mr. Welby's care after his death, which had occurred about a twelve month previously. One day I had gone to Mr. Welby's at his invitation to accompany his daughter, Mrs. Miles, and Miss Murray to some Exhibition—I think the Academy—and we were in an ante-room opening into the large drawing-room, about to take a biscuit and glass of sherry before starting, when a carriage stopped, and there came a very loud knock at the door. Then a servant brought in a card which Mr. Welby took. He became very much agitated, and told the man to show the lady into the drawing-room, and we could hear the *frou-frou* of her dress as she mounted the stairs. Mr. Welby held the handle of the door of the ante-room as if to prevent the visitor entering, and when she had reached the drawing-room, he left us. 'Some one on business, my dear,' he said to his daughter, 'remain here.'

We three sipped our sherry, and Miss Murray said she wondered who the lady could be. Presently we others also wondered, for sounds of most passionate entreaty fell on our ears, coupled with firm refusal from Mr. Welby. What the subject of the conversation was we could not tell, but evidently the lady was imploring Mr. Welby to tell her something which he declared he could not divulge. He had passed his word, he said, and he could not—would not—break it.

This went on for some twenty minutes, when Mr. Welby entered the ante-room looking very pale and distressed. Without saying a word to us, he took a glass of wine into the next room. Soon after, a bell rang and he escorted his visitor downstairs.

Mrs. Miles and I were a good deal disturbed by all this, but Miss Murray was differently affected. She laughed immoderately, and began to imitate the lady's imploring voice and words, 'For God's sake, tell me—do not be so cruel!' and she clasped her hands, and made no end of grimaces as she repeated the lady's words; then with a peal of laughter asked us if that was not a good imitation, and when we were silent, she became sulky.

On Mr. Welby's return he was evidently much upset. He said he must forego the little treat he had looked forward to in going to the Academy, and as evidently something very distressful had occurred, Mrs. Miles said our visit must be postponed, and I took my leave.

Some time after I learned that the mysterious visitor was none other than Miss Murray's mother! Her father and mother had separated for some fault of the latter—well, she had run away with Lord Somebody—and the father being ordered abroad, left his daughter under Mr. Welby's care with strict injunctions never to let his wife know where her child was. Mr. Welby kept the trust, and shortly after, Mr. Murray died; Lord Somebody also quitted the world, and the unhappy mother strove to find where her child was. Naturally, she applied to her husband's solicitor, with the result that I have told you More recently, I heard she died,—rather a melancholy end if I remember right, and Miss Murray married. I have often thought of that strange coincidence, the mother in her agony in one room, and the daughter in the other indulging in "taking off" the poor woman's distress.

We were silent for a while, and then Vann said—

"I don't think either of you were ever in St. Maria and therefore you don't know that Petit Sangaree lies opposite to St. Maria, of which it is a dependency. Between them is a deep channel which sometimes is as smooth and glassy as a mountain tarn, and at others, is a roaring sluice when the waves leap high and the "Bull," as a tall conical rock at the mouth of the smaller island is named, is covered with sheets of foam that rush up one side of it to fall on the other in silvery spray. One day the passage may be safely made in the smallest canoe, on another the pluckiest sailor in the smartest coaster shakes his head and "funks" it.

Once upon a time, I was staying with my friend Marchant who was a proprietor in St. Maria and owned another smaller island beyond Petit Sangaree where he grew sugar. I had never been to this place—it was called Mouchette—and so when he invited me to run down with him for a couple of days, I gladly said 'yes.' However the evening before the day of our departure, I was summoned elsewhere on duty, and next morning when we parted, I left him busy with his preparations and full of kindly regret at my inability to accompany him.

Two days after, I was riding homewards after a busy day, hot and weary, and envying my friend who as I thought was then enjoying the bracing breezes that at that time of the year blew over Petit Sangaree, and the adjacent chain of islands. At one point my road ran close to the sea, and on reaching the beach where a boat had just landed, the boatmen shouted, and as I halted, one of them brought me a letter—it was to announce poor Marchant's death!—he had been drowned the previous night on his return from Mouchette off the "Bull" in sight of his home which was perched on the opposite headland.

I was much shocked at the news and remembered how this was not the first occasion on which I had been prevented joining a trip that had ended disastrously for others, as this might have done for me.

Reaching home, I had to break the news to my wife, who was a relative of Mrs. Marchant, and the next day she went up to our poor friend's house where we learned that on the day of his departure for Mouchette, something had occurred to delay the sailing of the schooner, and Marchant had returned home to wait until it was ready. He expressed himself as most unwilling to go over to Mouchette but business compelled him; and ultimately he left. When about to return, he was advised not to attempt the passage as the weather was threatening, but he persisted. Off the "Bull" a squall struck his vessel and threw her on her beam ends; the crew at once took to the boat, and deserted our poor friend, who was below at the time, and who was thus miserably drowned. This happened at about 10 at night.

That evening, Mrs. Marchant who was an invalid, had gone to bed when she was awakened by her husband's voice calling for help. She aroused an old servant who slept in the same room and who also heard the cry. They concluded that Mr. Marchant had landed, and ridden up a short cut leading to the house where some accident had befallen him. As they listened, the cries were renewed, and the servant hastily dressing, roused the people in the negro yard. They turned out to look for their "massa," but could find no traces of him, and the next morning the cowardly crew of the schooner landed, bringing a garbled and confused account of the accident and how it happened.

As the St. Maria Channel is several miles wide and the night was a boisterous one, it is impossible that the cries heard by Mrs. Marchant and her servant could have been carried that distance; and yet was it another coincidence, strange but true?

THE COMMANDER-IN-CHIEF DEFIED.

IN the olden days, as a rule, there was not much work for the Governor and Legislature of a West Indian colony, if one may judge by the Statute Books, records of Councils and Assembly, and copies of despatches of the last century, but very often there was a good deal of fuss over what now seems a trifling affair.

I remember once coming across an old copy of the minutes of the Privy Council of a West Indian Island, for a portion of the year 1766. There were not many entries in it, and His Majesty's Council appears to have met at very long intervals for very short periods. There was an occurrence, however, which had evidently caused great excitement, and had to be dealt with promptly, and so the Council had met twice a week for a fortnight, and members had come in from North and East and West, and remained at their posts until the matter was decided. I wish I could transcribe the minutes of those meetings, for reading them would convey better than anything I can write, the importance of honourable members, the dignified language used, and the sense of relief at a crisis happily averted.

Following the Parliamentary usage of the day, the President who was administering the Government in the absence of the Governor, is described as His Honour B. B——n and the names of the other members are indicated by their initial and final letters.

At one of the meetings of His Majesty's Privy Council, composed of the Officer administering the Government and members of the Legislative Council, then nominated by the Crown, the proceedings at which are noted in the book in question, His Honour informed the members that he had called them together on a matter of the gravest moment. It would be unnecessary to remind them that on the departure of His Excellency the Governor, the Government of the colony had devolved on him. He had accordingly been sworn in and assumed that position which he was conscious he could not fill satisfactorily without the help of honourable members; and even at the threshold of his tenure of office, he was met by a serious difficulty, to extricate himself from which he relied on the support and advice of those, his constitutional advisers.

He had to inform them that on his requiring Captain James of His Majesty's 77th regiment of Foot, the senior military officer, to report to him and to receive from him the Parole, that officer had refused so to do,—adding that as a military man he had never, and would never take orders from a civilian.

Such embarrassing conduct, to use no harsher word, on the part of Captain James appears to have moved the Council, for they at once resolved that His Honour do write to Lieutenant O'Brien then "lying on detachment at Blooming Bay," directing him to repair to Head Quarters, to place under arrest Captain James and to assume the command of His Majesty's troops; and the Council adjourned, for a few days only, when they again met.

President B. B——n had then indeed a weighty matter to bring before them, and one can imagine the knitted brows of the grave and potent seigniors as they heard read a letter from Lieutenant O'Brien, who presenting his humble duty to His Honour, took leave to observe that he had never read in Military (or for that matter Profane) History, that an officer should be directed in affairs Military, by one (however Exalted his Rank) who did not belong to that honourable Profession, and that moreover, he could not take upon himself the charge of placing under arrest his Superior Officer save for certain matters when committed, as laid down in His Majesty's Regulations.

The minutes are dry records of what was done—not what was said,—and so the burning words in which the astonishment and resentment of the Privy Council members were couched are lost to us. But they were not to be done—for they resolved that His Honour do write to

Ensign Flaherty of His Majesty's 77th regiment of Foot lying at Cumberland Bay requiring him without delay to place under arrest Captain James and Lieutenant O'Brien, and take command of His Majesty's troops in that Island.

It is doubtful whether Ensign Flaherty might not have sprung into fame on this occasion, but at the next meeting of the Council, the President laid before his confrères a letter from that gallant officer, in which he says that he is "somewhat uncertain how far it would be competent to him as a junior officer, (who had but lately joined his regiment) to obey the orders of a Civil Governor and place under arrest his Superiors, but that for the present he must put forward as sufficient reason for not complying with His Honour's directions, a sharp attack of fever, which prevented his leaving his quarters and incapacitated him for duty."

This of course, left matters as they were, and possibly there was no other officer to whom President Brown could repeat his order. One rather feels for the old gentleman in his dilemma, and shares the gratification with which he subsequently announced to the Council "that he hath received advices of the speedy arrival of His Excellency Sir Ul—sses F—tzm—e" (which of course no one could take for Ulysses Fitzmaurice) and that as His Majesty's ship of war conveying His Excellency might be daily looked for, it might be expedient to defer until His Excellency's arrival, further action in this untoward affair.

THEY STUCK TO THE SHIP.

ONE of our Baratarian worthies was an honest straightforward gentleman of the olden school, who had raised himself from a humble position to one of wealth and honour in the little island, and some people who held that blood will tell, readily believed in the legend that Mr. Crooke's grandfather was a scion of historic family. who had fled to the West Indies from Scotland for political reasons, and had taken a different name to his own, which his descendants never resumed.

I don't know the why or wherefore, unless indeed, it were his Scottish origin, but old Mr. Crooke was of an extremely cautious—nay, suspicious character—and his unwillingness to go into society, or to meet strangers, was probably due to this. His wife was equally retiring, and the old couple were regular stay-at-homes, although to their acquaintances they were most hospitable.

Business and the recommendation of the doctors rendered it necessary for Mr. Crooke to visit England, and Mrs. Crooke, from whom he was inseparable, was not to be left behind. The old couple had neither of them ever been "at home," and the approaching journey was a very serious matter. Mr. Crookes scorned the idea of travelling in a "beastly, smoky, dirty steamer" since he owned, along with several other vessels, a clipper barque, the "Aurora," that made the fastest runs to London and was always kept in the trimmest, neatest order.

And as for time—was it not the sea voyage that was prescribed for them? and thirty days of it would not be too much. Well, the worthy couple left in their yacht, as they called the Aurora,—and in due time returned safely and improved in health, bringing with them no end of presents for friends, old and young. They were full of what they had seen, although for the three weeks they were on land, they appeared to have remained in London, to the description of which wonderful place their narratives were confined.

One of their friends, who was favoured with an account of all they saw and all they did, enquired about theatres.

"Didn't go to any" said Mr. Crooke.

"Not go to a theatre?"

"No."

"Perhaps you object to them on principle."

"Not that, but d'ye see the Dock gates close so confoundedly early,—six o'clock."

"I don't quite understand."

"Why, we had to be aboard by then. You don't suppose I was going into a dirty hotel, or stuffy lodging, while we had our own cabin in the Aurora! No thank ye!"

And so it was; the good old couple had "stuck to the ship" and had in consequence, never seen London by gas light.

MY FIRST "BIRTHDAY" BALL.

NOT long after my arrival in Barataria where I filled the responsible post of Private Secretary, it became necessary for the Governor to give a Ball "in celebration of Her Majesty's Birthday." I was young, and my inexperience relieved me of the duty of providing the refreshments, solid and liquid, which the

Governor and his wife undertook to supervise with the assistance of a most delightful old black man, who, from his long and faithful service, might have been Hereditary Grand Caterer, but the invitations, decorations, music, &c., were entrusted to me.

Of course, every one who had called at Government House was to be invited, and all who had omitted to pay their respects to Her Majesty's representative were, as a rule, to be left out in the cold, and so to work I went. There was a visitors' book, and a bundle of visitors' cards, and from these I had to make a list which at the outset, seemed a very hard task. When I had completed it, we thought we would submit it to one of His Excellency's official advisers who knew everything about everyone in Barataria, and a terrible criticism my poor list underwent in consequence. X. and Mrs. X. were all right, but young X. "was an awful young snob and was never asked anywhere." The O. family—well of course,—they must be asked, but "it was to be hoped O. would come sober," and so on. Some names were added because, poor people, the want of means of conveyance had prevented their calling, or they lived so far away, and though they wouldn't come, still they would feel hurt if omitted, and, in the same way, many additions and emendations were proposed and adopted. Then, being new comers, we took further means to ensure safety, and consulted some lady leaders of society, with the result that the advice of our first adviser was in some respects over-ruled and the list again altered. Ultimately I had a string of names, and sent out the cards, and before long in came the replies. Mr. P. (a gentleman who on political principles, never entered Government House, but as a matter of policy was asked) wanted to know why his wife was not invited. P. was a suggestion of our official adviser, who coolly told me "he had forgotten Mrs. P.," so I had to apologize and send an amended card. Q. "had great pleasure in accepting," but asked to be allowed to bring his wife's mother, formerly a constant *habitat* of Government House entertainments. I found the old lady was 80, and that Q. meant *habitués*. Then Mr. Theophilus T. accepted, but informed me that his son Grandison had completed his education at one of the best seminaries at Peckham, near London, and had come out to his native isle, and that an opportunity for Grandison to make his début in polite society would be acceptable. So Grandison was asked. I remember he got very tight at an early hour, and was sent home. Then Mr. C., who was an official of high degree, was indignant at Mrs. C. not being asked. S., our adviser, informed us it was *impossible* to invite Mrs. C., who had formerly occupied a position in the market where she sold cakes—and then had held what he called "an acting appointment" in C's household, and that in short, if she entered the room, every lady would leave it. Well, of course, I had to tell C. that the invitation he received was what was intended. Then he wrote asking for an interview with the Governor, who declined. Then he appealed to me to give him an opportunity of "dispelling the clouds that rested on Mrs. C.'s fair fame" as he eloquently put it. This could not be either, and there the matter dropped, but I was not very comfortable when the Governor told me his former P.S. in Cannibaland, (his last Government).

was called out by an indignant Artillery officer, whose wife, not being presentable, was excluded from Government House invitations. These are but a few examples of the troubles that beset me, and I was heartily glad when the invitations were done with.

Government House was an agglomeration of rooms, the result of extensions and additions by each of the dozen Governors who had inhabited it, but the two apartments that were to do duty as ball room and supper room were fairly spacious, and separated by a movable screen resting against two pillars, between each of which and the wall was a space closed by a sliding door.

The ball room was rather low, and from its ceiling and sides there hung bronze oil lamps of an antique description. In those days kerosine was unknown. The table lamps (moderateurs) were liable to sudden extinction by any gust of wind, and so as a rule, candles enclosed in tall glass cylinders or barrels, were the means adopted for lighting a room. On this occasion we stuck candles in glass shades round a wooden disc slung from the ceiling, and which to some extent, was concealed by a half balloon of pink muslin caught up below with rosettes and leaves, that gave the apartment a sort of circus-like air.

Inexperienced people, especially friends at home, always think that decorating a room in the tropics is easy, because "there is such beautiful foliage." Now-a-days, with gas and perhaps electric light, foliage is more effective than formerly, when masses of leaves, in a far from brilliantly lighted apartment, looked funereal; but on the occasion to which I am referring, the room that by day was a bower of greenery, by night was as lively as a coal cellar, at least it would have been so but for the flags which were draped here and there. Oh! those flags! they were borrowed from the mercantile marine, and were quite too awfully redolent of tar. They gave one the idea of a hop at a Dental Hospital where each of the guests had applied creosote to an aching tooth. I can smell them now! There being no garrison, there was no band, and so the music gave us great concern. We had clung to the hope that one of H.M. ships would have called in, and then we could have borrowed her band, but this was not to be. The only professional music obtainable was a fiddle, tambourine, and triangle, but this His Excellency would not hear of, as being low and common. There was a young man who played the flute pretty well, and to whom an honorarium would have been acceptable, but a Government House party could hardly be expected to dance for hours to nothing but a flute, and so we had to depend on the Governor's piano, and the kind help of guests.

The only vehicle, besides the Governor's carriage, in or near town, was a gig, and the majority of our guests had either to foot it for a mile and a half (for Government House was that distance from the metropolis), or to ride their horses or mules. It was in the days of crinoline, and when a lady was mounted, her capacious skirts swagged out, and had to be confined beneath a shawl, so that a procession of those lopsided figures in the moonlight looked weird and uncanny in the extreme. Behind some of them trotted boys, carrying on their heads baskets containing additional gear, to be donned at the last moment, and of course there were cavaliers escorting these damsels. Some of the prudent ones, who had ridden far, had their coat tails pinned up to their collars for the avoidance of contact with their perspiring steeds. Not a few of the animals had to repeat the journey many times, being lent by generous owners. And that gig—I think it was old B. and his stout wife who first borrowed it, promising to send it back to F., its owner, who was anxious to be early at the ball, but as the boy on his return approached the town, he was seduced by fair words and shillings, to convey pedestrians up to Government House, and this was repeated so often, that F. was very late, and Miss G. had given away all her dances, and the pony was unfit for work for weeks after.

At that time, the Baratarians did not consider it polite to be too early at a ball, and so our arrangements were all complete before the first arrivals made their appearance. The P.S. received them, and they stood about in silent groups of two and three. There were some enquiries after His Excellency and Mrs.——, in a manner suggesting fears that their nonappearance was due to ill health, and I heard old R., who had escorted his three daughters, mutter that in *his* time Governors were always ready to welcome their guests—but we were going on Cannibaland procedure. I was waiting for young Master S. who was reported to be very clever on the piano. At last he came, and pouncing on the obliging lad, I placed him at the Broadwood, whispered directions in his ear, and gave the concerted signal; a sliding door was drawn back, a voice announced His Excellency the Governor, and in walked Her Majesty's representative in full uniform, with his wife, bowing to the assembled company; while Master S. played the National Anthem with one finger on the piano. It would have been more imposing had we had a band, and somehow this opening ceremony fell a little flat, and I think in after years, we avoided the Cannibaland fashion in this respect.

The opening ceremony being over, the next thing was the first quadrille, to join in which was only permitted to the upper ten, represented by a rotund Chief Justice, with mutton chop whiskers and little *boucles* of rather frizzly grey hair, two Law Officers of the Crown, both small, but one agile and "chirpy," and the other grave and sedate, with a reverend specimen of the Muscular Christian, and the Colonial Surgeon, a dapper little man, with a head as bare as a billiard ball, who was much given to racing.

I forget now who their partners were, but you may be sure they had been carefully selected with due regard to precedence. Good tempered Mrs. M. and her daughter, excellent musicians, were seated at the piano, and the "British Navy Quadrilles" were played with great effect, and danced to with much solemnity. There were no frivolous gigglings and whisperings, but the dancers deported themselves as officials of high degree, engaged in a grave duty, might be expected to do.

I have not mentioned that what His Excellency wore was the now rarely seen Windsor uniform, a blue double-breasted coat with swallow tails, many silver buttons and a huge pair of epaulettes, silver laced trousers, and a scimitar shaped sword. It was the only uniform visible that evening, but on subsequent occasions Naval and

Military blue and scarlet frequently relieved the sombre hue of civilian dress. After the opening dance, the guests "went a head" and enjoyed themselves. They waltzed—none of the affectations and vulgarities one has witnessed in later years, such as Whitechapel wobbles and Limehouse lurches—but good honest trois-temps, and there were polkas and schottisches, galops, and more square dances. Everybody danced, young and old, for in my day, Private Secretaries and Aides took care that there were no wall-flowers, and it was an understood thing that the veriest old dowager, if she wished to dance, should be led out by the P.S. or one of the young men present rather than she should remain neglected. At one end of the ball room was a verandah looking seawards, and this space was pretty well filled with a double row of servant girls who had either accompanied their "missises" or attached themselves on arrival, and who, with their neat dresses and gay and jaunty handkerchiefs, added to the picturesqueness of the scene. Every now and then their eyes would sparkle and their grinning teeth gleam, as they recognized Missie This or Missie That when those ladies swept by; and their criticisms, expressed in under tones, were frequent and candid, so that while Miss Julia was said to look "too sweet," and Miss Tilda "really pretty," it was considered that Mrs. So-and-so, who was reputed an exacting mistress, "wid dem fedder on she head" would have been better at home "fo' nuss she mudder, than throw she foot dat fashion in gubnor ball dance." This creole custom of each lady guest having one or two females hangers on, was by no means convenient, but it was of long standing, and had become a vested right. Long after the time of which I am writing, the Governor at the period, objected to this fringe of unbidden attendants, and on the occasion of a Birthday Ball, ordered the gallery to be cleared of them. There were remonstrances and murmurs, and even some scuffling, but the command was carried out. Then the bandsmen began to mutiny. Clarionet openly stated that if Mrs. Clarionet was to go, so should he. Bombardon indignantly escorted his offended spouse and daughter down the steps; and the Drummer, who was a loyal, but weak-minded, man, was seen with his drum on his head, driven across the courtyard by Mrs. Drummer at the point of her umbrella. To recall them would have been feeble policy, and so His Excellency's guests were forced to content themselves with the music discoursed by the faithful first Cornet, and a bachelor and unattached Bassoon.

I wonder if any one plays now-a-days the music to which we danced that night some thirty-five years ago! Does any one remember the "Drum" and "Sultan" polkas called into existence, if I recollect rightly, by the Crimean war, and the "Agnes Sorel" and "Les Rats" quadrilles? Perhaps they may yet be found in some old musty collection of music, to turn over which is but sad work, recalling dear ones whose deft fingers have long been still, and whose melodious lips are silent for ever. Hearing these old pieces once more, one would almost expect to see them danced by spectres,—the ghosts of many of those gay guests of long ago.

I may record that throughout the evening liquid refreshments, sherry negus, claret cup, lemonade, tea, and coffee, were handed round. There was no "bar"; and as for Sodas and B., the Governor would have considered anyone requiring anything of the kind as in want of medical aid. We had tried punch, but as was often the case then, and is now, good old rum was not to be got, and the substitute was a failure, so much so, that old Marshall, who, on being denied brandy, had recourse to the mixture, was heard to indulge in language of the most disrespectful and insubordinate kind. Even in "Old Barataria" people could not go on dancing for ever, and as twelve o'clock came, and the "Roast Beef" was thundered out from the piano, the constitution of which instrument was considered to have given way from that evening, people hailed supper as a welcome break in the festivities.

Of course the guests went two and two, but not in any promiscuous haphazard way. Noah was not more careful in marshalling his guests into the ark than were we in seeing that people of like degree were linked together, and walked together in their places when entering the supper room. The table was a wonderful sight. In Cannibaland, where native chiefs were often regaled, besides sturdy colonists with appetites sharpened by some months roughing it in the bush, big feeds were the order of the day, and my dear Governor, who never quite realized the fact that West Indians were very different from the colonists of the island in the Pacific, provided as he used to do. The dishes were embedded in flowers and the joints were huge and various. Every kind of poultry was represented. Of pastry and sweets the examples were innumerable, and if our guests had been four times their number there would have been far too much. As it was, the inmates of the Poor House, and a crowd of dependants on Government House *largesse*, feasted for days after on the overplus.

We had no ice in those days, and consequently were free from those agonizing periods of suspense that nowadays, if the ship is overdue, drives thirsty lieges half crazy. We knew not the feeling that leads men to clasp each other's hands, and with parched lip and tearful eye, point their trembling fingers to the welcome, long-delayed signal, as castaways greet a sail on the horizon. We were spared all this. Moderate in our desires, we cooled our drinks in porous goblets or in bottles swathed in constantly moistened cloths, on window sills, or where a draught of air could fan them. With the humble or careless of appearance, the arms of discarded merino vests were used, but more often the envelope, daintily done in crochet, was an appropriate present from a clever damsel to a favoured swain.

No need to recount the speeches. The Queen was received as loyally as in any other part of Her dominions. And though planters were still smarting from the legislation of '46, which, as they contended, gave undue advantages to slave grown sugar, and though they had just gone through an epidemic of yellow fever which had thinned their numbers, and their labourers had been sadly diminished by a visitation of cholera, they still were brave and hopeful and true, and it was only one or two extreme radicals who, attributing all these evils to misgovernment, hinted at better things under another flag; and so the usual three cheers rang out lustily as ever.

And then they drank the health of the Governor and his wife, who were chorally declared to be jolly good fellows; and then followed the "Ladies" and a response from some bashful bachelor, I think Mr. S., the embryo pianist, and then more dancing till,—well in Barataria, clocks in those days stopped at 2 a.m., and took no count of anything after that.

At last, however, they went, those guests; ponies were brought round, and ladies, carefully shawled by their partners, some of whom must have been clumsy fellows they took so long about it, were lifted into their saddles. Some of the lissome girls of that evening still survive, but now it would take a stronger arm than that of their present historian to swing them on to their steeds. Then there were hands shaken, and words whispered, and many a lad and lass cantered away happily under the spreading boughs of a giant acacia, and round the corner of a dell filled with bamboos, and down the road chequered with the moonlight that streamed through the branches of overhanging trees, while the music of their voices mingled with the clatter of hoofs. And older couples trudged along on foot, with sometimes an ominous stumble, followed by a word of caution from the wife, until one by one the sounds died away, and the last guest faded from sight, as the Governor and I looked from the verandah across the garden, whence floated up the perfume of many a sweet-scented plant, and down the richly timbered ascent to the house, across the little town lying asleep, with its roofs glistening white in the moon's rays, out to the broad sea flecked with silver light.

"Well, thank God! that's over," at length said His Excellency, and his Secretary replied, Amen!

MUTUAL CONFIDENCE.

SPEAKING of St. Sangaree meteorologically, and with reference to its rainfall, one would say it was a moist island, but the people thereof are, or used to be, dry and arid. I remember being there once on duty with a superior Governor when it was arranged that there should be a levée. Such a thing had not been since St. Sangaree was a separate Government, with a strong garrison and a large staff of officials, Colonial and Imperial, but in our day the island had been sadly shorn of its pomp and circumstances, and there were only a quiet easy-going Lieut. Governor with an anything but energetic legislature, a slender and not well paid official surrounding, empty barracks, and ruined fortifications, the guns of which had gone to the United States as old iron. The building where the local parliament met and sundry officials were located was a rather pretentious building and evidently had been erected in the more prosperous days of St. Sangaree. It was here the important ceremony was to take place. A strong—numerically strong—body of police mounted guard. Their caps were of a bygone fashion, but it was explained that these were not worn except on very high occasions, and so had lasted a long while and were as good as ever. Boots, from the discomfort expressed on the wearers' faces, must also have been unfamiliar articles, and the firelocks were curiosities, but the Inspector General wore blue and silver and had slung to him a most uncontrollable and noisy sabre. There was an A.D.C., a civilian, who donned a blue frock coat with a rather mulberry coloured sash, quite eclipsing my evening dress. One of the principal persons with whom certain preliminaries had to be settled, was an official who, to meet the hard times, filled some four offices at what in the old days was the salary of one of them. His staff was not extensive and consisted of an old man who made up the mails, conducted the correspondence, answered questions, went messages, and acted as a bailiff in addition to other duties. He was a quaint old creature with round shoulders, on which hung a well-worn coat of a bygone fashion, the cuffs of which almost hid his long bony fingers.

I found my friend just entering his office. He was an active, handsome, young fellow, but as one glance could tell, had a lot of the devil in him.

"Glad to see you, my dear Sir! very glad. What can I do for you, eh? but here Mr. Winterbell, Mr. Winterbell!"

"Yes Sir," said his sub coming forward from a corner—

"Produce the brandy. We have no ice, but Mr. Winterbell! bring some cool water!"

"Nothing for me, thank you," I protested, for it was not later than 10.30.

My friend, however, would take no denial, and Mr. Winterbell, with trembling hands, put two thick tumblers on a table.

"Mr. Winterbell!" exclaimed Mr. Bingo, shaking his head, and holding up the bottle, which was half full— "You have betrayed my confidence Sir!"

"No Sir!"

"Yes! Sir—let me explain," added Mr. Bingo, turning to me—"the contingency vote of this department is employed, if not so intended, to provide two bottles of brandy a week. One-third is for me, another for persons like yourself coming on business and requiring refreshment, the remaining third is for Mr. Winterbell. We have barely commenced the week; this is Tuesday—and see—ah, Mr. Winterbell, even in apparent trifles like these, honesty should be observed."

I persisted in my refusal to drink, and Mr. Bingo mixed and swallowed a rather stiff glass.

I said what I had to say, and was about leaving when he detained me.

"Excuse me, Mr. Beke, but I think it is my duty to put you on your guard against Spiffkins, our Controller of Customs. He wants, I know, to get at the Governor to poison his mind against—well—myself and others who won't stand his nonsense. The Lieutenant Governor, as you know, is—in fact he's led entirely by McKenzie, a fellow I wouldn't—but you'll see for yourself. Adieu for the present."

With some excuse I got away from my friend and was going down the corridor, when I was beckoned to by Mr. Spiffkins whom I had known in another island.

"My dear Beke" said he, with outstretched hands, "I *am* so glad to see you. Come in, how well you're looking. Feel it hot? I dare say, but stop a bit,"—and he disappeared behind the flap of a desk.

When he emerged he had in his hand a bottle.

"Look here! This is real old St. Maria shrub, now have some, do—with some cool water, eh? you'll find it capital. No? *really* no? Anyhow you'll know where to find it, later on perhaps," and the bottle was replaced.

"Now," said Spiffkins coming up to me and holding my arm, "what I am going to say must be confidential—*sacred.* I saw you go into Bingo's office. Now beware of him, because—he's a snake in the grass—tries to undermine me with the Lieutenant Governor, who, poor fellow, is led by the nose by an infernal Scotchman, McKenzie—you know what I mean—Ah! that Bingo!" and Mr. Spiffkins drew in his breath in the style of a melo-dramatic villain, and shook his head as I left him.

I was about to descend the steps when the Hon'ble Mr. McKenzie, an official of importance, detained me; might he have one word?

"My dear Mr. Beke," said Mr. McKenzie shaking a forefinger at me in an impressive way, "let this be in confidence, but for God's sake don't let His Excellency trust either of those men, Bingo and Spiffkins. There's only one decent fellow here—that's Biggs, the Colonial Secretary, but Bingo and Spiffkins, my dear Sir, one is a rascal and the other"—McKenzie closed one eye and raised his thumb to his lips with a twist of his little finger—"awful Sir! perfectly awful! but that reminds me, you must be thirsty. I've got some 'Three Star' and—you won't? Ah! I will—you don't know how this climate takes it out of you. Well! now don't forget what I have told you about those two fellows. Au revoir! twelve o'clock's the hour."

The mention of Mr. Biggs reminded me that I must see him, whom I found in his office where we discussed some papers which had been referred to him. He was a tall, thin, young looking man, with a demure air, and his neat white tie and black clothes, with a measured way of talking, gave him quite a clerical air.

"I am glad of this opportunity, Mr. Beke," he said, with downcast eyes and a gentle voice, "of saying what may appear uncharitable, and which it grieves me to say, but duty compels me—and it is this: I pray you, keep the Governor from the machinations of three men in this community, in this building, I mean McKenzie, Bingo, and Spiffkins. They are deceitful men. It is not for me to say how their official duties are performed, but their chief aim is to ruin me. God knows what I have done to draw down their enmity, unless it be an humble attempt to do my duty, but I live, if I may so say, in fear of my life—my official life—of course I have not approached the Lieutenant Governor on the question because—well I must respect his position, but those three men"—

"I think," I ventured to say, "you misjudge them."

"Ah no"—and Mr. Biggs stretched out his hand to a glass of milk which stood on his table.

"You find that agree with you?" I asked by way of changing the conversation.

"Yes—the doctors prescribe it. Can I offer you anything? I find the oleaginous particles of the milk apt to disagree with me, and, under medical advice, I add generally" and he dived into a cupboard—"a little corrective stimulant. This" he added, holding out a bottle "is old rum, and here is a glass and some cool water, let me invite you to take some."

I refused—I would wait until the sun was over the yard-arm.

"Then I will add my usual modicum," and he poured

a good wine glassful into the milk and stirred it with a paper knife as I rose to go.

"We shall meet at twelve shall we not? Till then good day," and he opened the door for me.

When twelve o'clock came, and the two Governors in full uniform drove up, they were received with all proper ceremony. It is true they came in a small basket carriage, which was the only vehicle in the colony, and usually carried the parson and his wife, but to ride was for some reasons impracticable.

Now this levee was to be a great function, and due notice had been sent all over the island, but the St. Sangaree people were not a very energetic set and rarely came to the Town save on mail days, and I believe there were difficulties—at all events the affair was attended almost entirely by officials. The two Excellencies took up their station in the Court House, the fittings of which had been arranged to allow of those attending, to appear at one door, pass before the Governors, and make their exit into the passage beyond. The A.D.C. announced the names which were duly repeated by me. The Chief Justice and all the officials passsed in and out in a straggling intermittent procession, McKenzie, Bingo, Spiffkins and Biggs of course among them, and I was bewildered to see these four gather together outside, shake hands, laugh and talk and slap each other on the back as if they were the best friends, and I was wondering whether there had been a combination to hoax poor me, or if they were dissembling; when the Aide-de-camp called out "Mr. Webbels."

We had exhausted the official lists, no non-official had

appeared, and it was becoming necessary to decide whether it was not time for the curtain to be rung down, and the performance closed, when Mr. Webbels appeared. He was a very old man, much bent and feeble, supporting himself with a stick as he tottered from the door with a queer half-dazed look, turning his eyes from the Aide-de-camp to me, and then to the Governors. There was something grotesque and something very touching in this old man's appearance; a last link between the good old days of St. Sangaree and the present time. Suddenly he stopped and bowed, and then, lifting up both hands, he said, in a thin piping voice, "Bless me! haven't seen anything like it since '13;" and then he turned and tottered out at the door by which he had entered.

And when he had gone we went too. I have not heard of any levées in St. Sangaree since that one.

TREASURE TROVE AND NOT TROVE.

THERE are many well founded traditions of buried treasure in the West India Islands. The Buccaneers are supposed to have concealed much of their plunder which they never returned to recover. During the wars with France, and in those islands in which contests with the native Caribs were frequent, much valuable property was hastily hidden, and the places of deposit known only to a few with whom the secret died. In some of the islands, almost every estate shews traces where a search for money has been made. In one island, where the French were after a short resistance driven by the English never to regain possession, it is said that the French authorities buried a large amount of money (some thousands of pounds) before they took to their ships ; believing that they would soon return. The secret was apparently confided to few, but my informant, then an official of the colony, told me that he had been assured by an old coloured Frenchman that the money still lay undisturbed under the foundation of what had been, if I recollect rightly, a guard house, but which then formed part of a Hospital. The expense of the search, involving as it would, the destruction of some buildings, and the fear of being ridiculed if the search proved fruitless, deterred the authorities from making the experiment.

There is no doubt, however, that in some of the French colonies, records and plans exist shewing where treasure has been hidden in the islands now possessed by the English. The mystery is, why these clues should not have been fully followed up long ago, and how it is that only after many years have elapsed, people come and search apparently with success for hidden hoards. It now and then happens that a small vessel is seen to hover off the coast of one of these islands; two or three strangers land under some pretext, and after a day or so, the vessel leaves. Then some labourer reports having found a deep and recently dug hole in his provision grounds, around the brink of which splinters of decayed wood, flakes of iron rust, or pieces of broken jars, shew that some thing had been dug up and removed.

One manager I knew, who suddenly became possessed

of means with which he bought an estate, was supposed to have some such treasure trove which, buried in the face of a cliff, was disclosed by a land slip. But one rarely hears of an authenticated case of any such discovery by a resident.

Various are the marks which are said to guide the descendants of the French fugitives who made the *câche* to the spot where the treasure lies. Lines drawn so many paces from the apex of a triangle formed by three trees, or from a particular rock, are the most common.

One story tells of a stranger ferreting out an old negress, once the slave of former French proprietors, and asking to be shewn where the youngest child of her mistress had been buried. She shewed the spot; a stable had been built over it, but the stranger and his companion coming at night, dug up a portion of the pavement, took up a coffin-like box and carried off its contents, which were not bones but coin.

One common legend is that of a proprietor, before fleeing the country, employing a slave to bury the money he could not take with him, and then in order to keep the secret safe, murdering the slave;—but being himself taken and killed, all trace of where his wealth lies hidden has been lost. The result is that negroes go and burrow in the ground until the supposed place of deposit has become like a rabbit warren. Of course searchers are generally unsuccessful.

"Massa" once said an old negro lady to me "Wha' de good for dig for money? The deeper you does dig the furder de money sink."

The spot most often "prospected" is the site of the

mansion of some former proprietor. The house and garden have long since disappeared; a few old fruit trees and some old broken tiles are the only traces left; while of the family itself the only memorials are a field or two still called after them, or perhaps some old negro in whose name that of his former owner still survives. It is melancholy to note how the history of these former colonists is lost to us. Unfortunately, no records, letters or journals exist, from which one can learn any thing respecting the manner of the daily life of these old colonists, and one would gladly learn more of them.

It is difficult to understand how their wealth could have been acquired from their small holdings of 50 or 60 acres, and yet people must have lived in great comfort, if not in luxury, in those days. One has often heard of three or four balls attended only by white people taking place on the same night in "town,"—which now consists of a church, a grog shop, a small provision store, and a few tumble-down shanties. Of course all is now changed. As the French settlers have disappeared from the majority of the islands so the English and Scottish families who succeeded them have died out or sought occupation elsewhere. Field has been laid to field, and the homesteads where the former gentry of the land kept open house are either levelled to the ground or are inhabited by a far different class; and the money which is made in a colony, as a rule is no longer spent in it, nor is it buried except in the sense of being sunk occasionally in unfortunate operations on estates.

VOX POPULI.

SOME years ago the legislature of each West India island (as mentioned in another yarn) was modelled on that of the Mother Country. Queen, Lords and Commons, had their counterparts in Governor, Legislative Council, Legislative Assembly, the latter of course elected; but elections as a rule were tame, spiritless affairs. Of the few scores of electors registered, not a quarter ever came to vote unless there were some exceptional circumstances which aroused a transient interest.

Once upon a time, old Vernon, the returning officer in St. Maria, had an election at his own house where he had hospitably provided a sumptuous luncheon. The parish returned two members and the electors numbered under 20, but on the occasion referred to, only one of the two candidates put in an appearance, Dalziel, the owner of a small estate, and with this exception no electors were visible. I, who was a stranger on a visit, had no vote. After waiting a long while, we breakfasted, and the hour of nomination found us over cigars and sangaree. At length it dawned on Vernon that something must be done, so we put pens, ink and paper on a small table in the gallery, and the Governor's warrant was read; then the returning officer happily bethought him of a man who was shingling the stable and he was brought before us.

"Hepburn!"

"Yes, Marshal!"

"We have to elect two members to serve in the Assembly for St. Maria's Parish. You propose any one? You've got a vote I know."

"Yes, massa, me got vote, but me don't know any member."

"Well, you know Mr. McStiver, the attorney for *Belle Source.*"

"Yes, me massa, ob coorse, me know massa McTivah."

"Will you just say I propose Mr. McStiver."

"Yes sah, I propose Massa McTivar."

"And" said the considerate Dalziel, "I second the nomination of my friend McStiver; and I propose myself as the other member."

"Hepburn! you second that."

"Well, me Massa, you see dis buckra last time me wuk for him he cut my money too bad and me don't tink——"

"Ah! shut up! have a drink——"

"Tank'ee Marshal, well me second dat."

"And I declare" added the returning officer, "that in the absence of any opposition, Messrs. Edward McStiver and Roderick Dalziel are duly returned to serve as members of the Honourable House of Assembly of this colony."

AN OFFICIAL DILEMMA.

IN my time, thirty years ago, the gaol at Conquintay was not an attractive building. Its architectural beauties were nil. Whatever yearnings for æsthetic design the colonial authorities might have possessed, they resisted the temptation, so far as their prison was concerned, and thus the buildings with its four walls might be termed "bald." I once said as much to a worthy Executive Councillor whose ear failed to appreciate the value of an aspirate, and he, being facetious, retorted that I could not say the situation of the place was not "hairy." Of course I laughed; when councillors condescend to a joke, one ought always to look appreciative and amused.

The gaol had, probably still has, four walls, lofty, and topped with the regulation broken bottles, of which Conquintay could always furnish a constant supply; and being perched on an eminence on which nothing grew save some short grass, it was a prominent object, a landmark to mariners, and a warning to the evil-disposed of the town,—which was a collection of houses huddled together on the beach at the foot of the hill.

It was a bare uncomfortable hill; in dry weather the sun beat on it and browned it; the heat flickered above it and around the white-washed prison walls; and the half-starved goats that browsed there seemed glad to shrink away to any spot of shade. In the rainy season when it was green and pleasant with the springing grass, its surface was slippery and treacherous, while the pathways that scarred its front became small rivulets.

There was in the quadrangle of the gaol, a cocoanut palm that raised its leafy head above the enclosure, and when the winds blew, its pendant fronds would wave and toss as if it were some imprisoned creature striving to be free. When the air was still and heavy and hot, they drooped and hung as if condemned to death and despairing of all hope.

That tree had a history affording rebuke to all men

who think that colonial officials are hasty, heedless, and given to decide grave questions of state without consideration and consultation. As told to me, that history runs somewhat thus:

Of all the soldiers of the detachment quartered at Conquintay, Bob Johnson, a tall black man from Barbados, was the boldest and the bravest. He was smart and steady, an example to all young recruits who, seduced by the eloquence of a sergeant and attracted by a wide-breeched Zouave uniform, had forsaken hoe or fishing line to follow the drum. Bob was also a good servant, an excellent cook, and had a "lucky hand" with a horse, so that he was somewhat of a favourite. But alas! this paragon had one besetting sin; he was, not to put too fine a point upon it, a thief. He practised chiefly on a limited scale, picking up unconsidered trifles and evading detection by his skill, or escaping punishment through his otherwise good character. One day however Bob operated to a serious extent. A store in the town was broken into one evening when he was on leave, and a large sum abstracted. The evidence of an accomplice and other circumstances sufficed to convict Johnson and he was sentenced to imprisonment.

It was a serious affair and a source of regret to the corps. Johnson was missed terribly but "fiat justitia &c.," and there was nothing for it but that Bob should serve out his time in an unbecoming uniform, and in the performance of uncongenial and ignominious duties, and so time stole on until the day arrived when the detachment was to be relieved.

It was never clearly ascertained whether the authorities

yielded to the request of his officers to allow Johnson to accompany the outgoing garrison, or whether they were moved by the consideration that the cost of Johnson's prolonged stay in gaol would disturb that minute and exact adjustment of the Colonial finances upon which the prosperity of Conquintay depended; but certain it is, that it was arranged that Johnson should be liberated on the understanding that he left the colony, and the inhabitants be thereby enabled to "thank God that they were rid of a villain."

This plan somehow reached Bob's ears and displeased him greatly; perhaps because it interfered with his touching the fruits of the robbery which had never turned up and were supposed to have been concealed by him. On the morning that H.M.S. "Trooper" steamed into Conquintay, an order under the Governor's hand and seal for the prisoner's release was delivered to the jailor, who at once proceeded to communicate its contents to the person chiefly concerned; but he was nowhere to be found, until a group of grinning prisoners pointed him out, comfortably perched on the top branches of the cocoa palm.

The jailer ordered him down, but the prisoner only grinned; then he tried to coax him to descend, but equally without effect. The State document was read out or rather bawled out to him, but Bob only shook his head; and when his guardian lost temper and broke out into volleys of oaths and awful threats, the audacious fellow laughed to such an extent that he nearly lost his hold on the tree.

The only course left open to the jailer was to communicate these circumstances to the Colonial Secretary, and explain his inability to comply with the Governor's mandate; and this was done without delay.

When the letter reached the Colonial Secretary, he placed a minute on it to the effect that it was "embarrassing and unusual" and that he "presumed the jailor must compel the prisoner to quit the cocoanut palm," and sent it on to the Governor who wrote below it another minute "very much so, clearly" and adding his initials, sent it back to the Colonial Secretary. The document was then forwarded to the jailer, with a peremptory minute that Mr. Holdfast *must* (underlined) get the prisoner down. The jailer on receiving it, scratched his head and betaking himself to the foot of Johnson's retreat, renewed his orders, prayers, threats, and curses in due rotation, but his prisoner was as the deafest of adders, and so poor Mr. Holdfast had to contribute his minute, and say that with all he could do, the prisoner would not obey.

The Colonial Secretary who was a man of great resources, read it with a frown that changed into a smile, as an excellent expedient occurred to him, and he wrote to the Governor to suggest that the fire engine of the gaol might be made to play on the disobedient Johnson, until he either came or was brought down off the tree. The Governor however, when he perused this proposition, rather chafed at his subordinate writing about fire engines which clearly did not belong to his department, and so he wrote that it would be advisable to consult the Colonial Engineer,—firstly, as to whether the engine could send a jet to the height of the tree: secondly, whether the force of such jet could be sufficient to dislodge Johnson;

thirdly, as to the risk of depriving the gaol of water which would be necessary in case of fire. The Colonial Secretary read this with a shrug of his shoulders and wrote "Referred to Colonial Engineer for immediate report" on the letter which was speedily taken to that officer. The Engineer, who was a portly ex-Sergeant Major of Artillery, went up to the gaol followed by a negro boy laden with his instruments, and spent some considerable time in ascertaining what (perhaps from military associations) he called the Halt-itude of the tree, the cubic contents of the cistern, the bore of the engine's discharge pipe, with the velocity and volume of the jet, and then toddled down the hill back to his office, where he embodied the results in a minute (too long for insertion here) and added his opinion that in the present state of the hose, it would not be possible to throw water to such a height. The Colonial Secretary was half wild at the delay, and at the inutility of his suggestion, but on the principle of "least said soonest mended," he sent up the correspondence with a request for further instructions, to the Governor.

Now His Excellency was but mortal, and the envelope which was of a portentous size was handed to him while at luncheon with some naval and military officers, who, as the task of transferring the troops was all but concluded, had then some leisure. His Excellency read the Engineer's minute, and in a moment of haste scribbled below it "Damn the prisoner Johnson. Cut him down;" adding "of course, I mean the tree."

The Colonial Secretary was absent when this minute reached his office, and his head clerk, who wore spectacles and was a virtuous and proper young person, was horrified at this ebullition of temper on the part of Her Majesty's representative. Still he felt that what he conceived to be an order, rather than an objurgation, should be obeyed, and was considering who was the proper officer to anathematize Johnson, when his immediate Chief returned. Another minute was here added conveying a second enquiry of the Engineer as to whether there would be any risk to the buildings incurred by cutting down the tree. The Engineer, who was humane, observed that there would be no danger of damaging the gaol; but he added "how about injuring the prisoner?"

Thus it happened that the Colonial Surgeon was referred to, but he was out of town, and the Attorney General was in the meanwhile appealed to as to the legal liability of the Authorities if harm was done to the prisoner. When his opinion, which was an elaborate and explanatory one and touched incidentally on several points besides that in question, arrived, it was late in the day; and H.M.S. "Trooper" had to leave at a certain hour on account of tides and currents. The upshot was that Johnson did not embark, but had the pleasure of watching from his elevated post the ship go safely round the N.E. corner of Conquintay bay, before he slid down the tree and returned to his cell. Bob served out his term and then left for his native island where some years ago he was still alive and in easy circumstances. For years, however, any reference to him or that cocoa palm, in the official circle of Conquintay, was not considered to be in good taste.

HARD SKULL.

THE thickness of a negro's skull is proverbial, and in former times was, we fear, often made a subject of experiment. There was once a merchant who used to bet that one of his porters would run his head through a cheese, and this feat was frequently performed to the amusement of a delighted audience of loafers. On one occasion, after the "sangaree" had been passed round rather freely, the owner of the hard-headed porter had a grindstone wrapped up in canvas so as to imitate a "Double Gloster," and Mercury was desired to repeat the feat. The grindstone was set up on edge and the poor fellow sent his head with a bang at its centre; with a howl he fell back amid the laughter of the unfeeling fellows around. But he raised himself, remarking "Dat cheese well hard, 'spose he come last year; I think tho' he been bruck." And on removing the covering the stone was indeed found to be "bruck" or cracked through.

A few years ago at a county jail in England, a negro sailor who was undergoing imprisonment there, attempted to commit suicide by getting over the balusters at the top of the storey and throwing himself down the "well" of the staircase, a very considerable height. He was picked up senseless, but, strange to say, recovered in a few minutes and did not appear to have received any injury. Some weeks after, however, he effected his object by "butting" his head once against a wall with comparative little force, but the injury was fatal.

The "Black Caribs" of St. Vincent, who are the descendants of Carib and African ancestors, used to flatten the heads of their infants by means of a board strapped across the forehead to distinguish them from the African slaves imported as labourers, these lords of the soil having an aversion to work. But this practice of distorting the shape of the skull exists, or existed, among other Indian races.

A FISHY CUSTOMER.

IN Barataria the chief town is named, as any one can see on a map;—well—as it is to be so easily seen, I need not name it. In it, however, the principal store was kept by a firm styling themselves Mango and Co., but the original Mango had died out years before, and in his stead reigned Ratoon and Stump when I was stationed there. Ratoon had made money and had grown rather weary of the routine of business in spite of the variety presented by an establishment, where, on one side, bonnets, boots and dry goods were to be obtained, while at the opposite counter one could buy a ham, and a frying pan in which to cook it, to say nothing of there being a snug compartment where liquids of various strengths and qualities could be got. Ratoon had bought a sugar estate up the coast, and took pleasure apparently in watching how steadily he lost money by it, but it qualified him for a seat in Council. Mrs. Ratoon liked the prefix of Honourable to her spouse's name, and the precedence it gave herself at Government House, where His Excellency would take her down to dinner or supper before less distinguished ladies whose dresses she used once upon a time to make,—for every one in Barataria remembered Rosa Gussêt when she was a milliner. Mr. and Mrs. Ratoon therefore, were often absent from their Town mansion, which was the upper part of the premises where the business was carried on, and on such occasions Stump was the presiding genius of the mercantile establishment.

One day when I came into town, and was walking down the street that opened on the bay, I saw Stump seated outside his store on a barrel, kicking his heels in a desultory tattoo against its sides, and smoking a cigar of doubtful origin, as Stump's tobacco ever was. Stump I may explain, was a sun burnt, dried up old West Indian of 45, considered as the main stay of the business, and as good natured a fellow as one could wish to meet; and as I came up to him, he put out his hand and saluted me.

"Just come in?"

"Yes."

"Had any rain your way?"

"An inch and two-fifteenths." We were minute observers of rainfall in Barataria.

"When are you going out?"

"To-morrow—How's business?"

"Business be——"

"Slack?"

"Oh no—not at all slack"—and he grinned 'sarcastic.' "I'll tell you to-day's transactions and you will see. Take that chair. Have a weed?"

I declined the weed—for reasons.

"'Well, you know Ginger—up at the Garrison—Commissariat, Control o' something so;—well by Jove he's a fellow to trade."

"Sharp?" I enquired.

"Sharp! rather; to-day he came down on a flea-bitten pony he got out of a cargo from Tortola for $60, and rode up to the door here, as if he'd found a gold mine—'Ah!' says he 'Mr. Stump how *do* you do?' and he leant over his brute's neck and squeezed my hands as if I had been his brother. 'Do you know I want some good saltfish—really good you know—about six pounds. Any nice fish newly opened—eh?'

"'Well, I'm not proud, but we don't sell saltfish by retail, and so I told him."

"'Ah well! would you mind sending one of your lads to get some—Thank you!'

"'O course I had to call Peter and send him to the Portuguese shop round the corner, while Ginger kept smiling away and jabbering about his pony and the weather and Lord knows what."

"Presently Peter appeared with a whole fish. Ginger called him and inspected the purchase."

"'What does it weigh my lad' he asked with a bland voice like a sucking Curate."

"'A quarter, ten dog, and t'ree stampee' said Peter.'"

"'Which in English, Mr. Stump, means—?'"

"One and nine pence, said I—"

"'Ah! Yes, of course, but these barbaric terms'—and he began fumbling in all his pockets."

"'Dear me, how ludicrous—do you know I've actually come out without any money—positively penniless—may

I ask you my dear Mr. Stump to advance me this absurd sum of one quarter ten;—ah Peter! you're a sad wag'; and he began to aim a cut of his whip at Peter who grinned like a devil."

"Certainly, said I, with a growl."

"'Thanks! and may I ask our friend Peter to wrap it up in a sheet or two—we'll say two—of thick brown paper, for I must carry it myself, and the smell is not Eau de Cologne—is it? Thanks—ah! but Peter!' he went on as the boy handed him the parcel—'you forgot the string: just tie a bit here and then lash it to my saddle—thanks—and my dear Mr. Stump, you won't mind putting the quarter and ten—dear! dear! what a coinage!—to my account—thanks—Good morning.'"

"Good morning, I replied, in a rage at the fellow's coolness."

"Presently he came trotting back,—and pulled up at the door."

"'Mr. Stump!—Mr. Stump!' he called out as I tried to get away—'Ah! Peter! just hold Florizel'; for so he called his ugly brute, and off he slipped, and came into the store."

"'Mr. Stump—I've just remembered—I want to make some purchases for Mrs. Ginger. It's her birthday to-morrow.'"

"Well Mr. Ginger, I replied—I am very glad to supply you, of course, but your account is a little higher—"

"'Ah! of course, I know that—you've been very civil about it, Mr. Stump—very civil—and Mrs. Ginger and I appreciate your kindness, and we intend to settle before many days; but this is a cash transaction.'"

"That makes a difference! I observed—not that I believed the fellow."

"'Of course it does—*all* the difference—Well, I want to make Mrs. Ginger a present—some thing not very expensive yet something useful—I have a cheque for $120 —don't think I am extravagant, I don't mean to spend all in that way. Be just before you are generous, eh? —But it would be a convenience if you'll not pay it in until after the 1st——pay-day you know,—only 12 days off.'

"Oh well, said I, I don't mind—I presume it will be all right then."

"'My dear Sir? said Ginger, in a half injured tone, of course it will,—and if there are a few dollars over, your cashier could let me have them eh?—Yes! ah, will you just tell him—thanks.'

"I was glad to get rid of him, and did as he requested, and then off he went asking for and inspecting no end of things—presently he took his leave, and I pretended to be busy with a customer to escape his ceaseless jabber."

"Well Sir—just now I went to my cashier and what do you think Ginger had done?—Blessed if he hadn't bought a dozen handkerchiefs at $2.40 and got the balance of the cheque in cash. So that's a sort of forced loan of $118. Now that's the business I've been doing to-day. Of course I can't present the cheque and—" and Mr. Stump kicked his barrel savagely.

"What a sell," I remarked sympathisingly.

"Sell!—if ever that—but there! come in and have a a drink."

Some days after, I met Mr. Ginger who confided to

me that the Barataria shopkeepers were a lot of sharks and swindlers.

A STRANGE RIDE.

ONE day in our club old Sir Grey Charger, Bart, K.C.B., &c., who was always fond of talking of his West Indian experiences, and I were dining together. Putting down his glass of Chateau la Rose, he said "You've been in St. Fiddles where I was with the old 101st. Do you recollect old Sourwash and his two girls?—Of course not," he added after a moment's pause, "I'm thinking of 40 years ago;—but I'll tell you a yarn about them."

Sourwash—Simon Sourwash of Mt. Jupiter, in the Island of St. Fiddles, Esquire, had the reputation of being a very hospitable man, and so he was in a way. His invitations were frequent and sincerely meant, and one's three days' leave from garrison duty was generally spent with the old gentleman pleasantly enough. His daughters, Rosa and Rachel, were clever and cheery if not in their première jeunesse, nor very good looking, and we usually got up a little music and a dance on these occasions. On one point, old Simon was very particular, he never permitted a guest to bring his groom. He might as well said he, bring his own oats, and there were his own people to attend to the beasts. I did not quite like this arrangement, for on three or four occasions that I had been out to Mt. Jupiter, I fancied my horses did not seem improved by the journey and stay there, and and yet they were well fed and groomed; the stables were comfortable, and Sourwash always invited me to see the horses put up at sun-down. There were some six stalls in one building reserved for the riding horses, and in another long narrow stable or shed, the animals which Sourwash used on the estate's work, were kept. The mill was worked by cattle or horses, as is usual where water power is not obtainable, and where the position of the works precludes the use of a windmill. The crop, at Mt. Jupiter, was not a very large one, but Sourwash owned two or three estates adjacent and altogether he made perhaps 500 hogsheads. The works were in a valley not far from the dwelling house so that we could hear the creaking of the canes, and the lash of the whip as it fell on the backs of the unfortunate animals, which, harnessed to the long sweeps, went their weary round.

It was, as I have said, pleasant enough quarters. Of course I got chaffed about Rosa, who was the better looking of the two Sourwash girls, but I only grinned, for as yet I felt heart whole, and as the prospects of my succeeding to my father's estate was a near one, a share of Mt. Jupiter and a wife ten years older than myself, were no great temptation.

I soon found, however, that the Mt. Jupiter family were determined not to allow a baronetcy and a few thousands a year to escape them without a struggle, and the attentions of the old planter and his two daughters increased. I was inveigled into long rides up the mountain to see "such lovely views," and on these occasions I was left alone with one sister while the other lagged behind, until she too would take her turn. I was equally civil to each, and endeavoured to escape being betrayed into any expression which might be construed into an avowal of affection, and to tell the truth I rather enjoyed the fun; it pleased them and it didn't hurt me. One day we had been on an excursion, Rosa, Rachel and I. We started early on mule back with a boy carrying a basket with the commissariat, and had gone right away up to the head of the Carriacou river. I need not describe the scenery—we had a long ride up and down hill sides covered with canes in various stages of cultivation, the road passing three or four times under a confounded coulisse rope down which the cane bundles flew to the mill in the valley below, with a screech and a grunt,—no pleasant thing when you're on a skittish horse with a clear fall of 80 feet on one side of you; then a scrambling slippery climb thro' the labourers' provision grounds, past tall plantains and large tannias with diamond-like rain drops on their richly coloured leaves, or yams twisting round poles and reminding one of the Rhineland vines. Then would come a difficult bit along a narrow broken path, cut out in a groove by the constant tramp of the people, and only guarded from the edge of the steep precipice at the foot of which the river tumbled and roared, by a belt of tall bamboos with shafts as of polished glass, and huge tufts of feathery foliage.

A couple of hours of this work brought us to the source of the river, a small stream falling from a mossy nest in a cloven rock into a basin below.

Well, the lunch was good, and my two companions had famous appetites. The champagne—old Sourwash knew exactly what was good—was deliciously cool, and so with the bubbling brook and song of birds and the prattle of the two damsels—they were at least 28 and 30—time went smoothly. Presently Rachael went to a boulder within sight, if out of hearing, on pretence of sketching, and Rosa was left with me.

"Captain Charger," said she suddenly, (they always called me Captain, tho' I was only a Sub,) "I'm going to scold you," and she looked up into my eyes.

"My dear Miss Rosa," said I, "what for?"

"Well, it's about poor Rachel—I don't want to betray her—but you must have seen how—how—"

"How what?"

"How she loves you, there! I don't care—you know she loves you—and you if I am not mistaken, you—"

But here her voice faltered and as she bent her head a pearly tear dropped on to a morsel of chicken salad she was playing with at the end of her fork.

"My dear Miss Rosa" I began—but for the life of me I did not know what more to say—"my dear Rosa."

"Ah" said she dropping the fork with the salad and catching hold of my hand, "dont—I beg you, dont call me *that*. I am not—never can be yours. I know my duty too well to yonder poor sufferer my sister—no sacrifice can be too great for *her* dear sake," and she fumbled for her pocket handkerchief.

"Rosa!" said I, "There's some beastly—I beg pardon—some horrid mistake, I assure you."

She got up off the rock she was seated on, and rather struck an attitude as pointing with her fork to Rachel, she said—

"Mistake? ah! no, I will send her to you; may be the sight of the sorrow that is rending her—her heart may teach you your duty, oh! Captain Charger why are men so cruel?"—and off she strode.

Then I saw her plump down beside Rachel, who, after a few moments, rose and came towards me. Her arms and clasped hands were stretched down to her knees, and her head rested on her bosom, while her hair, released from her hat, which hung from its ribbons, fell in disorder. She came slowly towards me with a sort of theatrical walk, and I felt deucedly inclined to bolt. I was only 20, remember.

"Grey!" said she in her deepest contralto, "Grey, Rosa has betrayed me,—giddy, silly girl. I would my secret had died with me, but now you know all—yes! all."

"I'm awfully sorry Miss Rachel, I'm sure—but you see—or rather you dont see—that is—"

"I *have* seen! I *do* see" she cried, throwing her long and rather attenuated arms heavenwards. "I have seen your craft—your guile—I have marked the toils, the snares—"

"Good Lord!" said I jumping up and upsetting a plate and champagne glass, "Good Lord! what *are* you talking about?"

"I say" she went on "I have marked the snares, the toils, you have busily schemed with which to catch this weak unfledged fluttering heart of mine, or that of yon poor victim," and she spun round on her heels and dropped on her toes with a jerk, and held out her arms towards Rosa, who, to my surprise, was sitting with her head buried in her hands and rocking to and fro apparently in ecstacy of grief.

"Miss Sourwash" said I, after a pause "hadn't we better go home?—to your papa you know?"

"Never!" she replied spinning round and facing me—"never! till you promise here beneath that deep blue sky, and in the presence of these giants of the forest, and of Joe there the mule boy, to marry me, or that poor trembling child. I swear it," and she came down on my arm with a clutch that staggered me—"and you, Grey Charger, do you swear too."

"Damn it!" I ejaculated.

"Naughty boy!" said this queer woman, tapping me playfully on the bridge of my nose. "Naughty boy! Naughty word!"

I did not know what to think of her, or how to get quit of such eccentric companions. Perhaps, I thought, it will be best to humour them, so I said—

"Miss Sourwash, you must be aware I can't marry both of you."

"Then we'll toss for you!" she cried out. "Here! Rachel!"

"No, I wont toss," I said, "let's go home."

"Ah! You spurn me! Spurn me!" and the fair Rosa began to weep, and then tottered towards her sister who rose to meet her, and flinging their arms round each other they raised a dreadful row.

Well! I had an awful time of it pacifying the two ladies. I had to kiss one,—I forget which, but at last they seemed to be more reasonable, and I got them on their ponies. We turned homewards and a precious job it was conveying them to Mt. Jupiter. They never spoke a word, even when I tried to get up a conversation, and

I had to keep twisting round on my saddle to see if they were all right. A heavy storm broke just as we neared the house and we got wet through. Joe let the lunch basket fall over the bank into the river, and one of the beasts was lamed, so we were in a nice pickle when we got home.

Old Sourwash was at the door to meet us, and as I helped his daughters to dismount, each pressed my hand affectionately, and whispered her thanks and "You won't tell papa," as she escaped into the house.

"Charger, my boy!" said my host, "dinner will be ready directly. Have a bitter before you dress? That's right."

"Please Massa, de young lady say you mus' not 'spect them to dinner, they catch cold and no able for come down,"—so announced Pinkie, the sable handmaid of the Misses Sourwash.

"Ah! indeed," said their father. "All right, Pinkie. Then Grey, we won't dress, that is of course you can put on dry things but no swallow-tail, no white tie, you and I will dine comfortably. There's your bitter, now go and change."

As I put on other clothes, my thoughts of course continued to run upon the extraordinary conduct of the Misses Sourwash. There was only one solution. They were not accustomed to champagne and it had got into their heads. I remembered how at dinner they never took any thing but water, and that Joe when I asked him as to what was in the basket, told me with glee that Miss Rachel had put in the "pop" (in these degenerate days it is "fizz") and that her father did not know. Joe was entirely devoted to me thanks to sundry liberal tips, but of course I could not question him as to the peculiarities of his master and his daughters, but I made up my mind to sacrifice the remaining two days of my leave and get to barracks as fast as I could. I packed up my travelling bag and bribed Joe to have it sent down before day, while some other things were put in a small havresack which I usually carried at my saddle bow.

These and other arrangements made, I reached the dining room just as old Sourwash had ordered the bell to be rung, and down we sate. I noticed that the old gentleman's demeanour had changed and he was very grumpy. This I attributed to some thing he had heard from his daughters and I felt very uncomfortable.

"I hope" said I, "neither of the ladies suffered very much from their wetting."

"Well," replied Sourwash, "no, I don't think so. They're timid—shy."

"Very much so" I assented.

"What d'ye mean by 'very much so'?" demanded Mr. Sourwash looking at me very hard. "However, I want to have a few minutes conversation with you, but not now, perhaps to-morrow."

"Certainly" I said, "by all means."

"You seem to have anticipated it then."

"Not exactly" I replied.

"Look here, Captain Grey Charger, I like a man to speak out; but, as I said before, we'll wait till to-morrow."

I emptied my glass and talked on other matters. Sourwash seemed to get very excited every now and then, and had recourse to the decanters pretty often. If I passed the bottle he got angry, and so knowing that this sort of thing was going to end with my departure, I complied with his request and drank freely. Every few minutes he appeared about to talk to me about his daughters, and once or twice he mentioned their mother, but he always checked himself suddenly and changed the subject.

By degrees I saw he was becoming affected with what he was drinking, and I too, felt that my head was beginning to swim. But whenever I attempted to shirk the bottle, he became more and more violent.

Either from his indistinct muttered talk or my discomposed brain, I could not make out what it was he wanted to say to me. Some subject it was which he seemed anxious to confide to me, and what with his violent gestures and my "funk" at being in some foolish way compromised about his daughters, or one of them, I became very uneasy. The candles had burned down and gone out, but the faint light of the moon shone through the room. The servants had retired, and by a glance which I stole at my watch I saw it was between 10 and 11. Sourwash had put one arm on the table and rested his head on it, with the other hand he grasped a large glass filled with port. Presently I saw he was asleep and in a moment I felt there was no better time for me to make my escape. Rising from my chair and steadying myself for a minute, I gradually crept towards the door, supporting myself by the wall. When I gained the passage, my hat and whip were where I left them. West Indian outer doors in those days were rarely fastened, and so in a moment I was in the open. I peeped through the window and saw my host in the same position, and then I started for the stables. Presently I heard some one whisper "Captain! Captain!" and found I had been silently followed by Joe. I told him to get my horse. He seemed to hesitate, but I repeated the order and he left me. In my be-muddled state, and a thick bank of clouds having obscured the moon, I took the wrong path and found myself at the works. The mill was stationary, and in the uncertain light I could make out an animal standing there very like my horse Dobbin.

Joe has been precious quick, thought I, and when in a low voice I called to Dobbin, the faithful creature neighed in reply. I must tell you that the night air had increased the effects of the wine I had taken; in fact I was very drunk. Everything seemed in a muddle, but presently Joe appeared and saddled Dobbin. Then I heard people coming, and fearing lest it was Sourwash, I jumped on my horse's back. Joe attempted to say something, but in vain. I cracked my whip and off went Dobbin. I could hardly keep my seat, and we appeared to be going through very heavy ground. Dobbin could not manage more than a walk. Behind me I could hear other animals following in pursuit,—the cries of their riders and the lash of the whips as the horses were urged on. Fortunately, as I thought, I had a start of them and the same obstacles which impeded Dobbin hindered them; so on we went. The moon was behind the hills and the place where we were became pitch dark. I felt at length resigned to my fate; it seemed as if Sourwash must overtake me, and in his drunken rage he would be capable of any violence, but oddly enough, although it must have been the result of the drink I had taken, I seemed to have lost all care as to the result. I closed my eyes and took a firmer grip with my knees. Presently I heard the foremost of my pursuers call out, and his horse evidently halted, so did Dobbin. I had been met by a party coming from the other side. I did not care to look and see who they were; there was talking and some laughter as if in glee at my recapture, then Dobbin was led away and presently let go. He started at a feeble trot and I found I was free and without followers. As we rounded a corner, the moon again shone out and I seemed to recognise the high road to the garrison, so I left Dobbin, who at least was sober, to find the way.

I suppose I must have dozed off, for suddenly there was a stumble and a crash. Thousands of sparks flashed before my eyes, and I recollected no more.

"It'll be one o' Sourwash's friends. A sojer officer may be, eh! and well drunken. Bring a light, Cæsar." Such were the first words I heard, and opening my eyes, I found myself on my back close to the steps of a house, with a decent looking man and a girl bending over me.

They raised me and I found I was none the worse, perhaps, indeed the better for being somewhat sobered by the fall. I was led into the house and placed on a sofa while my new friend looked at me with a very inquisitive eye. Then he brought me some drink in a tumbler which he insisted on my taking. I complied, and in a few minutes I was asleep.

At daybreak my host revisited me, my head was quite clear, and I was anxious to continue my journey to town. I had first, however to satisfy the old Scot's curiosity, and I told him how that I had left Mr. Sourwash's after dinner, and that affected by the wine I had taken I fancied I was pursued, &c.

"Tut man" said Mr. McLean, giving me a rap on the shoulder, "I'll wager old Sourwash was up to his old tricks. Dinna ye ken that when a friend comes to stay at Mt. Jupiter that old deevil always puts in his horse for a nicht's spell at the mill, and it's possible when ye mounted your puir beast he was in the sweeps, and the sound ye hard as if o' pursuers, was no mair than ither five horses coming round and round with ye. Guid Lord! to think ye were sae fou as no to see that, and for you to be for a' the world like ane o' those inventions o' the deevil ye see at fairs at hame that they ca' merry-go-rounds, and grinding auld Sourwash's canes, and thinking yersel' a sort of Mazeppa. Eh, drink's a wonderfu' thing!"

I joined in the laugh, though at my own expense.

"It's a crazy thing too" went on my host, "for a man to do, for auld Sourwash, to gi'e the deevil his due, is a hospitable man and no' sparing wi' his liquor and maks his guests comfortable, but then puir man, he has plenty o' trouble with these twa dochters o' his. Sad thing, but they tak' after their mither wha died in an asylum, and if they get a drop o' wine in their head they're sair to manage."

Here then was the solution of the mystery. I left my good friend's house, first sending a note to Sourwash apologizing for my abrupt departure which I promised to explain when we next met. How I was to do it would have bothered me, but on arrival at the garrison I found

I was under orders to leave next morning, for—I think, Antigua; and so I never saw St. Fiddles or Sourwash or his daughters again.

TOO GRAMMATICAL.

I ONCE heard a sermon from a Bishop during his visitation of St. Maria, which was very different from those we were in the habit of listening to; it was, if I may say so, pitched in a higher key; and eloquent and heart-stirring as it was, it was "fired a long way over the heads" of the congregation who were almost entirely of the peasant class, and a very uneducated set. At St. Maria too, science was not cultivated, even by the wealthier classes, and so when at length the good bishop took advantage to employ the then more recent invention, the spectroscope, as a figure in his ornate address, his hearers were "nowhere."

Coming out of church I "met up with" (as we say in St. Maria,) two old dames shaking hands with great affection, and enquiring after after each other's health.

"Well marm, how you does like he Lardship? Me dear Mrs. Harcless (Hercules,) you ebber hearee better discoorse in you life marm?"

"Well, me dear, fu tell de truth, me like de Lardship v'ice, and he a nice lookin' man fo true, but he discoorse to my hearee been 'too grammatical.'"

REVEREND BERNARD BUMPSHUS.

WHEN the Reverend Bernard Bumpshus obtained a curacy in St, Sangaree, he made the mistake, common to many young men beginning their career, who consider themselves superior to everyone who does not happen to be of their own profession; and Bumpshus was a great sinner in this respect. He was an earnest, steady fellow, and in society was rather quiet and retiring, but once in the pulpit, or otherwise on duty, thought nothing of asserting the superiority of his order and his own attainments, and of course often with a ludicrous result.

"I am convinced" once said he in most self-satisfied tones, "that this is the duty of a Christian, and on refer- to the Epistle to the —— ch.—verse —, you will find that S. Paul *entirely agrees with me*." Another time he observed "I feel confident that Adam was endowed with scientific attainments of no mean order. I may indeed account him as the prototype of Owen and Darwin, for we learn that he was able to name each member of the animal world as it was created, and I have no doubt he did it correctly."

But poor Bumpshus once got a sad rebuff, and in this wise.

In Saint Maria in his time there yet lingered some of the 'old guard' of the former plantocracy, who had come out young, had fallen under the influence of evil example, absence of purer, better associates, and had taken to themselves, tho' not in marriage, daughters of the land and so some, in every other respect, blameless old gentleman would be surrounded by a group of dusky children who were unceremoniously sent out of sight, when visitors came, and whose mother never appeared in company. Of course, against examples such as these, precepts of moral tendency were of no effect; the people around reasoned that if the white man "the local magnate" so lived without shame and rebuke, so might they.

Bernard Bumpshus therefore one afternoon rode down to the estate of a Mr. Glenlivet, an old Scotch gentleman, who was, so far, a scandal and offender in this respect that two families called him father, while neither of the mothers could legally call him husband. Glenlivat had been ill, sick unto death, and his recovery was in great measure due to the assiduous care of the two dames, who as a rule sank all jealousy of each other, and did their best to nurse Mass' Andrew back to health. Bumpshus thought, not unnaturally, that a man who had stood almost within the portals of the grave, would feel better inclined to listen to his advice; and he counted also on the affectionate gratitnde which the attention of, at all events, Miss Bella, who was the mother of some half dozen of his children, would call forth.

"Mr. Glenlivet," said he, after some minutes' previous congratulations on the old man's restoration, and some general conversation, "I think it my duty to remind you of the uncertainty of life, of which you must have had some evidence, or rather I should say of the certainty of death, and as the clergyman of this parish, I call on you to amend your ways, and to live the remainder of your life in a proper way."

"And gude Lord! what'll ye ha'e me do?"

"I would have you repent, and show your repentance and desire of amendment by——"

"Jest hear to him!" said Glenlivet, addressing the chairs and tables, his only audience, "jest hear to him! and how am I to amend?"

"Why, sir, by marrying Miss Bella, I don't know her full name; Miss Bella, who has been a faithful helpmate to you for many years, and a tender nurse, and is, I regret to say, the mother of your six children."

"It's no sax, it'll be seeven, but let that pass," exclaimed Glenlivet. "I've nae doubt but ye mean weel, Mr. Bumpshus, and I'll be wullin' to follow your teachin', but——"

"There should be no 'buts' in such a case, Mr. Glenlivet, duty says——"

"Eh eh man! never min' what duty says, the difficulty is jest this, that if I marry Bella that's borne me seeven, what will I dae wi' Becca that's borne me ten? answer me that."

It *was* a difficult question to reply to, and Bumpshus perhaps did best when he fled from the house without a word.

"That's the warst o' sendin' boys, the like o' him, that does na understan' the customs o' the country," was Glenlivat's parting remark as he whistled back to his knees his little flock.

One day Bumpshus edified his congregation by informing them that "S. James shewed a keen perception of the frailty of human nature, when he coupled the two admonitions 'Visit the widow and orphan, and keep yourself unspotted from the world.' Indeed," he continued, "from my own experience, I know how difficult it is to visit a widow and not be spotted." Now the Revd. Bernard had been suspected of making love to a rather good-looking widow of thirty or thereabouts, who owned a small estate, and he had when twitted about his frequent visits, declared they were to the lady's aged mother; and so the remark was appreciated, and made some of the more profane smile.

AN OFFICIAL DUCAL FIRM.

MY acquaintance, Mr. Thomas Tinker, on the strength of being the owner of fifty acres of an abandoned estate in St. Molasses, and of keeping a small provision store at the village hard by, dubbed himself proprietor and merchant, and having been elected member of the Legislative Assembly of that island, by the votes of three electors out of a constituency of seven, became the leader of the opposition. He became also the *bête noire* of Governors and was a terrible fellow at correspondence. One day, however, Tom went home, to lay, as he declared, his many grievances at the foot of the throne, or at all events, at the door of the Colonial Office. He returned with grievances unredressed, with a keener sense of injustice, and of want of due regard to the important questions with which his patriotic bosom burned. "The Colonial Office" he shrieked out to an admiring knot of friends and admirers, "the Colonial Office! pah! Why, gentlemen, I went there—the underlings received me with an air as if they remembered who I was, and whence I came;—but I would have none of them, I wanted the fountain head, so I said, 'I wish to see the Dook—the Dook o' Buckingham.'"

"One flippant fellow said, says he, 'He's out.'"

"Then, said I, let me see Chandos."

"All I got for a reply was an impertinent snigger, till one clerk said, 'He's out too.'"

"I don't believe it, I never will believe it,—it was a subterfuge, a side wind to get rid of me; but I let 'em have it! I says. 'In business, gentlemen, this wouldn't do for both partners to be out at the same time, if, say Buckingham is out, why Chandos ought to be here and vicey varsus.' I wish you good day. And I shook the dust off my feet. That's how we're governed, gentlemen."

"Thank you!" Tom replied, after a pause, to some whispered enquiry from one of his friends, "I don't mind if I do," and the group moved towards the hotel.

A LOST LOVE.

WE—that is my uncle Jonas and I—were a firm of Solicitors. Our business was carried on in my uncle's name, "Jonas Spoonly." He objected to "and Co." as it was commercial, and as long as I got my share of the profits I did not object to *m'effacer*. Besides, my name was Jonas, also; and I reflected that when I became sole partner, there would be no occasion to change the style. It is true my second name was Maurice, but this my uncle bade me drop—at all events, in business, for, as he said it was too—something, romantic. The monotony of a Solicitor's life in the colonies is not usually relieved by startling incidents. Our business chiefly led us among titles, wills, and deeds, and now and then commercial squabbles. We did not care for criminal work, but there was one event of which an old letter or two, and a faded ribbon that I came across the other day, reminded me.

When I returned from England after a short leave of absence in 18— I found my uncle much more "chirpy" and brushed up than he was when I left. He moved about briskly and had contracted a queer habit of rubbing his hands together and smiling to himself, which I could not understand. If he saw me looking at him at such times, he would blush and resume his usual business manner with a somewhat guilty look. I knew better than to ask what it all meant, but I set about to watch and find out for myself.

One morning a week after my return, my uncle had as usual opened and read the letters which had been delivered at the office; it was a duty which he always insisted on performing himself, and he handed them over to me with some remarks or instructions about each. One, however, written in a feminine hand on perfumed rose-coloured paper, he clumsily smuggled into his waistcoat pocket as he watched me, apparently intent on the communication he had last turned over to me.

"By the way Jonas" said he, as I was leaving the office, "I think I shall have to go——but never mind; I'll tell you later on."

I went to my room and began work on the papers

before me and soon forgot all about my uncle's rosé-coloured billet. Presently, however, he opened the door and putting in his head, remarked "Jonas I am going out—back for dinner you know—just going as far as—but I'll tell you by and bye."

It was a common trick of my uncle to say "I'll tell you by and bye," but it was a promise he never fulfilled.

"Cannot I go for you, Sir?" I asked.

"Oh dear no" he replied, in a startled manner. "Oh! no. Goodbye. Thank you Jonas, no, I'll tell you"—and the bang of the door drowned the rest of the usual formula.

What has come over my uncle? thought I, as I resumed my employment.

I remembered that old Hecuba had welcomed me home with more than usual *impressement* and had said she was glad to see me back "for my uncle's sake;" but I attached no particular meaning to her words. Hecuba (or Mrs. Hecuba Romeo) was my uncle's housekeeper. When my father came over from England a disconsolate widower, with me then about five years old, he took up his abode with his bachelor brother Jonas, and Hecuba was employed as my nurse. When my father died, and I went to Europe for my education, she was continued as governante, and her affection and skill kept me well supplied with the jellies, syrups and "sweeties" that made me so popular with my schoolfellows. It is due to Hecuba's memory to say, her position in the house was unequivocal, and was understood and respected by all. I determined therefore to see if my old nurse could give me any information.

Scarcely had I come to this conclusion, when the door half opened, and a face appeared for an instant, and then was withdrawn too rapidly for me to see more than that it was that of a veiled female. "Come in," I called out, but as there was no response, I slid off my chair, and was at the door in an instant.

There stood a lady, in a riding habit of soft dark grey material, which set off her slight and supple figure, a single lavender bow at her throat was her only ornament, while a straw hat with a veil completed her costume.

"Whom may you wish to see, Madam?" I enquired.

"Mr. Jonas Spoonly," was the lady's reply in a gentle soft voice with a foreign accent.

"I am Mr. Jonas Spoonly," said I, adding, as something like a little laugh came from behind the veil, "that is, Mr. Jonas Spoonly, junior. I can, if you please, attend to you. I am my uncle's partner."

"It is with your uncle I have affairs."

"But he is out, and I——"

"When will he return?"

"That is difficult to say. Will you take a seat till he comes?" and I opened the door and invited my uncle's client into my office.

"Thank you, but he may not return till late, do you know where he has gone?"

"My uncle did not tell me."

"I wrote to him to say that I should ride in this afternoon, but I have come round by La Source. Yes, if you will permit me, I will wait for half an hour."

"Pardon me," said I, as she seated herself in an easy-chair, "you have ridden here, has any one taken your horse?"

"Thanks; my groom has taken it to the hotel, where I will walk when I leave here."

"May I ask to whom I have the pleasure of speaking? I have just returned from England and though I knew all my uncle's old clients——"

"I fear," said the lady, I am not to be ranked in so distinguished a company. I am not an *old* client."

"Of course not, Madam, not old in one sense—you know what I mean."

"I know what you wish to know, monsieur, and that is, who I am. Well, I suppose I may tell my business to your uncle's partner. My name is La Roche, and in your absence I have arrived in St. Molasses, I am a widow, my husband came here to receive some property; he died a year ago, and I have come to see about his affairs. I was directed to your uncle. I don't know that I have more to tell you, monsieur" and as she ended this statement she removed her veil.

I was prepared to see a pretty face, but I confess not one so perfect as that of my—or rather my uncle's—client. It was oval with large violet eyes and long black lashes, her hair was also black and worn off her forehead, her mouth was perhaps a little too small, but her smile was simply enchanting, at least to me, a somewhat susceptible fellow of twenty-five. I was so much struck with Madame La Roche's beauty that some moments elapsed before I could reply.

"My uncle has not mentioned your case to me, Madam" I at length said. "No doubt he will. I am not aware indeed that I have seen your papers. Is there anything I can tell him in case he does not return in time to see you?"

"I fear not, Monsieur Jonas" she replied. "It seems I must see him myself. He is so good, so patient, so responsive. You do not know how much I—I esteem your uncle, Mr. Jonas;" and she looked down at her little foot that peeped out from a fold of her skirt.

"My uncle is indeed fortunate" I exclaimed, "professional services are rarely so well repaid."

"No" replied Madame La Roche in a sarcastic tone, "professional men generally seek their reward in a fee, or in the professional success that attracts fresh clients. Your uncle does not value the one,—he does not require the other,"

"Then Madam" I remarked, "since his reward is your—your esteem, let me remind you we are partners, my uncle and I, and a share of the profits of every transaction is mine; may I then ask for my portion of your esteem?"

"When you earn it, Mr. Jonas."

"I will try to do so, Madame La Roche" was my reply.

She sate a little longer and then looking at her watch, said "Now I must go; your good uncle has not returned. I will write to him. Adieu! Monsieur, many thanks."

"Nay" said I, "you must allow me to escort you to the hotel" and I got my hat.

In the way it occurred me to suggest that we might call at our house and see if my uncle had returned. Madame La Roche assented, and on opening the door I found Hecuba about to go out.

"Mrs. Romeo," I enquired, "is my uncle here?"

The old lady replied in the negative, and as we turned

to leave she gave Madame La Roche a searching glance. We had gone a few paces when I turned, looked around, and saw Hecuba gazing after us, and slowly shaking her head in rather an ominous way.

I escorted Madame La Roche to the hotel, where her groom was waiting with her horse, or rather pony. Having assisted her to mount, I bade her farewell. I fancied there was some slight pressure of my hand, and then I walked slowly home.

Of course for a lawyer, love at first sight is a most unprofessional folly, but there was something in Madame La Roche's manner, something in the tone of her voice, that, to use a modern vulgarism, had "fetched" me, and there arose in my breast a feeling very much akin to jealousy of my respected uncle.

I had not forgotten my intention to enquire of Hecuba the cause of my uncle's manner, but it suddenly occurred to me that perhaps it was owing to some absurd infatuation of his with respect to his pretty client. Any doubt on the subject was dispelled on my enquiring from Hecuba if my uncle had yet returned, by her remarking:—

"No indeed, Mr. Jo; no indeed. That Marm Laroosh that you been walking with—well—she's a scheming woman for true. Take care she no fool you uncle, but here he comes; my father! I never think he so stupid—he eyes so clean and he no see dat woman's tricks—she scheme till—me never see such a ting!"

When my uncle came in, he looked tired and annoyed. He answered me sharply, and was deaf to Hecuba's enquiries. I asked where he had been and he replied that he would tell me by and bye, and to my remark that Madame La Roche had been at the office, he snapped out :—

"Yes, so I heard, I met her and she told me."

"I did not learn what was the business about which she wished to see you," I replied.

"No, I dare say not," said my uncle, "it was private business—nothing to do with office work."

"A good-looking person," I remarked in a cool indifferent tone, "rather young for a widow though, not more I should say than twenty-two."

My uncle glinted at me from beneath his bushy eyebrows.

I continued—"Tidy figure, very good eyes, nice hair too, a very decent foot and ankle, nose perhaps a leetle too——"

"Confound it!" shouted uncle Jonas, putting down his knife and fork, "Confound it, you talk like a demonstrator of anatomy, or a Judge at a cattle show."

"Well," I explained, "I was only enumerating the several items that went to make up a rather charming woman. Don't you agree with me?"

"Madame La Roche" said my uncle, "is a lady who demands sympathy and respect; I confess she possesses mine and—"

"So I gathered from what she told me," I interrupted, "she said you were good and patient, and responsive (whatever that may mean) and she also intimated that I could not imagine how much she—she—esteemed you. I congratulate you uncle Jonas!"

The old gentleman only replied with an angry glance; I fortunately kept my countenance.

"I thought" I went on "she might have come on that wild-goose chase that brought her husband here, about that estate he fancied he was entitled to. You remember uncle, you upset all Monsieur La Roche's hopes by showing that his title was bad, and then he caught the fever and died."

"I may have been mistaken" said my uncle.

"You were quite right though."

"The opinion of so experienced a practitioner as Mr. Jonas Spoonly, junior, is of the greatest value to me," sneered my uncle; "perhaps we may drop discussing M. La Roche, his widow and his affairs."

I said no more, at all events on that subject, on which my uncle seemed peculiarly sore, and we finished the meal in silence.

For some days after, my uncle's old manner returned; his unusually brisk and vivacious habit in great measure gave way to a preoccupied determined air, and in addition he appeared to have become suspicious of me, and to transfer much of his confidence to our clerk, McInroy.

We had, as it happened, a good deal of work to get through just then, and I was fully occupied, not so much so however, as to exclude all thoughts of Madame La Roche.

She lived, I found, at a pretty little cottage about five miles from town, with an old servant and a lad who groomed Madame's little pony and ran messages. I was anxious to see her again, but was deterred from riding out to the "Retreat," as her house was called, more by a disinclination to cause gossip, than by any fear of my uncle's displeasure. He, however, in his rôle of professional adviser, and as an old staid gentleman, was not so liable to be talked about, and I suspect he occasionally turned his grey nag's head toward Madame La Roche's residence. I ascertained moreover, that old Hecuba's mistrust of the pretty client arose from a fear that if my uncle were so weak, and Madame La Roche so crafty, as to marry, the old lady's despotic rule of the Spoonly ménage would be over; and she therefore conceived a hatred to Madame La Roche, that was—except for this reason—perfectly unjustifiable.

One afternoon, I was riding leisurely out of the town when I saw Madame La Roche going up the hill in the same direction. She was mounted on her pony, and her boy who had a basket or packall on his head, was holding on to the animal's tail, as is the habit of boys in St. Molasses.

Of course I was soon at her side. In St. Molasses where the roads run up hill and down dale, and are not in tip-top order, one's pony does not travel fast, especially with a boy tugging at his tail, and so five miles is really a long ride; hence there was plenty of time for a long conversation.

Now I cannot be expected to remember, much less to repeat all "I said" and "she said" but I found out that Madame La Roche had, as I guessed, come to try and recover a property which once belonged to her husband's relative and that my uncle had not only not informed her of the all but hopelessness of her case, but had rather led her to expect success.

Madame La Roche had received money from my uncle on the uuderstanding that they were advances for which the latter would recoup himself when he recovered her property, and that she had no present means of repaying the sums so borrowed.

I learned also that my uncle had made her an offer of marriage, which Madame La Roche had declined, alleging that her sentiments toward him were only those of gratitude &c. for his own exertions on her behalf.

As time went on, my uncle became more and more soured, he never enquired where I went of an afternoon, and of course Madame La Roche's name was never mentioned. I, however, began to work upon the case of her late husband's claim and had opportunities of seeing her. My attachment increased. I hoped to become Louise's (that is, Madame La Roche's) successful champion, recover his property, and so deliver her from obligation to my worthy uncle.

In one of our interviews, Louise told me that my uncle's last advance had been a sum of 300 dollars for which sum he had directed her to draw on him, that he accepted the draft, and that she had taken it to the Bank and obtained the money. I concluded that he adopted this course so that the transaction might appear more business-like than giving her his cheque.

One afternoon I was going for a ride and found my uncle at the door mounting his horse and so we rode side by side out of the town. My uncle asked me where I was going. I replied "Nowhere in particular;" and we jogged on together until we reached the foot of the hill where the road divided, a somewhat narrow track leading up to the Retreat, Madame La Roche's cottage, while the highway ran along the level. Here my uncle pulled up.

"I suppose," said he, "you are going to visit your interesting friend" and he pointed with his whip towards the hill top.

"No," I replied, "I am not, perhaps *you* are, in which case——"

"Look here, Sir," he burst out, "I want to speak to you. I believe some formalities are usual when a client changes his lawyer. You have thought fit to advise Madame La Roche independently of me, your partner. We cannot both act for her, she must choose between us.

"You seem to forget," I replied, "that you alone acted for her, and denied to me, *your* partner, that her visit to our office was on business."

"No doubt," continued my uncle, "you think your good looks supply any deficiency in experience and knowledge of the case, however we shall see who succeeds."

"Uncle," I replied, "let this cease. I had no desire to cross your path as Madam La Roche's professional adviser. If you hope to occupy another position, one which——"

"I *will* occupy, my dear nephew, in spite of your superior attractions, and your visits on the sly to this good lady. You have some advantages over me, perhaps, but when the time comes, you'll see. I'll shew you by and bye."

"You are unjust" said I—"whatever my sentiments may be, I have never presumed to—"

"Well here she comes" observed my uncle, "let her choose between us now."

We sate watching Madame La Roche on her pony

slowly descending the hill, her boy as usual following her. My uncle and I never exchanged a look or word, until we suddenly saw her animal bound forward and galop towards us. Madame La Roche had dropped her reins, and lost all command over her steed. In a moment I leapt from my saddle, and rushed up the hill to her assistance, fortunately coming up with the run-away just as its mistress fell from its back. Fortunately I was able to break her fall and to place her on the ground, and support her head against my shoulder, for she had fainted.

Her wretched pony continued its course down hill, indulging in a kick or two, till cannoning against uncle Jonas's charger, the shock dislodged my relative from his saddle, and I saw his white-trousered legs describe an arc in the air while his head came on the grass with a thud. He was not however hurt, and regaining his feet he came towards us.

"Uncle, some water," I shouted, pointing to a little spring in the hillside.

The old gentleman improvised a cup out of a leaf, and having filled it brought it to me.

"Drink, pretty creature drink," said he unconsciously quoting Wordsworth, and putting the water to Madame La Roche's lips. "Louise! do, do, drink"—and he patted her on the shoulder as he popped down on his knees. Under other circumstances my uncle's distress might have been touching, but I confess to me it was ludicrous in the extreme. His hat—he wore a tall white felt, bell-topper,—had been crushed in his fall, and he had put the mis-shapen affair on the back of his head; his coat was all over dust, and the knees of his trousers had a pitch of vivid green on them, while a sprig of acacia had scratched him across his nose; so that altogether he looked a most deplorable figure.

As Madame La Roche opened her eyes, and saw this apparition intently gazing at her, she started and gave a scream.

"Madame La Roche" began my uncle.

"Oh! go,—take him away" she said, placing her outstretched hands before her, "take him away!" then looking up at me, murmured "Maurice, dear Maurice," and bending down my face to hers, our lips met.

"Well I *am* d——d" ejaculated Uncle Silas regaining his feet, and attempting by no means of vigorous knocks with his fist to restore the symmetry of his injured hat, "you're a nice couple you are—and you madam adventuress, you think you've got the whip hand of me do] you? but I'll show you by and bye. "Yes;" he repeated as Louise smiled, "yes, you may grin, but who wins, laughs."

I will not dwell upon the tender words that passed between Louise and me as my uncle stalked away, and how I saw her to her house. I was very happy, so happy that I only gave her boy half the thrashing he deserved for having caused the accident by "chooking" the pony with a stick to make it go.

A few days later, I was in St. Molasses Bank on business of my own, and while at the counter heard my uncle's voice in the manager's office.

"Well," replied my uncle, "I won't be sure of course, but I can soon tell. I have sent to enquire, and the messenger will soon return. I'll tell you by and bye."

"Forgery" said the manager "is severely punished. Look again, Mr. Spoonly. Of course I ought to take your first denial, but—pardon me—it seems so like your handwriting, I venture to ask you to be quite certain."

As the manager spoke, a boy ran into the Bank, and handed me a note in Louise's writing addressed to Jonas Spoonly, Esqr. The boy was wet through, for it was raining, and he chattered something about the river being down and the bridge carried away, but my attention was engrossed by the note. I don't know that I did wrong to open it, although she usually in writing to me used my second name Maurice, but I feared some catastrophe. As I ran my eyes over the letter, I became aware of the cruel plot my uncle had laid. Louise had written—"You know you accepted the bill or paper or whatever it was you told me to sign, in order that I might get the money you advanced me. You know it is no forgery. You threaten to involve me in a crime of which I am innocent. I know the penalty—shame—imprisonment, worse than death; but I reject the alternative you propose. My heart is no longer mine, it is Maurice's. I never could love you,—this last act of yours makes me hate you. Maurice will help me—if he cannot, God will! L. L."

"Boy" said I, carefully refolding the note and resealing the envelope, "this is not for me, give it to Mr. Spoonly in there."—I pointed to the door.

I could watch my uncle as he tore open the note, and I marked the demoniacal expression that came over his face as he crushed the paper and thrust it into his pocket.

"That acceptance," said he, "is not in my handwriting."

"Then I have only one course to pursue" returned the manager, and he rung a bell. "I will send for Mr.———" naming the Inspector of Police.

"Spare yourself the trouble Mr.——" said I, walking into his office, "I have overheard part of what you were saying, I hope you will excuse my intruding. Be so good as to let me see the paper you speak of."

"You have nothing to do with it, Sir, I protest"—began my uncle.

The manager however placed before me Louise's draft for $300, and across it was what was evidently my uncle's acceptance. I looked at it for a minute and then said:—

"My uncle is right, this is not his writing, it is mine, I accepted it as my uncle's partner. Here is a cheque for the amount."

"Do you know you're telling a lie, Jonas!" said my uncle, "a lie! Sir" and he walked out of the bank in a towering rage.

The manager who knew all about the rivalry between myself and my relative, looked much relieved at my action, and when my uncle was gone, he glanced enquiringly at me, but I could not stay to satisfy his curiosity. I longed to see Louise and relieve her anxiety, so in a few minutes I was cantering towards the Retreat.

It had been raining heavily, and the road was much cut up. As I proceeded, I could hear the roar of the torrent into which the small stream which crossed the road at the foot of the hill, had been swollen by the rain.

In fine weather, the ford and its surroundings formed a picturesque scene. The road turned abruptly to the right, past a large rock partly covered with ferns and moss, above which towered a clump of bamboos, throwing the water beneath them into deep shadow only broken by the ripples, as they danced over stones and pebbles. On the left of the road was a similar boulder stretching across the bed of the stream, and damming the water into a narrow space; gliding past this obstruction, the brook then fell first into a broad and shallow pool, and then, separated into a dozen little rills, it leapt and skipped down the face of a large rock into a dark deep basin, round and round which the water swept in circles crowned with bubbling eddies. The people called this spot "Deadman's hole," and even in a bright sunny day, to gaze down at it below the thick foliage which cast a sombre shade over it, half gave one the idea that the place was haunted. There was some dismal story connected with the place, and it was generally avoided, the more so, as the strongest swimmer could not hope to escape from its almost ice-cold waters.

On the day of which I speak however, the scene was indeed changed. The brook had become a river, and over-whelming the road, it dashed impetuously along. At each obstacle its waves were tossed high in the air; the roar of the waters was mingled with the shock of the stones which it bore in its course along with boughs and trunks of trees. The place where the boulder in dry weather presented a barrier to the stream, was marked by the waves dashing over it, and from the precipice overhanging "Deadman's hole" clouds of spray were thrown up in quick succession.

To cross the stream was of course impossible. The fragments of a foot bridge, built of slight materials had been swept away, and one of its white beams still fastened to the bank tossed in the water like a straw.

There were one or two people on the other side who pointed down the stream, and appeared from their gestures to be calling to me, but their voices were drowned by the roar and noise of the current.

I stood for a while trying to understand them, but in vain. At length, fastening my horse to a tree, I walked in the direction they indicated down the brink of the river bed, and they followed my example, keeping of course, on the other bank. After some scrambling and a fall or two, I came to "Deadman's hole." At first I only saw that it had been converted into, as it were, a boiling cauldron. The river dashed down the face of the boulder above it in one large sheet of foaming water, and the basin was full of tossing waves, dashing against its sides. It was a fearful sight, but one more dreadful awaited me. Under the further bank, I saw what at first seemed part of some up-rooted tree, but in a moment I recognized the form of Louise. She lay, nearly covered with water, in a little recess of the rock around a projecting portion of which one arm was twisted, the other, bent upwards to her face, which was turned towards me, seemed as it obeyed the motion of the waves, to beckon to me. At a glance I saw the truth. I knew that she I loved was drowned,—was dead.

For some moments I gazed,—spell-bound—and then,

as her arm once more appeared to beckon me I prepared to leap into the boiling water and reach her; but as I stood up and stretched my arms for a plunge, the strong grasp of some man who had followed me to the scene, dragged me back from destruction.

I knew no more till weeks after, when I awoke to find old Hecuba bending over me. In time, I was able to leave my bed room, and thence travel to England. Months—two years—passed before I regained my strength, some said my senses; and then I learned how Louise had perished in her attempt to reach me, that I might protect her from my uncle's base and cruel scheme. She and her pony had been swept away while crossing the ford, and had been carried down to the spot where I had seen her. Then too, I learned that uncle Jonas was no more; that with a few words of contrition he had left me all he possessed, which was more than enough for my wants.

They never let me return to St. Molasses, nor do I care to go; so here I live in a quiet English home, waiting till I am called to rejoin my lost Louise. Of her, all I possess, save the sweet memory of her love, are a few letters and a long tress of hair tied in a lavender ribbon which old Hecuba, who has just handed me my pipe, gave me the day I left St. Molasses for ever.

THE MAJOR-GENERAL'S YARN.

I SUPPOSE it is only grey-headed fellows like myself, who were quartered in Barataria in the forties, that recollect Mary Gordon—"Miss Mary," as she always insisted on being called, and who kept *the* hotel of the place. There was another, an opposition affair; that succeeded chiefly in attracting the mercantile marine; but was considered only a second-rate establishment. Some times with fresh paint and a new flag, it strove to put on an appearance of superiority, but it never enticed any desirable customer from Mary. Her *clientèle* consisted of the "landed gentry," who, if they had no town house of their own, made Mary's their headquarters when they came in on estates' business, or to attend the Legislature or Law Courts, and who always brought their families on the rather frequent occasions of a ball at the Governor's or some other house. The Hotel was also the rendezvous of naval officers, while there was often a transient official guest awaiting the preparation of his house or the arrival of the homeward packet,—then of course a sailing vessel. Miss Mary therefore, could afford to look down on the neighbouring hostel, and indeed to regard it as a sort of convenient receptacle for guests whom she did not care to receive or retain.

In those days Gordon's hotel did a big business. There was a strong garrison in Barataria, and we young fellows, when off duty, usually found ourselves within Mary's hospitable walls for an hour's chat and a sangaree. By the way, that is a West Indian institution that somehow seems to have faded with Emancipation and has given place to cocktails, swizzles, juleps and other Yankee innovations; but it was very pleasant of a blistering hot afternoon to be seated in a well-shaded verandah, and have a white-clad black fellow at your elbow with the amber sherry or madeira in a big class, "mantled o'er" with grated nutmeg, and the thin rind of a lime gracefully curling over the brim and giving out a most delicious odour; besides, there was no sangarees like Miss Mary's.

At that time Mary Gordon was a tall, handsome woman. Her splendid hair and eyes and her perfect teeth excited the admiration of the men and the envy of the women of the place She was about thirty-eight—at least she owned to that—but one never got much information as to her birth and origin, and our respect for her prevented our asking impertinent questions. There were stories which we hoped were untrue, or, at the worst, exaggerated, about Miss Mary's earlier days; and new arrivals as yet unlearned in the ways and customs of the West, were greatly scandalized at there being in her household a very attractive young girl of eighteen who called Miss Mary "mamma," and bore a name other than Gordon, for it was Cassidy. Still, Miss Mary's honesty and good heart and (at all events in recent years) irreproachable character won her warm friends from the Governor down to the youngest sub in the garrison, and in return Miss Mary never allowed the good name of any of her favourites to be impeached. Any backbiting of the sort she put down with a firm hand, or at all events a stern tongue. It cannot however be said that she was silent as to the peccadilloes or shortcomings of her own enemies and rivals, of which latter the lady who presided over the opposition "Phœnix" was the chief. Mary's retentive memory, aided by a somewhat active imagination, was a very armoury of offensive weapons which she brandished and hurled on occasions with great effect, and, to tell the truth, it was not an uncommon pastime with us to 'draw' our hostess, and beguile her into battering to pieces the reputation of someone she disliked. Miss Mary on these or other occasions, when excited, would give vent to her feelings in pure Creole, although at ordinary times she used precise, not to say prim language, and the transition to a flood of broken English added all the more to our enjoyment of the fun. I have often seen a negro slink away perfectly cowed by one of Miss Mary's impassioned addresses in the vernacular.

The principal room at Miss Mary's was a long scantily furnished apartment opening on to a broad verandah overlooking the bay. Its floor was bare, but scrubbed and scraped as white as white could be. There was a long table made up of many leaves of mahogany which age and frequent polishing had made like ebony, and a spindle-legged sideboard with drawers gaping from long and rough usage, and covered with the oddest of all odd lots of glassware.

Art was represented on one wall by a large portrait of a military hero in a scarlet uniform, with very blue eyes and sandy hair. The back ground was made up of soldiers, horses and smoke. This was always declared to be the likeness of the late Captain Cassidy—'my papa'—as Miss Norah Cassidy called him or 'poor Peter' as her mother, when in a very confidential mood, described him. The military records of the station did, I believe, make mention of some such officer being at one time quartered in Barataria, and there was a tradition that a wild fellow of that name had been rescued from debt and disgrace and death by Mary, and had rewarded her with broken faith and desertion; but to Mary he was still 'poor Peter,' and I have seen her big black eyes swim with tears when she talked to me as she sometimes did, about him.

There was another room which I remember, and this was the drawing room,—a small apartment sacred to Miss Mary and her daughter. I was rather overfurnished and looked like a museum with its various ornaments. There were shells from all parts of the world, small corals from the Baratarian and other seas, large fan-like masses of gorgonia, a cocoanut shell covered with barnacles that had been washed ashore on the island, a shark's distended jaws, and sea monsters more or less artistically stuffed were among its principal curiosities, and there was a piano, the maker of which had lived in a far remote period. It was never in tune, and had suffered much from the amateur tinkering of myself and others who undertook to restore its failing powers. Norah however used to extract a good deal of music from it, and it supplied the accompaniment to many a little ballad which she used to sing to us. I can shut my eyes and still see the little room and its queer contents and hear the girl's contralto voice and—by Jove!—smell the guava jelly Miss Mary was always making, and the fumes of which at times used to pervade the whole house.

I was then eighteen and an Ensign in the Buffs, a fair haired boy fresh from school, very quiet and shy, and a good deal teazed by my brother officers to whom my rather unfortunate name, Theophilus Talavera Tompion, was the subject of endless fun and ridicule. Of course it was no fault of mine that I was christened after an uncle from whom we had great but vain expectations, and that my father desired to connect his son's name with that of the famous battle at which he lost his leg. On such occasions, Miss Mary stood my champion and defender, and would warn my assailants to "leave off badgering Theophilus Talavera." She always in a motherly sort of way called us by our Christian names.

I have said that Norah Cassidy was attractive; to me she was especially so, and no wonder, for I was of a susceptible age, while she was simply the most lovely girl I had ever seen. Norah had the pliant, graceful figure so peculiar to creole girls. Her features without being regular had a charm of their own, and whether in repose when her dark violet eyes were half concealed by their long lashes, or lit up with fun, with her musical laugh rippling out from lips that—but there! you will only laugh at an old fogey trying to describe the girl who was his idol long, long ago!

I think we were all more or less in love with Norah, except perhaps a young artillery sub of my own age called Busby, who had been cruelly thrown over for an elderly and somewhat inebriate Major by a siren of twenty-eight, the daughter of the Controller of Customs at St. Sangaree. Busby (Augustus was his christian name) went moping about, bewailing his unhappy fate, and was for a long time faithful to his cruel enchantress.

I used to think that Norah cared a little for me, but I could not be certain, and boy-like I was afraid to speak out to her. Whenever I could, I sate by her side, and tried to talk, but I was stupid and *gauche*, and if I caught, as at first I often did, a glance of what I took to be suppressed merriment at my diffidence, I used to blush and shut up. I never dared to ask her to come for a ride or walk. Her mother and she too much respected Mrs. Grundy, and so my only chance was when Norah and I if there were no guests in the house, used, to sit in the little drawing room, singing duets out of an old well thumbed book. Even then Miss Mary would keep popping in and out of the room, or would bring her work, usually consisting of house linen, to be marked or mended, and keep us company. Again, if Miss Mary was otherwise occupied, we were rarely alone; there were almost always people staying at the hotel, and my brother officers were all fond of a little flirtation with Norah and took delight in spoiling our tête-à-têtes. Miss Mary, I suppose when she heard us singing or laughing, felt that all was going on correctly, and that Norah was safe without her presence and protection, but anyhow my love-making was difficult work, until one day plucking up courage, I managed to let Norah know how dear she was to me.

That day Mrs. Cavally's hucksters came to Fort Frederick, offering their wares to the doctor's wife and the married women of the garrison. I may explain that in those days shops there were none, only wholesale stores. Mrs. Cavally was the wife of the President, and though a Member of Council of that era would sooner have thought of cutting your hair than selling you a single shirt, he had no objection to his wife employing a string of black girls who, tray on head, wandered all over the island selling her goods. Mrs. Cavally's Rosa had some brand new jewellery to sell, and so at a price that made a big hole in my month's pay, I bought a ring with a pearl in it for Norah.

That afternoon Busby and I rode down into the town to the Hotel, and found Miss Mary downstairs standing over a big pan of guavas which were boiling away on a coal-pot. She was busy with two lady customers, and so with a nod we went upstairs, where as luck would have it, we found Norah in the drawing room alone.

Busby was good nature itself, and after some conversation he began to work away at the piano, keeping his eyes like a discreet dear fellow straight before him, thundering in his deep but indifferent bass whenever Norah and I, who were seated on the sofa behind him, allowed our voices to rise. I don't recollect what we talked about, but I managed to get possession of Norah's hand, and to slip the ring on to her finger, when she made some little fuss about it at first, but presently put up her face to be kissed.

"Well! well, my patience! Theophilus Talavera! Norah! You Miss!" and, in rushed Miss Mary (preserve-ladle in hand) with astonishment and a big smear of smut on her features—"Go along to your room," and she gave Norah a push—"Go along! and you Theophilus Talavera, and you Augustus Busby, sit down there," and the ladle was pointed to two chairs.

"My dear Miss Mary," I began—

"Don't dear me, Theophilus, don't dear me, I am ashamed of you."

"Perhaps I'd better leave you and Talavera, Miss Mary," said Busby, and he sneaked out of the room.

"Oh, sonnie," said Miss Mary, flopping down on the sofa beside me, "if any one been tell me you would have behave so, I'd have tell them they lie. It is a real advantage (egvantage she called it) you take of me; my father! look my trial!" and she wrung her hands.

"But Miss Mary, I love Norah."

"My goodness, Theophilus, don't let me hear those words come out from your mouth. You love her—yes that is how the trouble come."

"There's no trouble. Of course, I know my pay is not much, but we could wait, Miss Mary—we wouldn't marry till I was"—

"You does know what you talk?" and Miss Mary shook her head and smiled.

"And why not?" said I "Norah's a dear good girl—and she's clever, a deuced sight cleverer than most girls—than Mrs. Fausip's (our doctor's wife)—and I'd try to make her happy—I swear I would—"

"Yes buddie! that's all very well, and if I was a schemer sort of woman like that wretch there" and she jerked her thumb in the direction of the hotel over the way, "I'd have said yes, and perhaps as poor Peter always said his family were Kings in Ireland once, Norah's as good by her father as most girls,—but no, buddie! Chicken hawk never build nest with ground dove! no that you are hawk, Theophilus—I don't mean so—but you know you family—you uncle Sir John and them, how they like to hear you marry a girl who, good as she be, have for mother, this poor sinner—Miss Mary as keep a hotel? and God forgive me she no lawful born—no, sonnie! beggin you pardon, you is a fool but that no make me a villain. Don't cut me in, Theophilus Talavera! hear me discourse and consider to youself—"

"I have considered, Miss Mary—I have thought of it—of nothing else for weeks past."

"You think Norah could be comfortable with all them big fashioned people in England? I must think for she, Buddie, and I no able to let she be ashamed."

"But——"

"No, my son! this 'ting must stop. Poor as I be, t'ank God I am able to see what is right—what is best for my child—and for you too, sonnie."

"Miss Mary," said I, "I don't think you are right—I don't, indeed."

"I don't t'ink either, me friend—I *know*—" and she rose from the sofa.

"Look me good, sonnie. 'Member I ask you—I beg you—do—don't you see Norah any more—little bit more and you forget em—don't tell me no—young people heart like sand at bay side, you go scratch name in em, first wave come wash em out—and now, go—look you hat—there, buddie!—come!—go."

Miss Mary went on in this way for a long while, without allowing me to speak half-a-dozen consecutive words, and there was therefore no resisting, so at last she led me out of the room and down the stairs till I found myself at the door.

"I must see Norah! Miss Mary—I couldn't live if I did not."

"Theophilus Talavera!" she replied, "I don't say no, as to your seeing her again, but not now—I must first see she and have discourse with she. Another day—and now please go."

She took up her station at her guava jelly which had

been in the meanwhile under the care of a half-clad black imp, and stirred it round and round with a grave air, slowly shaking her head as if it were some terrible witch-brew she was compounding, and I—well there was no use my stopping—so off I went very sheepish and perplexed towards the Garrison.

The next day, or day after that, I think, it was, the Colonel put me in orders to go to Barbados in charge of some men in the place of another officer. I was of course much annoyed at any arrangement which removed me from Barataria and Norah, but I dared not rebel. I did not know, by the way, until long after that Miss Mary had got hold of my Colonel, told him the whole story of my love for her daughter, and besought him to get me out of the way. However, I was informed that the packet might arrive any hour, and so I set to work to get all ready.

As to going without an interview—a parting word with Norah, that was out of the question. I arranged after a good deal of manœuvring to meet her as she went to evening church. A tête-à-tête in the street was not to be thought of, so I had secured the services of a mulatto boy whose boat was a safe and comfortable little craft. Everything went well. I intercepted Norah and her little black attendant on their way, and we three stepped unobserved into the boat, which Julius had prudently brought ashore, where the shadow of the hill on which the Fort was perched fell darkest on the beach. It was a lovely night. There was a moon and it seemed to me as if I had never seen the bay and its back ground of tall richly clad hills look more attractive. The batteries above us stood out sharp and clear against the sky. I could almost see our sentries as they paced to and fro. The houses on the beach were lit up by the soft rays, and here and there lights shone from them. The music and the bells from the churches and chapels floated in a dreamy way across the water, and so with Jane Ann curled up in the bow, and Julius sculling in a desultory way so as to keep his boat as much as possible under the overhanging cliff, Norah and I sat and whispered—well, if you like—nonsense to each other. Of course, we promised and vowed all sorts of things—constancy and never dying remembrance, and above all a determination to overcome all obstacles to our union. In this, as it now seems, very ridiculous way we talked, and the boat drifted on and on, till we came to the low rocks which once formed part of the cliff which was the eastern boundary of the bay, but had fallen in a rugged heap at its foot. Then there was a sudden confusion, and a cry,—a large boat with five or six pullers shot round the point and before Julius could get out of his way, it crashed against us. I really did not know what happened after, only that Norah and I clung to each other as we sank into the dark chilly waters—I did all I could to keep her and myself afloat—I managed to get her near the rocks—and felt her drawn from my clasp—then a rough hand was laid on me, but I recollected no more. To cut it short, it seems I had saved Norah's life, though, if the men in the other boat had not helped to haul her and myself on to the rocks we must have gone. They took me to the town, and Miss Mary insisted on my being put into her best bed then and there. I had fever, which, in a few days developed into genuine Yellow Jack. They did all sorts of things to me. I believe I was bled, blistered, dosed in every possible way; I know they shaved my head. Miss Mary never left me, and they say but for her and Norah, I could not have pulled through. The attack left me fearfully weak, and I remember as if it was yesterday, when Miss Mary came to my bed side with tears of joy running down her brown cheeks, and thanked God I was out of danger. Then she brought forward Norah, and at her mother's bidding, she bent down and kissed me. I didn't know it was the last time I should ever see her.

They packed me off as soon as they could to England. Miss Mary first gave me a scolding for my nearly losing the lives of Norah and myself, and then with as tender a leave-taking as if she had been my own mother, prayed God to bless me, and asked me never to forget her.

"Never! dear Miss Mary," I said, "never—but Norah, where is she?"

"Sonnie! never you mind, where Norah be, she be."

The boat shoved off, and I could ask no more questions. Afterwards, I used to write to Miss Mary, but I never got a reply, and so in time, my recollection of Barataria, and my pretty Norah almost died out; and, then you know, I married the present Lady Tompion.

Well, years rolled on, and brought their wonderful events and changes. By the death of my uncle, the Baronetcy came to me. Years and years after, I was appointed Governor-in-Chief of the islands of which Barataria is one. Of course I was glad to see the old place once more, though all the fellows who were in garrison with me then, were dead and gone, save some two or three, and they were scattered over the world. Still, the lovely island and its well remembered barracks and fort were interesting objects as H.M.S. —— steamed in, one midday some four years ago. I had Lady Tompion and the girls on deck, and pointed out to them the several points of interest.

It was a good deal changed, there was no garrison there, and the hill below the barracks, once so trimly kept, was overgrown. Through my glass I could see that the batteries were no longer armed, while the buildings looked worn and dilapidated. In the town, too, the houses had gone to decay, though there still seemed some little life in the place, and one or two of the stores I recollected appeared to be yet tenanted and busy.

There's always a lot of fuss landing at these places officially. A governor has to wait until an inspector of police or some civilian A.D.C. in a nondescript uniform clambers awkwardly on deck, and in a half-shy, half-conceited way goes with a sword he doesn't know how to manage, clinkety clankety all over the deck in search of "the Governor;" and one's own Private Secretary, in my case, was never ready, being always chatting and chaffing with one of my girls. Then you're "Your Excellencied" and asked when Your Excellency will land, and how long Your Excellency will stay, &c., &c., all of which I used to cut very short I assure you,—in fact, these chaps generally found me reading a newspaper, and got my replies like minute guns. I've no doubt they thought me pompous and all that, but it taught them discipline.

On the occasion I'm talking about, I had to get into my full fig, and the Captain sent us ashore in his barge with a Union Jack at the bow. As we left the ship, they banged a salute, and as I landed, bang went the guns from a small battery they hadn't dismantled. They didn't do it badly either, not, of course, as it was done in the old days, but still very creditably for a set of policemen. Then my Lieut. Governor in his official blue and gold received me, and I had presented to me all the local people, old chaps that never been out of the island, some of them in clothes that might have been built a score of years ago, and one with a white felt hat and big bulgy white cotton umbrella; I had to grin and shake hands, and appear as if they were each of them a long lost brother. Then a second boat brought miladi and the girls, and another introduction had to be gone through. Some wanted to shake hands, but trust my lady for that! She knew her position, and so just gave them one of her bows and icy smiles—I know them—and our friends drew back. However, we in time started to walk to the Lieutenant Governor's Office to wait for his carriage which wasn't forthcoming. Very often the carriage is not, and he has to borrow from some one in the place as was the case on this occasion, when our party was rather large. Then, we formed a sort of procession. I went first with Bagges my Secretary; and then came Lady Tompion and the Lieutenant Governor; the girls and some officers from the ship completed our party; and of course, we were followed by a small mob of the local people. I had determined when all this parade was over, to seek out my old friend Miss Mary, who I heard, still kept the hotel, but had suffered from the change of fortune which had come over Barataria, and to which the withdrawal of the Garrison had contributed; but my intentions were frustrated, for as we passed the old well remembered doorway, who should rush out, but Miss Mary, grown very stout and grey, but still wearing a handkerchief tied as jauntily as in the old days. She stepped in front of me, gave one long steadfast look, and crying "Me God! Theophilus Talavera; you come to bless these old eyes before me dead. Ah! Sonnie!" and quite disregarding our altered circumstances, and ignoring my official position, she flung her arms round my neck and kissed me in a most—well—embarrassing way. I couldn't remonstrate, I was so taken aback, besides being mortified at the ridiculous figure I must have made—my cocked hat had fallen off—and the nigger boys yelled with delight, while to complete all, her ladyship rushed up and in her deepest, severest tone said, "Tompion! Sir Theophilus Tompion, *may* I ask who this is?"

"Beg pardon ma'am," said Miss Mary quitting me and curtseying to my wife, "beg pardon; but when Theophilus Talavera been here in the Buffs, he like my own pickney, and I never, never see him till now. Excuse my feelings, ma'am." But it was evident that Lady Tompion did not excuse poor Miss Mary, from the manner in which, after observing to me 'If Your Excellency has quite done with this interesting person, we will proceed,' she swept past my old friend.

"Good morning" said I, raising my hat which a small boy had handed me, "good morning, Miss Gordon—glad to see you looking well."

"Morning, Miss Gordon!" Miss Mary repeated as she retreated a pace or two, holding up her hands.—Morning!

and that all! Well! Well! Theophilus Talavera! you do right, Sonnie, you no more the boy as swear you never forget me nor my poor dead Norah, you Governor now—big man—but I 'spect you got Governor over *you*. Well! well! Morning you Excellency, Morning Missis" —and she dropped us a very low curtsey and then strode off to her door.

I am sorry to say I did not see her again; but Lady Tompion raised some objections, and perhaps she was right. Her ladyship reminded me, that evening after we had retired to bed, that 'one of the chief duties of exalted rank is to discipline one's emotions, and to subordinate to the exigencies of one's position, every impulse which may lead to inconvenient or derogatory results.'

But still I should have liked to have seen old Mary once more, and asked her about her poor dead Norah.

PRINTED AT THE "ARGOSY" PRESS, DEMERARA.

LaVergne, TN USA
18 September 2009
158274LV00004B/42/P

9 781120 053336